Detail from 'The Moving of the Address to the Crown on the Meeting of the first Reformed Parliament in the old House of Commons on the 5th of February 1833', by Sir George Hayter, 1848. W. E. GLADSTONE, M.P. for Newark, on the left and, on the right, JOHN GLADSTONE, M.P. for Portarlington.
*Reproduced by permission of the Trustees of the National Portrait Gallery.*

ROYAL COMMISSION ON
HISTORICAL MANUSCRIPTS

The Prime Ministers' Papers:

# W. E. GLADSTONE

II: Autobiographical Memoranda 1832-1845

EDITED BY JOHN BROOKE
AND MARY SORENSEN

LONDON
HER MAJESTY'S STATIONERY OFFICE
1972

# CONTENTS

# CONTENTS

# INTRODUCTION

It was Gladstone's habit throughout life to write accounts of events or conversations which seemed to him important or worth commemorating. They were purely for his own use and never intended for publication. They supplement his diary and give a fuller account of events than was possible in a daily journal. For the most part they deal with politics or religious affairs, only occasionally with his personal life. They were invariably written on the day the event or conversation took place or shortly afterwards, and are an important source for Gladstone's biography and for the political history of the nineteenth century.

This volume contains all Gladstone's autobiographical memoranda from his first election to Parliament in 1832 at the age of twenty-three to his resignation from Peel's Cabinet in 1845.

The first memorandum and one of the most interesting is an account of the canvass Gladstone undertook at Newark in September 1832 in anticipation of the first general election of the reformed Parliament. Gladstone had opposed the Reform Bill as a revolutionary measure, but it had made little difference to the way in which elections were conducted at Newark. The constituency had increased in size from about 1,000 to 1,500 voters, but candidates still stood on the interest of the Duke of Newcastle (whose family had held one seat at Newark for over a hundred years) or on the independent interest. Party names were not used, and the candidates were distinguished by their colours. 'Are you the Red?' Gladstone was asked by one old lady. 'God Almighty bless your eyes and limbs and every bit of you.' Women, though without the vote, had to be canvassed because of their influence over the men. 'The enthusiasm of the Red wives and widows was boundless', writes Gladstone. 'The women generally take a lively interest in politics.' The first moral dilemma he encountered in his political career came when he was instructed by his agents (in the Eatanswill style) to kiss the women. He solved it by deciding that he appeared in a public capacity, that kissing was not only 'conceded but expected', and he did it 'not apparently either to the displeasure or the detriment of the parties concerned'. The difference between the personal canvassing of Newark and the oratory of Midlothian is a measure of the change that came over politics during Gladstone's life.

Political issues played little part in the election. Gladstone estimated that 1,100 of the 1,500 voters 'had properly speaking no knowledge or notion of politics'. Slavery was the issue on which he was most frequently questioned. He seems to have made a favourable impression on his constituents (due possibly as much to his good looks as to his politics), and at the election (12–13 December 1832) he came top of the poll. He held the seat throughout the period covered by this volume.

Gladstone's patron, Henry, 4th Duke of Newcastle, was on the extreme right wing of the Conservative party, one of the 'diehards' who had rejected the Duke of Wellington's advice and had voted against the third reading of the Reform Bill. Gladstone was charmed with his visit to Clumber, Newcastle's residence in Sherwood Forest, and by his conversations with the Duke (3). They agreed that the world was in a sad state. 'We seem to be approaching a period in which one expects events so awful that the tongue fears to utter them', he said to Newcastle. (A similar remark could well have been made by Gladstone's opponents at the end of his career.) He placed his hopes of averting revolution on what he termed in his autobiography 'the religious mission of the Conservative party'. Liberalism he believed to be essentially irreligious. His wish had been to enter the Church and he hoped to achieve in a lay capacity in Parliament something of what he might have done had he been allowed to take orders.

He was greatly troubled in his conscience at having to travel to Newark on a Sunday, and it was some comfort to be able to express his feelings in verse (4). (Throughout his life when deeply moved he relieved his emotions by writing verse which rarely rises above the pedestrian level of this example.) The young Gladstone would have been an acceptable visitor in the drawing room of Mrs. Proudie. His early religious views were Evangelical and strongly influenced by those of his eldest sister Anne (who was also his godmother). When Peel became Prime Minister in 1834, Gladstone rejoiced to learn that his leader had promised to have no political dinners on Sundays and as far as possible to avoid Sunday Cabinet meetings (20). He noted anything he could discover about the religious ideas or practice of the Conservative leaders (22), and was delighted when Wordsworth asked to be allowed to join him in family prayers (31).

When Peel formed his first ministry in December 1834 he offered the young Gladstone the choice of a seat at the Treasury or Admiralty Boards, recommending the Treasury. 'He gave as the reason', Gladstone writes, 'that I should be there in confidential communication with him, and that my relation to him would there afford me much general insight into the concerns of government' (13). After a month at the Treasury, Peel invited him to become under-secretary of state for the colonies and spokesman of the Colonial Office in the House of Commons. This was great promotion for a young man of only twenty-five who had been but two years in the House, and the strongest mark of Peel's confidence. 'I give you my word', he told Gladstone, 'that I do not know six offices in the State which are at this moment of greater importance' (15). The ministry lasted only five months. It gave Gladstone his first experience of the practical work of government and raised him to the front bench of the Conservative party.

Peel and Aberdeen (his chief at the Colonial Office) were Gladstone's mentors in politics. By January 1836 he was sufficiently close to Peel to be invited to spend a few days at Drayton Manor, Peel's house in Staffordshire, together with the Duke of Wellington and other Conservative leaders (26). In October he stayed with Aberdeen at Haddo (33). The short-lived Conservative ministry had united the party behind Peel's principles of support for moderate reform and opposition to radicalism. The adhesion of Lord Stanley, Sir James Graham, and Lord Ripon, who had left the Whigs on the question of the appropriation of the revenues of the Irish Church, strengthened the Conservatives. From 1837 the Whig ministry was in decline.

Gladstone was one of the inner circle whom Peel consulted on policy and parliamentary tactics (43, 44, 46, 68). He seems at this time to have been considered as the Conservative spokesman on colonial affairs (53). These years also gave him his first insight into the problems of Ireland (52, 55, 57). Religion, however, remained his main tie with politics, and his book *The State in its relations with the Church* (1838) laid down the principle that the State was bound to support an established church and no other. As Gladstone later recognised, this ideal was by 1838 completely impracticable. The publication of the book did not forward his political career. Peel had no sympathy with the ecclesiasticism which Gladstone assigned as the role of the Conservative party.

In May 1839 the Whig ministry resigned, only to resume office after the farce of the Bedchamber crisis (62, 63). It was, however, clear that they could not continue much longer. They were a spent force, clinging to office only through the favour of the Crown. Gladstone was now admitted to the shadow Cabinet and it was borne upon him that he would receive high office in the next Conservative ministry (80). There is a vivid description of the decisive division in the House of Commons in which the Whigs were defeated (81). At the general election of 1841 Gladstone was again returned head of the poll for Newark with another Conservative as his colleague (Lord John Manners, who in 1898 as Duke of Rutland was one of the pall bearers at Gladstone's funeral). He also canvassed on behalf of his brother-in-law Sir Stephen Glynne in Flintshire (89, 90). The general election gave the Conservatives a majority, and after being defeated on an amendment to the Address the Whig ministry resigned.

Gladstone tells us in his autobiography that he wished for the office of Chief Secretary for Ireland. His contemporary memorandum shows that he also expected to be in the Cabinet (98). He had been one of the leading members of the party whom Peel had consulted on the amendment to the Address (91), treated on the same level as Stanley, Graham, and Goulburn, who were to be the chief figures of Peel's Cabinet. Because of his opposition to the Chinese war and his dislike of the opium traffic, he had consulted his father as to whether he could conscientiously enter the Cabinet and had resolved to explain his difficulties to Peel (93, 94). Much to his disappointment, he was offered the vice-presidency of the Board of Trade without a seat in the Cabinet (95). It was an office for which he felt himself to be totally unqualified, and he speculated as to how he could have offended Peel.

Gladstone was slow to realise that Peel had given him one of the key offices in the ministry. Trade and finance were to be the important subjects in the politics of the next few years, and with the President of the Board of Trade in the Lords Gladstone held a rank in the House of Commons above his official stature. Peel did well to steer him away from the politics of ecclesiasticism. Had he gone to Ireland, he would probably have ruined his political career in the attempt to make policy conform to his religious principles. As he admits himself, there was a touch of fanaticism about his religion at this period which confirms the wisdom of his father and Peel in steering him on to secular matters. What Gladstone wanted was a hard spell at practical business and a rest from theorising. He buckled down to his work, and though he never mentions it he soon became the effective head of the department.

Peel was the first to recognise Gladstone's abilities as a financier and administrator. Perhaps the similarity of their social backgrounds disposed the master to sympathise with his pupil: both came from families which had prospered in business and only recently joined the ranks of the gentry. Certainly Peel must have thought highly of Gladstone to put up with his naivety and gaucherie. He had hardly been in office six months when he submitted his resignation because of his disagreement with the details of the sliding scale under the new corn law (102–104). This was not a matter of principle, though it rose from Gladstone's belief that the government was proposing a greater degree of protection than was necessary. He did not understand the real point at issue. The Duke of Buckingham and Chandos had resigned from the Cabinet because he thought the corn law did not give sufficient protection to the landed class: if Gladstone were to resign because he thought too much protection was proposed, Peel's position would be difficult indeed. He told Gladstone that his resignation would endanger the ministry—a consequence which had never occurred to Gladstone and which he could hardly credit when he related the episode in his autobiography fifty years later. Asked by Peel why he had not stated his objections when the matter was discussed with Ripon and Graham, Gladstone naively replied: 'I had remained silent, not conceiving myself a party whose consent was to be regarded as of necessity or authority' (104). He had taken care, he told his wife, 'not to *look* assent', but felt it was not for him to give an opinion unless specifically asked.

He saw that Peel was 'annoyed and displeased' with him, and that night (5 February 1842) 'sick at heart' he told the whole story to his wife—perhaps the first of the many political secrets which he revealed to her. His memorandum concludes: 'May my sense of weakness lead me unto Thee, o fountain of all strength.'

The end of the story appears in the documents printed in volume i (appendix 5). The next day he withdrew his resignation. Peel in return gave him his first lesson in the art of politics:

There are probably few persons who are not very much in the same position in which you are who would not (if their single voice could determine the question) modify the plan which I propose for the settlement of the corn question.

They consider, however, that alteration of the law is necessary, that the proposed alteration is an improvement, and they look to that point which must always be looked at by the members of a government, the prospect of carrying the measure they propose.

'The great art of government', Peel once said, 'was to work by such instruments as the world supplies, controuling and overruling their humours' (164). It was in the House of Commons and at the Board of Trade that Gladstone's education really began.

On 13 May 1843, as part of the changes following the death of Lord FitzGerald, Peel offered Gladstone the presidency of the Board of Trade and a seat in the Cabinet. Here was an advancement which most young men (Gladstone was only thirty-three) would have accepted with delight. One can hardly imagine Disraeli, who had been panting for office ever since the Conservatives came in, hesitating at such an offer. But Gladstone was troubled. He drew up a memorandum for an interview with Peel (126), stating his doubts about the government's policy on the opium trade, the factory bill, the ecclesiastical courts bill, and above all on the proposal to suppress two Welsh bishoprics. He began a long letter to Peel (128), but after consulting his friends Hope and Manning decided that he could in conscience join the Cabinet (127). It is curious to reflect that the advice of two men, both of whom were shortly to enter the Roman Catholic Church, on a point concerning the estabishment of the Church of England, might have deflected Gladstone's political career.

On 15 May 1843 Gladstone took his seat in the Cabinet. (His Cabinet 'life'—from his first meeting to his last—was to extend over fifty years, a record only surpassed by that of the 3rd Marquess of Lansdowne.) To the historian, the reports of Cabinet discussions will probably be the most valuable documents in the book. The subjects most frequently discussed were Ireland, India (the forward policy of the Governor-General, Lord Ellenborough, was strongly disliked in London but could not be disavowed), factory legislation and the education of factory children. Foreign affairs—except certain matters concerning foreign trade—are not noticed by Gladstone as having come before the Cabinet. One wonders if Peel, Aberdeen, and Wellington formed a small committee for the business of foreign policy? The Bank Charter Act, one of the principal measures of Peel's ministry, receives only two brief mentions in Gladstone's notes (150): 'In Cabinet on Tuesday Sir R. Peel opened the Bank question'; 'In

Thursday's Cabinet the Bank question was discussed as to its general principles'.

Consideration of commercial policy seems to have taken place largely outside the Cabinet, and the decisions were made by an ad hoc group consisting of Peel, Graham, Ripon (until his transfer to the India Board in May 1843), and Gladstone. Gladstone and Peel were moving fast in the direction of free trade, and Gladstone's speeches had aroused the suspicions of the Protectionists. Peel as party leader had to be more discreet, but his views were known to his colleagues. In December 1843 he 'expressed *obiter* a strong opinion that the next change in the Corn Laws would be to total repeal' (147). When the decision was taken, Gladstone had left the Cabinet.

In February 1844 Peel proposed to increase and make permanent the government grant to Maynooth, the Roman Catholic college in Ireland for the education of priests. The proposal was contrary to the principles Gladstone had laid down in *The State in its relations with the Church*. He wrote a long memorandum against the proposal (151), which drew arguments from practical inconveniences as well as from principles. He stated his objections to the Cabinet on 12 February but found no support. 'The rest went with the proposition, on which I fear that Peel's mind is set' (151). 'Depend upon it', said Peel a week later, 'the attack upon the Church of Ireland *can only be staved off by liberal concession*' (152).

Peel was loth to lose one of his ablest colleagues for what seemed a love of consistency and a punctilio of conscience. He had regarded the publication of Gladstone's book as 'political suicide', and now it seemed that his fears had come true. On 2 March he said to Gladstone: 'What are the words you have used which you consider to pledge you? no one would remember them' (155). This of course was quite the wrong approach to induce Gladstone to change his mind. Stanley on 4 March (158) suggested that when a statesman was reduced to a choice between two alternatives, both of which he disliked, he must take the least unpalatable to avoid the worse. Such was Gladstone's position. Gladstone replied:

Even if it be so yet how different is your position from mine—you have made proof of your fidelity—and have already arrested by a decisive and welltimed act the course of spoliation—you are like an old general that can in the view of the world well afford to refuse to fight a duel: I am one whose courage never has been tried—I have no position, no rank or stake of property in the country—the public may very fairly regard me as a mere adventurer, if I should part company with character—and I have never had the opportunity of demonstrating that: I came into Parliament while my party was in opposition, came with it into place, and have quietly remained there with it—it is not therefore that I should be suspected, but I should be fairly and reasonably suspected—the solemnly recorded, systematically explained pledges I have given would cover me with disgrace—nay my disgrace would even impart itself to the Government of which I acted as a member and instead of strengthening I should weaken it.

Gladstone was always sensitive to the demands of conscience in public life.

The decision on Maynooth was postponed to the following year. By 1844 Peel was beginning to feel the strain of office. He complained to Gladstone of 'a sense of fatigue on the brain . . . a physical sensation' (175). 'He then spoke of the immense multiplication of details in public business and the enormous tax imposed upon available time and strength by the work of attendance in the House of Commons.' He was losing touch with his followers in the House, and in March 1844, after a defeat on the Factory Bill, 'spoke bitterly of the treatment of the government by the party' (160). In June the ministry was defeated on an amendment to its proposals for changes in the sugar duties, and Peel, supported by Graham and Stanley, put it to the Cabinet that they should resign (167). 'It is evident', wrote Gladstone, 'that Peel's mind and the others leaning the same way have been influenced not principally by the difficulties of this individual question, but by disgust with the immense, uncheered, unrelieved labour of their position and with the fact that their party never seems to show energy except when it differs from the leaders.' Long before the repeal of the Corn Laws split the Conservatives Peel had become disillusioned with his followers, and perhaps he was not sorry to break with them.

The Cabinet resumed its discussions on Maynooth in November 1844 (171, 172). Gladstone informed his colleagues that 'considerations of personal honour' and the need to make his conduct as a politician square with his theory as a theologian would oblige him to resign. In reply to Stanley, he said that he did not consider himself bound to oppose the grant as a private Member. His resignation speech puzzled the House of Commons. 'Parties do not understand', he reports Hope having said to him, 'whether I repent of my book—or if not why I have left it—or why meaning to support the bill I disturbed the public mind by quitting office' (174). The ultra-Protestants thought of him as a possible leader (Sir Robert Inglis, M.P. for Oxford University, even as the next Prime Minister if the government should be defeated), but Gladstone said that 'no religious ground of opposition could be maintained in practice'. The last document printed in this volume (176) is a defence of his apparent inconsistency in resigning from the Cabinet and supporting their measure.

When Gladstone took office in 1841 his experience of government amounted to no more than a few months as a junior minister: in May 1844 Stanley told him, 'You are as certain to be Prime Minister as any man can be if you live'. (No one in 1844 would have imagined that Disraeli would become Prime Minister before Gladstone.) Such was the measure of his progress during these years. One of his remarkable characteristics was his ability to learn and to profit from experience. At the Board of Trade he shed his ecclesiasticism without losing his religion and became a practical statesman without ceasing to be a thinker and a scholar. Such was Peel's contribution to his development, and he would be proud to be known to posterity as Peel's greatest disciple.

The sources of these memoranda are as follows:

1. ADD.MS 44819. This is a quarto note-book containing reports of conversations and discussions, 1832–1843. On f. 2 it bears the title, in Gladstone's hand: 'Notes or memoranda of politics and men'.
2. ADD.MSS 44777 and 44778. A series of 125 political and autobiographical memoranda from 1832 to 1861.
3. Memoranda of a personal or autobiographical nature taken from ADD.MSS 44722–44776.

One peculiarity of Gladstone's system of dating should be explained. In some documents the date appears, e.g. in the form 'June 5/10. 1843'. This indicates that the transaction narrated took place on June 5, and the account of it was written on June 10.

The Commissioners wish to express their thanks to Sir William Erskine Gladstone, Bt., for permission to print these writings of his

great-grandfather. We wish to thank Professor M. R. D. Foot, Miss
V. J. Langton, M.V.O., Registrar of the Royal Archives, Mrs. F. W.
Parish, and Miss Mary Sullivan for their kindness and assistance. The
publication by Professor Foot of the first two volumes of *The Gladstone
Diaries* has enabled some additions and corrections to be made to the
dating of these documents.

# AUTOBIOGRAPHICAL MEMORANDA

## 1: ADD.MS 44777, ff. 1–12

Private. A visit to Newark[1]

September–October 1832

On Thursday, September 20, while I was reading quietly at Torquay, Mr. Handley and Mr. Serjeant Wilde suddenly commenced a canvass at Newark; both I am informed made haste to be first in the field, and the winner in the race, I forget which, is stated to have succeeded only by ten minutes.

An express, sent to Leamington for me, found my brother John there and brought him instead. I was aroused while in bed at Torquay on *Sunday* morning, and off in the space of an hour—the Exeter Mail brought me to Town, and the Highflyer (York coach) landed me in Newark at midnight on Monday, September 24. It was painful to sacrifice the Sunday to the purpose of travelling: but under the circumstances it appeared to be called for. I very soon afterwards however found reason to apprehend, that among the many dangers and temptations attaching to anything like political life, not the least would probably be, the preserving inviolate that rest which God's mercy has ordained for his self-wearying and self-afflicting creatures.

I had heard much of the extreme violence of Serjeant Wilde's party in Newark and on seeing a man waiting, evidently on the look-out for me, at the hotel gateway, I was in no way inclined to suppose him a friend but thought it at least equally probable that he might be a spy stationed there for any purpose whether of violence or of fraud. He addressed and shook me cordially by the hand, proving to be the landlord of *our* hotel, Mr. Lawton, and assuring me that the three days' canvass which had already been completed were of the most successful character. Ten yards from the coach I met my brother Robertson who had arrived the night before, and Mr. George Hutton, an active friend, with him. John had just gone to bed, and was speedily roused, when we had reached the Clinton Arms. By and bye were brought in some dozen friends from one of the clubs, who gave three cheers, and all shook hands very heartily, saying, 'What, are you *the* Mr. Gladstone, the candidate?' It appears that rumours had been circulated of my not intending to appear.

I retired to bed late, and with notice that I must be up to breakfast

---

[1] WEG began writing this on 17 October.

at 8 a.m. and address the people before commencing the day's canvass. Thoughts however of the scenes which lay before me, exciting enough to a young person startled at the transition from the soberest prospects and the most retired habits, to the noise, the animation, and the aims, of a contested election, passed in hurried succession through my mind, and kept me from sleep for three or four hours, notwithstanding the fatigue of my journey. I had been pleased with the accounts I had heard, and the zealous spirit, manifestations of which I had already witnessed. I was perplexing myself with endeavouring to collect my thoughts and arrange some topics for an address to the people from the windows in the morning—but the spirits were too much inflamed, and their influence too strong upon the restless mind, to admit of my doing so to any good purpose. However, much time, as I lay in bed, was fruitlessly spent in endeavouring to prepare the framework and as much more as I could of a speech—but when the time came I found my labour lost—that I was more perplexed by struggling to make an effort of memory, than I should have been by committing myself to the excitement of the moment, and being borne along with and by it.

I found, or thought I found, that such a speech as is required on these occasions might be easily put together with premeditation of five perhaps noisy minutes, or delivered with none: not because I have any pretensions to superior fluency, for I am confident that I am most deficient in this respect: but because, in the first place, you address an audience prepared to applaud very indiscriminately and universally, and thereby affording both time and encouragement of a highly stimulating kind; in the second, there is no long and intricate chain of argument to be introduced, requiring circumspection at each transition from step to step: in the third, the subjects are generally of a popular character and such as must have been resolved so often in the mind as to have become familiar, when in consequence observations on their more broad and palpable points lie near the surface of thought, are easily seized and readily enunciated. In the debating societies at Eton and Oxford, I used to undergo most uncomfortable sensations both previous to speaking and sometimes during it from apprehension of losing the cue—but at Newark I felt for the most part perfectly at my ease, and was content to be borne along upon the tide of feelings suggested by the circumstances of the occasion. The absence of adversaries too no doubt contributes to this feeling of security.

My rest was short: and as I awoke I saw on my bed the pink gauzy hue refracted from our flags waving at the windows, which recalled the full sense of the novelty of my situation. Events ordinary to others were strange to me, while, being new and numerous, they fixed themselves in the imagination, as all such clusters do, and made me believe myself in a kind of fairy world, notwithstanding the well-known forms of my brothers (now more than ever kind, and more than ever welcome) and the businesslike aspects of agents and supporters.

Next morning at breakfast-time I was introduced to Mr. Godfrey, Mr. Tallents, and many other friends. About nine, the band played under the windows, and Mr. Godfrey introduced me to an assemblage of perhaps 400 or 500 persons, to whom I addressed some sentences which just sufficed for their purpose, and no more.

I was immediately launched upon our canvass: well supplied with directions to shake hands with every body, whether they would or no: and to kiss all the daughters. This latter was for me rather a novel occupation, and certainly I had doubts of its desireableness: for I trust it was far from my desire to do anything that would either encourage a forward or embarrass and distress a retiring person. I found, however, before proceeding far, that I was considered to appear in a sort of public capacity, and therefore I availed myself of the privilege whose exercise was not only conceded but expected, and that as I thought not apparently either to the displeasure or the detriment of the parties concerned. I fancy however that my performances were considered to be rather sparing: for a report was circulated, that I was a married man. On this and other subjects I am sure it is a sacred and solemn duty to be cautious, and to manifest a marked coolness of manner where there is anything like forwardness exhibited in a female: yet it is here perhaps an easier matter than would be conceived, to observe delicacy without fastidiousness. As regarded shaking hands, my rule was, always to be *ready* to do it, and distinctly to seek it whenever *anything* favourable was said—to do it without this is I think overdoing it, for it is a sort of *sign* accompanying and signifying thanks, and so it would convey a suspicion of insincerity: except where it is done by way of saying goodbye, when I used to offer it invariably. I think a hand was refused me about eight times, out of perhaps 4,000: principally by *women*: indeed I *remember* only one man, Franks the tailor: to whom I offered it twice separately and distinctly: as a matter of principle: not indeed at much sacrifice to myself: for, though full enough of pride on most occasions I am, perhaps through cowardice, singularly indifferent and insensible to what many people consider insults. Of course the hand was almost invariably accepted with readiness: often enthusiastically volunteered. On the whole my canvass went to prove, that, even in Newark, there was little ill feeling entertained in cold blood against us; especially when compared with the mass of general goodhumour: for, God be thanked, it is not characteristic of the English people to let the sun go down upon their wrath. And my impression certainly is, that the more intercourse there is between different classes in this country, the better they will understand, and the better they will love one another: for though there are everywhere a few spirits of determined malice, ignorance and consequent prepossessions constitute the *bulk* of the feelings which are wrought upon by the designing: and it was to me a sensation of lively delight to find, how often these impressions were wholly dispelled, how generally they were materially mitigated, by free and candid communication. Of the poor I would say in particular, that their objects are in general most moderate and reasonable, while they are liable to deception as to means and instruments for attaining them: and they often will tolerate no difference of opinion here, not however from pride *in most cases*, but rather perhaps from dependence on those who have been their teachers, or from a sense of weakness, and consequent suspicion of intention to deceive them on the part of a candidate whom they are taught to dislike more or less for his opinions and instinctively dread as a 'scholar' at least enough of one to confound their artlessness.

But these same persons, when they are congregated in large masses, assume a much more faulty and much more formidable character. In the first place they become inspired with a consciousness of overbearing physical strength, which naturally and strongly tends to indispose the human mind towards candid and patient hearing of unpalatable opinions. In the second they are necessitated by the circumstances in a great measure to go along with the speaker, and few can exercise sufficient quickness to discern *on the instant* a flaw in the reasoning, when they are already favourably inclined to the conclusion. Moral perverseness ever turns to its own account intellectual impediments and imperfections. In consequence, they must receive impressions rapidly and as it were with an impetus, or not at all—of course they incline to the former and act upon it for the minds of few can bear protracted suspense, and when they have come expecting confirmation to their inclinations, can endure the disappointment of going away without it. Next, the sights and sounds are of an exciting character: and stirring up all the passions of the soul from its very base, they disturb and precipitate by illegitimate impulses the calm action of the understanding. Deeper than all these reasons lies one which it is less easy to unfold, the magic power of sympathy, whereby opinion, unexamined and unweighed opinion, is propagated, if there be a sufficient predisposition, through the minds of men with the velocity and effect of an electric shock—and it seems as if, analogous in some sort to the laws which govern the motion of matter, it gained momentum by that velocity, and again, like the rolling snowball,[1] as if it brought the force which it has acquired by adoption in the mind of one, carrying that mind thence-forward along with it, to bear upon the next and so strengthen its claim to repeated acceptance and renewed augmentation. I am aware that these illustrations may be indistinct, and are certainly imperfect: inasmuch as the gathering of opinion is not, it may be said, progressive from one to other in turn, but simultaneous upon all—yet we may perhaps acknowledge a virtual validity when we recollect, that it is in fact the nascent *sense* of the admittance of an opinion in the minds of others, which mixes itself with and hurries and confounds the reasoning process in our own[2]—and this action taking place in the mind of almost every individual throughout a large assembly, each feels himself borne along by the power of the *belief* that the sentiments enunciated are acceptable to those around him, and he is then likewise acted upon by apprehension lest he seems to lag and lest he be anticipated by others in adoption of those sentiments, in fine lest he fail of keeping pace with the march of feeling, and we all know that there is nothing more painful to our mind, than when warmed by the contact as it were of many minds, and bound up with them in one sympathetic action, to make that strong revulsive effort, under a thousand unfavourable circumstances, by which alone it can be restored to individual *separate* and impartial action. Again, the sense of shame is almost lost by subdivision *ad infinitum*: the notion of *responsibility* cannot be kept

---

[1] 'Und jedem einzelnen Wächst das gemüth im grossen strom der menge' [sic]. [Die] Piccolom[ini] [Schiller], 2. 6. [WEG] Translated by S. T. Coleridge: 'And every individual's spirit waxes, In the great stream of multitudes.'

[2] And the φαινόμενον ['appearance'] is for all practical purposes equivalent to the ὄν ['reality']. [WEG] The reference is to Plato: cf. *Republic*, x, 596–7.

alive and present, among so many: the indolence too of the human mind here finds a favourable opportunity to substitute the reasoning of the speaker for the labour of an investigation of its own:[1] the heated spirits overleap all bounds: and here are surely enumerated a most formidable number of more or less efficacious powers, each and all independent of reasoning, and each and all therefore tending to absorb its action, and adopt conclusions by inclination and not by judgment. And now be it remembered, that in a multitude, where the action of the judgment is hindered, nay where the judgment is as it were smothered by these hot and turbid excitements, the active strength of inclination is augmented in a fearful proportion: for it not only exists unfettered and mettlesome under the sense of security in each, but it is multiplied by the propagation of sympathy pervading all, and uniting them (who has forgotten the fable of the bundle of rods?) in a common bond for the attainment of a common object. The principle of combination here applied to the faculty of *will*, not to that of *judgment*. The judgment derives no additional clearness or coolness from such a hurried consciousness that others are likewise *judging* the same thing: but the will derives immense additional impetuosity from this rapid assurance, for rapidity is not alien but akin to the natural action of the simple will. Delay is always the suggestion of another faculty.

It was impossible, as we walked through some of the poorer districts, chiefly inhabited by Serjeant Wilde's supporters, to avoid being struck by the reflection that many persons who by their own firesides were peaceable, nay friendly, might nevertheless soon figure in a Blue mob as brickbat and bludgeonists.

The women generally take a lively interest in politics, though with more of local than of public feeling. On the Tuesday as we were marching round the town at the close of the canvass, we saw a struggle between a husband and wife at a window, he bearing a *blue* ribband and *she* a red. 'Brute force' prevailed, but perhaps the worsted party was consoled by the cheers of our procession. On the next occasion that we came by, the husband had retreated altogether, and the red

---

[1] A clear proof of the superior *moveableness* of men when congregated—that comparatively poor writing would often appear impassioned and effective speaking.

In reading speeches, the imagination always helps us, by picturing the scene with more or less vigour in which they are supposed to have been delivered. [WEG]

ribband floated in triumph. It seemed pretty generally admitted that the women were with us, particularly those in better circumstances— but where they were hostile, they had less scruple in displaying their feelings, than the men. 'We don't want no slave-drivers'—'We're slaves enough here, we don't want there to be no others'—thus happily *splicing* their feelings of private and public wrong, their pique and their patriotism. One saucy body shut her door and rowed us from an upper window—another tore my card and flung the pieces at my feet—a third on hearing 'Well Ma'am, shall we have a vote here?'—'I wouldn't give you one to save your life if I'd a hundred.' This was the worst by far. Of the men, only two or three were at all insolent. On the other hand, the enthusiasm of the Red wives and widows was boundless. 'One? aye he shall give you two' (i.e. a plumper) 'if I've anything to say to him.' 'God bless you Sir, God Almighty bless you—I hope we shall win this time'—'Ah Sir, I can't do nothing for you—but my poor dear man, he *was* a good Red always, he sarv'd the Duke for fifty years'—a widow would say. One poor old creature seized my hand and said, with a warmth and earnestness not easily to be forgotten—'Are *you* Mr. —— I forget his name, the Red?' 'Yes I am, my good woman'— 'God Almighty bless your eyes and limbs and every bit of you' ejaculated the old dame and kissed my hand before I could tell what she was about. These people, and *their* ancestors, have received kindness from the Duke and his—and they know, they feel, they return it. Among our opponents we met with many verbal and some substantial goodwishes: 'Well Sir, I've promised both mine: I can't give you one, but I wish you luck!' Once I got *pity*—'Well Sir, I do assure you I'm sorry for you from the bottom of my heart, for you're among bad ones'—'Why didn't you come *Blue*' said one woman, 'and then we'd all have voted for you?' My great strength, it is gratifying to say, lay in the palpable and acknowledged worth of Messrs. Godfrey, Tallents, and others my supporters—and it was pleasing among much interested feeling, to trace sometimes the workings of simple gratitude. Harsh acts were *once or twice* charged against Mr. Tallents, but, if he were present [he] effectually refuted them. 'How can you ask for a vote', said a woman to me, 'when Mr. Tallents turned us out of our house at a moment's warning?' 'That is *untrue*', said Mr. Tallents, looking fixedly at her. She said not a word! Mr. Tallents afterwards explained to me the circumstances.

In the course of personal applications to so large a number of persons, applications of a kind too, so remarkably calculated to draw out the lurking sentiments of selfishness, any man ought to find materials for augmenting in no small degree his knowledge of human nature, that acquirement so valuable to all men, to politicians, I would rather say to πολιτικοί[1] most of all. My own impressions may be briefly recorded as follows.

Of this constituency which may be called 1500, I should say 1100 had properly speaking no knowledge or notion of *politics*. And of the remainder, while some will have had the means of becoming informed on one question, some on another, very few indeed[2] could be set down as having competent means for forming opinions on the *general range* of questions now likely to come into discussion. What knowledge is conveyed, commonly comes either from a *single* newspaper, or from a party leader recommended by a local lodge. Many persons ask questions, which are proved to have been merely put into their mouths, by the fact that when they receive an answer not decisive but such as ought to suggest *another* supplementary question, they do not perceive this, but have no more to say, whether satisfied or not: so that in fact they do not ask, but merely transmit them. Some Radicals, who had a string of interrogatories prepared, made no comments on any of the answers, when not categorical, and did not appear at all able to pursue the subject beyond the ready-made phrase: and those who *did* talk largely were by no means the most sensible—as at least it appeared to me. On the other hand there were cases of decided acuteness and intelligence, formed chiefly upon meditative habits, and not accompanied with great volubility of speech.

Nor is it highly desirable, as I conceive, that the people should learn to take an interest in general politics, except in as far as such is necessary to secure their good government. In the abstract, I think politics a misfortune rather than otherwise to persons whose time and attention should be fully occupied by the demands of their spiritual being and their physical necessities. Not that it is desirable to exclude the feelings of patriotism, associated perhaps with some great question of the day—

---

[1] This word has more implications than any one word in English can express. No doubt that is why WEG used it. The meaning uppermost in his mind was probably that of responsible citizens, conscious of their place and of their duties in the government and maintenance of the πόλις or State.

[2] One tenth? [WEG]

they are lofty and ennobling—but the detailed and habitual entertainment of questions which pain and perplex the wisest heads of men *wholly* devoted to them, and which without that general devotion, and the mental *habits* which it will have formed, it is impossible to comprehend.

We number (October 22) about 930 promises.[1] Of this total, I think we may set down to the account of the respective feelings of gratitude, custom, and interest, not less than 750—and these three motives will be mixed in proportions which it is very difficult to determine in the minds perhaps of the entire number. Those actuated wholly, though indirectly, by interested feelings, with perfect general indifference, will probably be few—those influenced by the other feelings in an unmixed state, more numerous. But in about 500 these motives are blended. About 100 may be persons who have distinct opinions on politics, formed not without inquiry. And the 80 besides may have distinct opinions on particular questions—mainly slavery, and moral feelings requiring to be satisfied. This is perhaps the most religious and in this view respectable class of any.

The tendency of the newspaper system will be I fear to pervert the minds of the people by introducing excitement into them: thrusting out domestic habits to make room for political opinions: irritating the entire mental constitution and feeding it on a stimulating diet at the expense of its permanent tranquillity and happiness.

But I know not how a man can move among such a mass of human beings in such a condition—can see how much alloy mingles with the motives of the better voters—how much sordid interest and unmitigated baseness exists among the worse—can contemplate the results of political struggles in embittering feelings and debasing conduct and in its relation to man's highest interests—and can still regard popular representation as something *per se* desirable, instead of maintaining that it ought to be fixed, for the sake of the people themselves, at the minimum point consistent with infusing such a portion of popular feeling into the legislature as shall effectually prevent oppression. And certainly my canvass has brought home to my mind a deeper and more sincere hatred of the Reform Bill, on this account, than I had before entertained.

Selfishness, as well as zeal, appeared in every form: from the lowest,

---

[1] November 26. 955. [WEG]

who hinted intelligibly that 'something to drink' would be found useful in disposing them to promise: to those who *after* speaking the word endeavoured to advance a plea of equity in the proper quarter for some additional accommodation or indulgence in their tenantship. Indeed, *this* is to be expected—nor is it necessarily blameable. One wife spoke out very fairly. 'Will your husband give us a vote?' 'He is a poor man, and has a family, and must look to himself and them.' 'And how will it be, Ma'am?' 'Why I'll tell you how it is—if M*e*ster Tallents there'll let him have a house with a pigstye, he'll vote for you—and if he won't, why then he won't. That's how it is.' Again. 'Yes, Sir, you'll have one here.' Then 'M*e*ster Caparn (to the agent) do you think young so and so could be appointed a flagman, for he's been out of work etc. etc.'

I am in no degree ashamed of votes given through attachment to a landlord, and I think that they will bear the most rigorous scrutiny in cases of this kind, where circumstances are such as to preclude the voter's forming an opinion for himself—it is then, I think every way natural and proper, that he should look to those from whom he has received kindness and in whom he therefore reposes confidence—and act upon their recommendation. It is the πίστις ἠθικὴ[1] in one of its most spotless applications—and it is a motive which has place, *mutatis mutandis*, in the scheme of religion itself. Next to those who have sound understanding, are those who have an unperverted instinct. When I speak of forming an opinion, I do not use the phrase in the newspaper sense, which is, *adopting* one: but I mean the capability of conducting the intellectual process, which first thoroughly examines and then deliberately decides.

Of course in canvassing the town thoroughly, we came from time [to time] upon scenes of poverty and affliction. The former I am happy to say were rare[2]—and I was astonished as much as pleased by the cleanliness and comfort generally prevailing. But there was something awfully admonitory in those occasions, when amidst the forced exhilara-

---

[1] 'Ethical proof', persuasion or conviction through trust. The hearer accepts the speaker's proposition, not because the speaker has demonstrated its truth, but because the hearer trusts him. WEG no doubt had in mind Aristotle's *The Art of Rhetoric*, especially 1.2: κυριωτάτην ἔχει πίστιν τὸ ἦθος: 'moral character . . . constitutes the most effective means of proof' (translation by J. H. Freese, Loeb edition).

[2] Say twenty? [WEG]

tion of these active excitements, I stumbled upon dwellings visited by the hand of Providence. A poor woman once heartily wished me success—and the hand which she spontaneously extended was withdrawn from the body of her infant child who lay extended upon her knee, the lips already livid and the eyes already glazed, the spirit in the very jaws of death. Again, a nice little girl in black stood by a closed cottage door—'my dear', said some one, 'is your father in?—we've come to ask for his vote.' 'My father died last week Sir' replied the little one. At these moments the mind recoils from the essential earthliness of its occupation, and at least, God knows, for the moment, they bring home to the inmost heart a living consciousness of the unreal character of all the immediate objects of pursuit, and teach him who covets a blessing, to look through them and beyond them for his motive and his reward.

I give the *questions* on which communication with me was sought, and as nearly as I can the *numbers* who interrogated me.

| | |
|---|---|
| Slavery | About sixty |
| Ballot | eight |
| Abolition of taxes on knowledge | three |
| Universal suffrage | two |
| Abolition of impressment | two |
| Currency | two |
| Tithe commutation | one |
| Corn Laws | one |

This is I think a faithful account. Of our opponents on the ground of slavery, there are two—Mr. Williams[1] and Mr. Simpson (grocer), whose hostility I much regret: there may be many others—but certainly as regards Gillson, Andrews ( if all I hear of him be true) and one or two more, I care not a jot. It was impossible to help respecting the moderate and conscientious views of the Methodists, as far as I came in contact with them. They acted as men who had a duty to fulfil, and knew it, and who discharged it.

When the offer concerning Newark was first made to me, I had no reason to suppose ejectment would in any case be resorted to. It was gratifying to infer the same from all Mr. Tallents said—and to hear it spontaneously confirmed from the Duke's lips at Clumber.

---

[1] Mr. Williams is I believe uncertain. [WEG]

Yet I should have been ashamed to accept his proffered kindness, with the *possibility* (in the first instance I mean) of contemplated resort to ejectment, had I been prepared to admit the justice of the charges made against the Duke of Newcastle on this head—although they have now been so often reiterated, and the facts so much misstated in compliance with the democratical feeling of the day, that it is generally considered nothing but the most extreme tyrannical feeling can advance a word in their justification.

The question is, whether a man may in any case eject his tenant—not whether he may in every case—and here was perhaps the *flaw* in the argument of the Duke of Newcastle's expression, 'May I not do what I will with my own?' A man may not always do, morally, that which he may do legally. The Duke's argument *seemed* to be, that the legal right in itself conferred the moral right: such it would be drawn out into syllogism. And yet this is a proposition from which I believe his own kindly nature would recoil much more strongly, than those of many who revile him.

I believe I am correct in alleging, that the Duke's houses in the town are let at low rents: the relation therefore between him and those who hold them is one not strictly of equivalents rendered in marketable commodities, but one of favour on his part, of gratitude on theirs.

Nor will it be deemed by moderate men of any party audacious to advance, that the desirable state of things would be that in which the tenants, not by compulsion, not even by stipulation, but acting from spontaneous gratitude, should make a freewill offering of their political influence to support the consequence of their benefactor, and of the order to which he belonged.

If the houses were not let at low rents, then where would be the disadvantage incurred by leaving them?

In the pretended harshness and suddenness of ejectment? No: they were yearly tenants: six months were therefore legally necessary—and almost all of them could have moved with as perfect facility in six days—I had almost said six hours?

Then why all this soreness? Because the people feel they have in general lost a better landlord than they have got in his place.

But as to anything like personal distress, I do not believe it was caused in a single case—and this is enough.

What the Duke did, was simply, to simply withdraw a favour. Has he not a right to confer favours on whom he pleases? Regarding certain principles as essential to the happiness of this country, may he not use his influence for their promotion, provided it be without either corruption or cruelty? which in this case it was.

But the withdrawal of a benefit is *pro tanto* equivalent to the infliction of detriment. It *may* be so in its results upon the party from whom it is withdrawn—but we must contemplate the act also in relation to the party active as well as the party passive, and particularly in relation to the laws of social justice—and here we see that there is a broad and essential difference.

But would you even, says a moderate antagonist, withdraw a favour on account of a political difference? Is a man to force his conscience? Or is he to be a loser for not forcing it?

To this I reply: that in none but a case of very extreme necessity would I withdraw a favour from a thoroughly conscientious man—and then, the moving cause would be, not the desire to take it from him, but the urgency of circumstances compelling me to give it to another.

But I do not think that these were in general cases of that description: that most of those ejected were competent to form an opinion: or that they voted from mere regard to the call of conscience. I see how mixed and how equivocal in such matters are ordinary men—and I think that in some cases pique, in others (e.g. Gillson) pride and a fractious temper, in others that vague but strong appetite for change with the expectation of preponderating advantage by it—in short the persuasion that the material augmentation of their physical comforts was involved in their voting for Wilde—would constitute the moving spring of opposition to the Duke. In the cases where it might not be so, no sufficiently positive hardship was inflicted, to render it binding to alter the general rule.

I have here I think assumed no extreme principle, and yet the Duke's conduct appears to receive satisfactory vindication. Nor has it been necessary to defend him either by alleging (however true) the very indifferent motives which actuate too many of his accusers nor the circumstances that the same thing is done by Whigs as well as Tories.

As an example of a Radical opinion, I would mention the case of a respectable man named Perkin, who was my fellow passenger on October 24 from Wakefield to Sheffield, and who professed that political creed. He had workmen under him (where be it observed the equivalent is *strictly* rendered, and no six months' notice required). A Tory with us named —— said, 'Mr. Perkin then would discharge any workman who did not vote as he pleased.' 'Is that true, Mr. Perkin?' said I. 'Why certainly it is, Sir' he replied, 'I always let them know what is expected of them.'

So much for the ejectments: of which I would say that while no rightminded man would lightly resort to them, yet they may receive a full vindication under urgent circumstances, just as the declaration of martial law by a government. A great deal of the old, substantial English character remains yet, one may hope and think, both in the country and in towns like Newark, which have known the aristocracy not as enemies but as fostering friends. A large proportion of the population appear attached to the Duke and his family: and it is alleged among the Reds of property, that the cottages of their party are as a general rule inhabited by a more tidy and orderly class than those of the Blues.

We met with many cases of genuine kindliness and warmth, some of which I shall ever remember. It chose different modes of manifestation —from a tankard of ale awaiting our arrival in due form and state, to a glistening eye of anxiety for our success.

The English population, where strong feelings of subordination and attachment to the wealthier classes, differs so much from that same population in districts where the connection is none at all or one of *mere* profit and loss, that it is difficult to believe they belong to the same nation.

The Dissenters are strong in Newark, but not actuated by the spirit of Dissent. The division of political parties by no means corresponds with that of religious. This happy circumstance may be owing partly to the circumstance that as there are no Church Rates in the town, illdisposed men have no handle to use for the creation of hostile feeling. Probably the majority of the Dissenters are opposed to me. The Baptist Minister however is favourable, and the greater part of the Wesleyans, I think: including certainly some of our most active supporters: as Eggleston— Boler—and Butler.

It is melancholy to see how men take advantage of a canvass or an election to get drunk, even upon their own resources, and independently to those facilities which are in too many instances afforded by the candidates. Mr. Tallents, though an experienced electioneer, is not a *hardened* one, and, under the influence of sound principle, is resolved to prevent the opening of public houses so far as we are concerned.

Of course incidents queer enough often arise out of these unhappy circumstances.

One afternoon as I was walking rapidly home, and alone, a man called out in the dialect of the place, much akin to broad Lancashire, 'Gladstone! *are* say, Gladstone! come here.' 'Well, friend', said I, and waited till he worked his way up to me. 'Are say, Gladstone my man', said he, 'are say, do you think now, do you think—as you're a proper man to go to Parliament?' This was rather a difficult question— and I referred him to Mr. Betts, a chemist, and a highly respectable supporter of ours, as a more competent and impartial witness—'Ask Mr. Betts, who is good enough to support me.' 'Mester Betts! aye, Mester Betts—he is a proper man—if Mester Betts would put up, are'd give him one.' Mr. Betts interceded for me in vain.

I found the use of firm, not to say strong, language, answer very well in one or two cases. A man named Harrison, a sawyer, when solicited, said he knew that if I went to Parliament I should go to vote against the people, and perpetuate the miseries of the country—as being the protegé of the Duke of Newcastle. After disclaiming such intention, I asked him what he thought was the cause of our miseries—and whether he did not think there was a good deal of difficulty about the inquiry. 'No, he did not see what difficulty there was—he had read a good deal' (looking up from his saw) 'within the last seven years, and he knew that the cause of all our miseries was, the change in the currency.' I congratulated him on the facility with which he seemed to solve so intricate a problem—he did not seem at all aware that there was any kind of difficulty in the question, and maintained his opinion as pertinaciously as if he had been capable of understanding or even of defending it. He was however surprised when I told him that on this question the Duke and he were *agreed*, at least as to the desirableness of a paper currency.

'There would be blood in the country soon', he said. I said, I feared there might: but not unless men forgot the command of the Bible, that every soul should be subject unto the higher powers. 'There's a great part of the Bible I don't set no more by than any other book', said he, 'I don't hold with it.' I was disgusted at this avowal of the unfortunate man—for the tendency to infidelity is surely very rare among our peasantry. I said, perhaps illnaturedly, 'I am exceedingly grieved to hear that, on your own account—and if that be the case, I think I had better have no more to say to you.' Here I was surprised by his calling out, as I walked sharply away, 'Mind, I don't say as I shan't vote for you: I think as I shall.'

I was thoroughly disgusted with one man named Kingdon, who on receiving my request, launched forth into a regular speech of sounding phrases accompanied with ample gesticulation behind his little counter, the quintessence of conceit painted on his brow, and that of affectation embodied in his tone. The evils of society were his theme. Seeing it was a hopeless case, I expressed agreement with him that it would be difficult to overestimate those evils, and walked off. It was a cooperative shop.

Another man said to me—as if he believed electioneering was the only object of life—'You've kept away from us.' 'I have been in Devonshire.' 'What, have you been canvassing there?'

Talking with Gillson about slavery, I lost my temper completely, and very foolishly: not, however, when he talked on the West Indies question, but when he took upon him coolly to assert, that the slavery of the Christian era was entirely different in kind from that of our days. The old dog kept his temper, and said to me, 'I'll tell you what, Mr. Gladstone, I hope you'll keep your temper a little better than that when you're on the hustings, for if you don't I'm afraid you'll get into a great scrape.' Sour was his charity.

It was gratifying to see the degree of comfort which existed in a great majority of the houses—indeed in almost all. They were generally well supplied with Bibles and religious books. There were often pictures representing the Crucifixion and other interesting scenes in the life of our blessed Lord. And there was even an *approach* to images, in a bas-relief crucifix, cast at a foundry in Newark. Little evil is to be apprehended from this: and on the whole I was very glad to see these pictures, as indicating a fondness for and sense of religion.

Once I saw a small print framed, with 'Golfo di Napoli' written beneath it, and recognised a scene I had so lately quitted. A Naples gig was represented trotting along with three persons, one a padre.

I have now recorded many of the little incidents that struck me during my first electioneering expedition.

It was impossible not to foresee, that political life must in its infinite varieties include an immense mass both of temptations and advantages. It is full of 'the knowledge of good and evil'. And therefore it is evident that it may be most beneficial to a mind of right will and adequate power—it must be pernicious to one wicked or weak—how strongly then ought to the contemplation of its weighty stake and fearful risk, to bring home to my mind the consciousness of helpless incapacity, that I may throw myself on Him from whom all light and strength proceed.

18

I am as yet, amid many perturbations and shocks upon my mind, firmly persuaded, that there lies involved among the possibilities of that life which I have adopted, a purpose of the very highest utility— namely the endeavour to keep the principles of society right so far as they are right, in opposition to the deadliest foes of man—and yet more especially to oppose to the increasing wordliness of modern political principles, an increased, or rather a restored, unwordliness: to maintain the principle of Church and State is *one* part of political duty—but a higher branch, nay I think the only hopeful instrument to effect the former in defiance of the extraordinary energies now brought into action against it—is, to *unfold and apply* it—to show how high are the moral responsibilities of governments, as well as to teach the religious duty of submission on the part of subjects—to show particularly, how infinitely extended are the means of good which Providence has put into the hands of the rulers of this nation, and under God and with his blessing, to struggle for their effectual use.

This high province lies far beyond and above not only the narrowness of party feeling, but the entire scope of all material interests, how good or desirable soever. Restrict the sphere of politics to earth, and it becomes a secondary science. Its perfection and its end lie within the sphere of beggarly elements. But admit the duty of governors to maintain the laws of Him by whom they govern—admit that the intellectual and the spiritual nature of man are legitimate objects of their solicitude, and then if you can estimate the moral dignity of him who is taught of God and enabled to apply the most powerful engines and the most extended resources of which our wordly condition admits, to the promotion of the benevolent and lofty purposes of God in the redemption of mankind.

Much, in the present day, is to be done on the *defensive*, but more yet, in my mind, the Christian ought ever to desire to do, on the offensive. If the preservation of the spirit of our institutions is desirable, it is only because they contain a root of essential good, and are improveable, by their nature, to the very uttermost. The object of the faithful politician should be, not to restore a state of spiritual deadness ill compensated by the mere absence of toil and anxiety, but to wrench from the hands of the foe the existing elements of power, and to seek not only to check his impetus, but communicate one in a contrary direction.

No doubt this is a difficult object. The prospect is distant: it may be visionary. Notwithstanding, is it worth the trial?

So long as my conscience replies in the affirmative, and hope lives and burns within, I need not repent that I have cast my humble lot into the lap—that I have committed myself, my hopes, my desires, my destinies, to the rude and tumultuous ocean.

If that conscience should ever reverse my judgment, a principle not another but the same will dictate my retirement from a world which short of the objects I have described, can scarcely be hoped to prove other than a world of preponderating dangers. I desire not to set out with ambition for my stimulus, or fame for my polestar and reward: when my mind becomes conscious of being ruled by such a guide and such an object, it will be a duty to remember that in the Almighty alone our efforts can be legitimate or truly blessed, and to seek a humbler and a safer sphere, desiring rather to have little and that little his, than much, if it be apart from Him. For the poverty of the former condition is wealth: and the abundance of the latter is but too true and too substantial destitution.

Thus I have recorded, without art, perhaps without discretion, the sincere feelings of my *soul*, and the *especially guiding* principles of my present conduct. I feel the difficulty of choice, in a case where my own interests and affections are intimately involved. I have always deeply felt, as though the great power and weight of the subject bore heavily upon the mind, impeded the free action of its powers, and perturbed all its conclusions. Therefore it is, that with a view to that noble study, the study of the heart, having thought it would be powerfully promoted by the acquisition of a more *distant* and yet scarcely less faithful and minute view of itself. I have sought to minister food for some future contemplation, and the material, as I would hope, of advantage, by recording one state of mind as a subject of study for another. And I have striven to express a secret of my heart, as it shall be developed in that great day, when the secrets of *all* hearts shall be made known. I have scarce ever been able to get farther into the subject than I have here, though hastily, endeavoured to go: but it broods over my mind in frequent and long visitations—and the knowledge of this circumstance may perchance serve to render the difficulties and the doubts which recur from time to time, the ministers of a more effectual discipline of humiliation. *November 27. 1832*

## 2: ADD.MS 44777, ff. 13-14

The thoughts recorded in the latter part of the foregoing paper, gathered successively into numberless combinations, and appended to numberless hypothetical pictures of the probably approaching life, swept over my mind during my stay at Newark, through no small portion of the hours alloted to repose, with a vehemence which effectually repelled the present sensation of fatigue. I felt as if the life of strong and overbearing *nervous* impulses had been substituted for that of regular and habitual sensation, and could ill believe that even a change of situation would ever control the impetuosity of the excitement which seemed to have carried me beyond the bounds of reality.

Such was the effect of circumstances not more than ordinarily stirring—but flowing in upon a mind thoroughly quiescent.

No reflection ever comes home more powerfully to my thoughts, than that of wonder at the fact, as I believe it to be, in how many of its faculties, when energising singly and not combined, the human mind appears to find an independent, entire, and adequate subsistence.

And not only is this exemplified in the devotion of different classes to their different occupations: but in the *various* tendencies of the same individual mind, at one time finding a full and satisfying existence in the exercise of the religious affections: at another, in the laborious investigation of high general truths: at another in the soft or thrilling delights of the imagination, whether in its joyous or its mournful mood: at another, reaping full satiety from energetic entrance into political discussion, and sharp collision with the passions and the prejudices of men. In each *for the moment* there seems to be involved, that which the ethereal activity of mind desiderates: a full occupation—a stimulus to action on the one hand, and a province of action on the other: the first, able to rouse the whole mind: the second, to employ it. The sense of languor and the sense of destitution are then alike excluded.

But these phenomena tend to show, how much yet remains to be done, before the organisation of the mind, as a single whole, composed of distinct but conspiring and converging faculties, can be said to be completed. It explains to us, it realises the conviction of the extreme facility with which a slight additional impulse communicated in one direction, may enable it, where forces were already so nearly balanced, to overbear every other—and brings home to us something of the process by which many of the great men of the world have become naturalised in a single pursuit. For we have only to suppose the extension of that full satisfaction which any one of many can communicate, over a considerable space of time, and the problem is solved. But the results can then only be effectually blessed, and stamped with the character of permanence, when the supreme rule of the entire being is placed in the hands of the ruling Christian principle of love—there is no other, which can harmonise and blend together the whole man—there is no other, which can realise to him the benefits of the lessons to be learned in this world, or secure to him the precious vision of peace which is opened in the other. Independently of this, one faculty wars with another—and one world wars with another. Immense then indeed is the work which Christianity has to effect, before in a powerful mind all strongholds can be cast down and brought into captivity to the obedience of Christ.

Of course these subjects were present to me, as I went from Newark, like one emerging into another element, to Clumber. Hilarity had been on my countenance during my canvass and visit—hilarity, which repulsively contrasted with the deep gloom that tinges my views of politics and apprehensions for the destiny of the world at large. Sometimes the thought shot across my mind, that it was both dishonest and directly degrading to indulge a boyish mirth, resting upon a foundation of not only anxious but painful presentiment. I thought the time was perhaps not very far distant, when politics should have poisoned nature to my eyes—for even now, the first idea suggested by joyous or tranquil scenery is that of contrast, by gloomy landscapes and lowering skies that of comparison, with the appalling symptoms of the moral world. Yet as this mirth was not forced but spontaneous, I would not check its effusion, while youth still fed the flame of hope, and gleams of bright prospects shone at intervals—I thought it was cruel to cut off its term, which might in the decrees of God, and restrict perhaps the means of utility by generating a premature moroseness—and dwelling on some of our happier signs, I remembered the singularly benevolent saying of our Saviour, that the children of the bridechamber could not weep so long as the bridegroom was with them. May that Bridegroom be with us and His Church!

The road to Clumber lay through Sherwood Forest, and the fine artless baronial park of Lord Manvers. In the Forest, every oak was a model of ancient grandeur: each one might have served Robin Hood for his Trysting Tree. I never saw so fine a collection—and it was impossible to check the influx of the ideas suggested by this thoroughly aristocratical domain. Those ancient oaks, which had themselves seen the lapse of many generations, and so were monuments at once of permanence and of change, yet stretched forth their proud branches, some bare and blackened to the blast, others still green and pregnant with the promise of future years. Feelingly did they suggest by their strong similitude, the image of that ancient aristocracy, than which the world never saw one more powerful or more pure. Wealth—authority —ease—the reciprocated influence of example—the proud and exclusive spirit generated by the sense of high birth and till of late resistless power—and the dissolute temperament of mind resulting from their mutual intercourse and association in London—have wrought indeed upon their character as a body with an influence as penetrating as pernicious. Why? Because they were men. It does not follow, that they are to be rooted out. Birth, wealth, station, are as well as talent and virtue among the natural elements of power, and we must not war with nature's laws. Moreover there are many among them still strong not only by bulk of property and influence, but by lofty understanding or unblemished character. To this latter class I am persuaded belongs the nobleman, whom I was then on my road to visit.

His family seemed to be strictly domestic—but as there was no other stranger present than myself and I of course little accustomed to the society of persons so highly born, the conversation was neither domestic, nor *social*, as contradistinguished from domestic: for my presence was able to restrict the one: but not to supply the other. It therefore partook in my eyes of the character of formality— notwithstanding the extreme kindliness and freedom of the Duke's manner. The Ladies Clinton entered the room together—left it together: sat together: rose together to play: performed in duets: one worked sampler—the other worked embroidery. The twin brothers are amazingly like in figure, and generally in countenance: and I scarcely ever saw them farther apart than the Siamese youths. The younger *branches* went off to bed in relays at stated hours. I feared I was in their way— and this of course made one's blood run cold. But never did I receive or could I detect, the smallest degree of what is properly called *hauteur* in their manner. They have not seen much of the world—may the knowledge of it come in its own power, and a purity not its own.

*November 28. 1832*

## 3: ADD.MS 44777, ff. 15–22

*Memoranda.* October 9 and 10. 1832.

October 9.

*Gladstone*: It must have been a very exciting period in London, your Grace, when Lord Lyndhurst's motion was carried.

*Duke of Newcastle*: Yes it was. I never gave the Duke of Wellington credit for great talent till then.

*G.* How did it appear, my Lord?

*D. of N.* In the extraordinary clearness and self possession with which he explained his views at the meetings which were held. Nothing seemed to disturb his coolness in the least degree. I can give you an instance—at one of those meetings, the Duke of Buccleuch, I think, fell into a fit or fainted, when the Duke of Wellington was delivering his opinions—he sat down for a moment, not moving towards him, and said, 'What, what? what's the matter? get somebody—give him some assistance'— by this time they were carrying him out and the Duke resumed his sentence.

*G.* No doubt he was governed by highly honourable motives in his conduct during those trying times.

*D. of N.* Ah! but if he had but adhered to what he set out with—

*G.* Your Grace thinks then that he was misled?

*D. of N.* Not that he was *misled*, for he was the leader.

*G.* That he was mistaken in his views, then.

*D. of N.* Certainly I do.

*G.* So it appears to me: but still one need not doubt that he acted upon high motives.

*D. of N.* He was worshipped by everybody among the Conservatives at that time, and lauded to the skies—whereas Peel had little said in praise of him for its consistency, and it seemed as if their deserts were the other way.

*G.* Peel's speech appeared to me not to assume sufficiently high ground— he pursued the right course, but apparently rather from a desire to maintain the uniformity of his own conduct than any other reason, and he seemed to be perpetually thinking and to have exclusively thought of what other people would say of him instead of driving right at the question. Now the Duke's conduct appeared to be of a very chivalrous character even if he was mistaken in the line he proposed to adopt.

*D. of N.* What you mentioned with regard to Peel's declaration was just what struck me. And so it happened that the Duke got all the credit: but I am persuaded it was not from romantic feeling in excess that he acted—he is a calculating man—he thought he could bring us through by those means—but, to turn round upon all his own previous declarations! Why, if he were *convinced* it was all very well—but he was not, and did not profess to be. He is a calculating man, and indeed Mr. Gladstone (I speak this privately) he is not a *safe* man. He would upon occasion yield anything from motives of expediency.

*G.* I suppose your Grace thinks, that he would resist manfully up to a certain point, and then make the best terms he could, and that he would deal with all questions alike upon this principle, and that there is nothing which he would not give up under sufficiently urgent circumstances.

*D. of N.* I do think so. Peel saw his former error, and avoided the repetition of it: but it is a great misfortune in the Duke of Wellington, to whom however I look up very much, and from whom in his private capacity I have received far more kindness than he either got or had reason to expect from me. But this kind of conduct will not save the country. In my mind this is what a man should do—he should make up his mind, with as much moderation as he chooses, to the objects on behalf of which he deems it essential to make a stand: and when he has done this, no extremities should induce him to swerve. People must get into their right positions, and act upon their own principles, and rigidly adhere to them—nothing else will do for us, and I believe the time is not far distant when this will be the case.

When I heard Stanley in the House of Commons, I thought him the very cleverest man I had ever seen—he seemed quicker than thought itself—he is too good for them: I wish he were with us.

I am a very bad patron—for what small pieces of Church preferment I have, and they are very small, I give only to those who will reside, being always willing to assist them in building. I made two rules about Church preferment, of which this was one, and the other, never to give away a living for election purposes.

October 10. (At breakfast).
*D. of N.* What we want is the union of character with talent in our public men—when that takes place, I do not know what can resist it, nor

do I see what else can carry us through. Mr. Pitt perhaps had more of it than any other.

*G*. Mr. Perceval, my Lord.

*D. of N*. Yes, Mr. Perceval was a striking instance: he was an excellent man, but his reign was short—and his wisdom has not descended to his son.

*G*. No my Lord certainly not, as regards one occasion up to that time I think Mr. Spencer Perceval had displayed a good deal of judgment and in very difficult circumstances.

*D. of N*. Yes, he had. His religious turn has now overset what abilities he had—I fancy he is quite mad.

*G*. Certainly it was not the act of a sane man to speak as he did—all the useful sentiment of his speech might have been conveyed in a very different manner—but he seems to have selected that style and language which was most estranged from what men are accustomed to. And yet I think, that the madness of Mr. S. Perceval would well bear comparison with the wisdom of the present age.

*D. of N*. Yes it would: that is lamentably superficial indeed. You may see by Mr. Perceval's eye the turn of his mind—it has something very wild in it.

*G*. Yes my Lord. I met him at dinner lately at Sir R. Inglis's, and he spoke then like an able and a sensible man—but his eye is wild.

(Alone.)

*D. of N*. I was saying, in reference to Mr. Perceval's conduct, how unwise it was to talk so much about religion to persons who you know beforehand will only despise it. Let a man keep God in his mind as much as he pleases—and let him remember his God in every action of his life—but it does not therefore follow that he is to be always talking about him. If we have a King whom we show every day, we soon learn to think very little of him, but by his remaining a little secluded the reverence due to his office is preserved, even though his person may have little claim to it.

*G*. It seems to me, my Lord, that there is a kind of indelicacy in the religious feelings of the present day.

*D. of N*. Yes, I think that is the point. When Lincoln started for the county, they wanted me to retract some things I had said against them in a little pamphlet I put out the other day—but I would not do it. I have a relation near whom I appointed to a living, having first promised his father that I would do it if he were inclined to be diligent and conscientious, but desired him not to let the son know of it—however, when the father, who had been the incumbent, died, I presented the son supposing him to be attached to what are termed the orthodox principles of the Church of England. (Mr. F. C. ) By and bye I saw in a paper language purporting to have been used by him at a Bible Society meeting, when I could not believe my own eyes—and I wrote to him to say that language was there attributed to him such that I believed there must be some mistake in the name. He wrote back to me that there was no mistake—that he had used the language—that he used such language for the benefit of the Church of England itself—that by these means the people were drawn back from the meetinghouse to the Church —for that they would go to church when the clergyman preached evangelically but they would not when he did not preach evangelically —and indeed I think no wonder, for doubtless the people will be ready enough to come to church if you will preach for them there the doctrines which they hear in the meetinghouse.

G. I think my Lord it is a great misfortune that preaching should be connected with any term which bears a party signification of any kind. It is quite true that the Church of England should be at unity within herself, for she has foes enough.

D. of N. I wrote back to Mr. C. to say I knew I could not help it now, but I was very sorry I had put him there—he does all sorts of strange things: he congregates numbers of labourers in his kitchen; I am persuaded it can do them no good, it must degrade religion and make it common in their eyes—last time I came by there I saw the church illuminated at ten o'clock at night.

G. I do indeed think it is most desirable to keep as nearly as possible to the ancient and authorised methods of proceeding.

D. of N. I do not know what they teach them, I am sure. I believe many of them teach them Calvinistic doctrines, and I am confident though I am not a great theologian, that if they do it must be very bad for them.

G. As far as my experience goes I should say that the tendency of the Low Churchmen in this country is not, except in a few cases, to preach Calvinistic doctrine. Some indeed there are, very few, who go as far as Calvin—but on the other hand I do not think there are in other quarters those who fall short of what the Church of England teaches.

D. of N. For my part, so far as I can judge, I can conceive nothing more entirely and perfectly in accordance with the spirit of Christianity, than the principles of the Church of England universally.

*D. of N.* You think not?

*G.* I do indeed, my Lord: I think that there are few who enter into the whole *spirit* of the Church of England and take up the proper ground as regards her. But this I think, that we are now rapidly obliterating the distinctions of party within her pale—and it is high time.

*D. of N.* Doubtless, speaking of her clergy, there may be cases of abuse among them, but speaking of them as a body, I do not think the world has their equal, so far as my experience of them goes.

*G.* And they will have need of all their strength, and more. But I do rejoice to see that we are forgetting our internal quarrels—and that a large class of men are springing up, whose names cannot in any way be connected with party, but who stand on the broad ground of the Church of England. A magazine which your Grace may have seen has lately been established in London on this principle, called the *British Magazine*, and I believe it succeeds very well. It is edited by Mr. Rose.

*D. of N.* I know Mr. Rose—a very excellent man, and a beautiful writer: an exceedingly fit man to be a bishop. I think our bench of bishops is but ill served now.

*G.* Indeed, my Lord? I should have thought many of them were exceedingly valuable men: and some have mainly contributed to make extreme opinions approximate within the Church. I might name the Bishop of Lincoln as one: the Bishop of London as another.

*D. of N.* Do you think that of Blomfield? He sometimes appears to be but a worldlyminded fellow.

*G.* I say nothing of his politics, your Grace—but in them I should at least hope he had been mistaken not corrupt—I speak of him as a bishop.

*D. of N.* And have you heard him spoken of as a good man? I had not been aware of it.

*G.* I have my Lord and when living in his diocese of Chester—he got much abuse from all sides: for he would neither tolerate bad practice on one side, nor extreme opinion on the other: and I have heard many testimonies to his merits.

*D. of. N.* Indeed. I myself know nothing of him as a divine, except that I took my children to be confirmed by him in town, and then I heard from him I think the very best discourse I ever heard—it was admirable.

*G.* He is an admirable preacher—and his example in this respect, so totally unconnected with a party tone must be of infinite value. For my part I cannot help thinking our state within the Church rapidly improving—for some thirty years ago I imagine there was much on both sides that could not be approved.

*D. of N.* Certainly not.

*G.* On the one hand indifference to religion and to the performance of duty, on the other extremes in opinion and want of candour in controversy. As regards Bishop Blomfield I had a very pleasing testimony from Mr. Spencer of whom no doubt your Grace has heard.

*D. of N.* Ha, have you seen him?

*G.* Yes your Grace—he was the Bishop's Chaplain, and he told me that he had by nature a most violent temper—but he said by discipline and the exercise of Christian principle he had subdued it. Mr. Spencer is now a Roman Catholic priest, and so an unexceptionable evidence.

*D. of N.* I confess I have a great notion of the horrors of enthusiasm—I think it is one of the worst things that can be—because it gives so much occasion of speaking against religion, which every one should maintain.

*G.* Your Grace, I think we must expect to see enthusiasm in the present day, for when after a long period of prosperity and ease the minds of men are disturbed in their slothful habits by some great convulsion, as was the case at [the] French Revolution, it naturally happens that opinion starts forth in every variety of form which it can possibly assume.

*D. of N.* Yes it is so. There can be no doubt that if we desert God, as a nation, He will desert us.

*G.* Yes, my Lord. And we seem to be approaching a period, in which one expects events so awful, that the tongue fears to utter them, particularly as they are yet uncertain and we can only discern them in their rudiments.

*D. of N.* Yes, it is necessary to be very cautious in expressing such opinions, when we entertain them as I do.

*G.* I think your Grace has adverted to these prospects in your pamphlet.

*D. of N.* Yes—I ran a great risk of being called a fool for doing it, but those persons considered me a fool before, so it makes no matter.

*G.* It is no disgrace to be called a fool by persons who look upon such views as folly.

*D. of N.* Still I do not give the reins to my fancy—of fancy indeed I have little or none—but I do not give way to a disposition to speculate on these points.

*G.* And yet it is impossible wholly to exclude them, nor does it appear that the study of unfulfilled prophecy, though difficult and peculiarly dangerous, can be altogether rejected. The only point is to give to these considerations strictly practical results.

*D. of N.* Yes, I see nothing for it but that a man must struggle to the last—one is always undergoing defeat, it is true: and there are powers in operation against us too strong for man to cope with: but still we must go on in our course, and who knows what may be the issue? At least we trust that, by God's mercy, all will ultimately turn out for the best.

*G.* Yes my Lord of that there can be no doubt, although the intermediate region is full of darkness and danger—one seems to see in all quarters the silent working of opposite forces, sweeping off to one side or the other, and thinning the neutral ground which lay between, so that all seems to be in preparation for the grand struggle between the principles of good and evil. The way to this seems to be in preparation by the approaching downfall of the Papacy.

*D. of N.* Yes, Popery is attempting to rally its forces, but I think only preparatory to its utter defeat and extinction.

*G.* The present government of the Pope is so bad (October 9) and yet the difficulty of finding a better to succeed so great; and in the same way the Roman Catholic religion is so bad, and yet the prospect after its overthrow so very dreary, that one scarcely knows whether to wish for its continuance or destruction.

*D. of N.* O, I think there can be little doubt that one ought to wish for its destruction.

*G.* The question as to what is to succeed is full of interest beyond calculation.

*D. of N.* I fear that infidelity must succeed—for a time at least.

*G.* It appears to me that those are right who think there are great evils in the state of society—but wrong when they think them so superficial that they can be cured by legislation.

*D. of N.* Yes, all depends upon individuals, and the matter cannot be reached by Act of Parliament.

*G.* In all classes of life from the highest to the lowest we see bad symptoms—among the former indifference to the duties and responsibilities of their station—among the latter a feverish desire to push onwards, and to affect an appearance beyond the scale of the means they have to support it.

*D. of N.* That ambitious affectation is I think nearly at an end owing to our present declining state. But I am of opinion that we shall have to pass through the fire, and be purged thereby.

Errors excepted. WEG.
October 10. 1832.
1832. October 10.[1] 'I don't know—I wish to be charitable—I form my own opinion and think so and so—but I don't say that the man who thinks otherwise is wrong.'

October 9.[1]
*Duke of Newcastle.* I need hardly trouble you with saying so, but I do not mean to touch any of them: they will vote as they please without any notice being taken by me. Indeed I was reminded by a good thing either in the *Standard* or the *Morning Post* the other day, from a correspondent at Newark, of a fact which I had totally forgotten—namely that the notices for which I was most abused were served on Lord Middleton's account and not on my own. I had quite forgotten it, but so it is.

October 10.[1]
Our Premiers in succession for a long time past have been doing nothing but struggling and making contrivances to keep themselves in office. And in the meantime the interests of the country have not been regarded.

I liked several of Lord Grey's speeches made about the time he came into office.

Some things there may be still to correct—but let a man only look how much has been done within the last thirty years and he will then see that we ought to set about it moderately.

## 4: ADD.MS 44722, ff. 57–58

A Sunday Journey. September 1832.

> Full boldly each contending horse
> The even causeway trod:
> Small hindrance was there to his course—
> It was the day of God.

---

[1] These were apparently added afterwards. They appear separately on f. 15.

Echoed aloud the circling wheel,
 The hoofs rang loud and clear:
Those breezes, Autumn-leaves that steal,
 Lay gently on mine ear:

And Devon's purest sky above,
 Around, her brightest green—
But yet in vain that heaven of love,
 In vain that liquid sheen:

In vain that peace was poured around,
 As on a glassy sea,
For I was as a jarring sound
 In Nature's harmony.

I marred the motion of her still
 And tranquillising breath,
A rebel to her kindly will
 And love for all beneath

Its week day labours to beguile
 God bade the ear to rest,
And hark,[1] to learn a little while
 The[2] music of the blest;

If haply we might catch from far
 Faint echoings of the strain
That hymns on high the Bethlehem Star,
 The Slayer, and the Slain.

The Lord He bade each seventh morn
 The downward eye to raise,
From tasks of pain and looks of scorn,
 And thitherward to gaze.

Where it espies, though far the land,
 Soft hues, and forms of grace,
The angel-forms, in Heav'n that stand
 Before the Saviour's face.

---

[1] 'Hearken for' written in ink above the line.
[2] 'To' written in pencil above the line.

But I displayed to human eye
    The signs of earthly care,
And forced them from their feast on high
    Back hither to repair.

But I was charged with meaner thought:
    With common din and rude
Strong discord to their peace I brought,
    And idle marvel strew'd.

One tranquil fielded horse, and still
    Another and another,
Each o'er his gate, looked out his fill
    Upon his straining brother.

I heard, I heard the village chime,
    Some distant and some near
But all in concert told the time,
    The Mystic Word to hear.

And rosy damsel, little maid,
    Grave sire and matron sage,
And youths robust, and forms decayed
    Of calmly waning age—

Each journeying in his proper pace,
    Our speedy coursers past:
(May each one run the Christian's race,
    And win his prize at last!)

Peace sat upon each open brow,
    In every gleaming eye
Peace nestled, and diffused below
    The joy that dwells on high:

But me: within my heaving breast
    A restless craving lay:
It swelled and would not be repressed
    Even on that holy day:

> If it were sin, thou knowest, Lord!
> But thankfully I know
> At least, it brought its own reward,
> Its pain and proper woe.
>
> *October 1832*[1]

## 5: ADD.MS 44819, f. 3

July 26. 1833.

The day before yesterday, Mr. H. D., a West Indian proprietor, said to me that he thought Government would not hold by their engagement to the West Indian proprietors to make the twelve years' apprenticeship an essential part of their plan for emancipation. I said with more eagerness perhaps than was consistent with respectful manners to a senior, that the idea of their departure from it could not be entertained for a moment. He quoted a pledge about London police, which he said they had broken: but I answered, their engagement in this case was too close, definite, and personal, to admit of their retracting: it was a part of the express condition of West Indian cooperation, nay more, it was the basis upon which alone the West Indian body determined to give up the idea of formal secession and protestation.

Yesterday I for one had a painful and severe lesson taught me, and I feel that I ought to have retired to rest, if not with an untroubled mind, (for there is no mental perturbation more fearful and oppressive than that which follows the utter frustration of a strong and undoubting *reliance*) yet wiser than I was twelve hours before. In the morning sitting, on going into committee, Mr. Stanley declared he would propose seven and five years' apprenticeships, instead of twelve and seven.

His reason was, an inference from the division of the previous night—158 to 151—on a general resolution of Mr. Buxton's—that Government could not carry the twelve years' apprenticeship clause. We did not know that the battle had been fought. No West Indian had spoken against Buxton—they rested on their arms, expecting that *the* struggle would come afterwards, when people would really know what they were voting about. Stewart intended to speak, but saw that the debate

---

[1] Written at Thornes, the home of his Etonian friend James Milnes Gaskell, 14 October.

was so vague and general, that he thought he had better not waste his labour.

## 6: ADD.MS 44819, f. 3

July 9. 1834.
Introduced to Lord M.[1] He said most of his family had broken with him on account of his political principles: his brother Henry (I think) had not spoken to him for two years.

## 7: ADD.MS 44819, ff. 3–5

July 10. [1834].
Went with G. Sinclair and O'Connell in an open carriage to Coggeshall to examine Mr. Skingley. A good deal of conversation.[2] O'Connell said, amongst many other things, that the heathen were in a state of reprobation, he believed necessarily, while of Protestants etc. he deemed it his duty to hope that they were internally united to the true Church— that absenteeism was the great bane of Ireland—that he could see how every question might be adjusted but that—that taking half the Irish Church property placed us in a state of transition, and was a prelude to taking all—that it would compel us to divide the Church property in England—that it would make the Protestants repealers—that the *resident* Protestant proprietary would be able to preserve their estates after the repeal—that there was no truth in the story that the descendants of the ejected Romanists looked to a recovery of the estates lost by their ancestors—that the rental of Ireland was 12 million of which 5–6 went to permanent absentees—the land 15 million [acres]—of which 9 were cultivated and 3 more might be—that the subletting Act had driven 25–30,000 Protestants out of Sligo in (I think) one year, that, however, being the vent for three or four counties—that Protestantism was on the decline everywhere as well as in Ireland—that resistance to payment of impropriate tithes was at least as great as to clerical: for the

---

[1] Perhaps Lord Melbourne, although he did not have a brother Henry.
[2] I sent to my father a fuller account of O'Connell's conversation on this day. [WEG]

people retained some notion of them as an ecclesiastical imposition and at the same time saw there was no pretence of duty done, also they were in general more severely exacted—till latterly, no cases of severity among the clergy personally—that Littleton had told him much more in the conversation than he ever revealed—that Sir R. Peel prepared his speeches to a very great degree—that he would recommend Hume *in the first place* to learn to finish one sentence before he began the next but one—that Strafford did nothing for Ireland: also some opinions on Christmas, Tennent, Young, Sheil, Colonel Perceval—that Graham regretted his present position and was to have gone to India as Governor General—that he himself made above £7,000 the last year he wore a stuff gown in Ireland—that he often forebore to advise appeals to Lord Brougham as Chancellor from his incompetence, and its being a mere matter of accident which way he decided: that many intellects were fit for comprehending law and fit for nothing else—and *vice versa* —and that the intellect thoroughly legal was of a subordinate description —that his politics became fixed upon hearing the trial of Hardy—he had many connections who had all sided warmly with the Bourbons, and he himself had come over from Douai in January 1793 a violent aristocrat—that the French liberal party were infidel in general, but that the religious liberals headed by Montalembert were greatly increasing in strength—that the Archbishop of Toledo had between £2,000 and £3,000 a year—that Brougham was received ordinarily and of old in the House of Commons with cries of Question! Question! on rising, though he would after a time when he came to his subject reclaim the attention of the House.

O'Connell subsequently spoke *very* highly of Sir C. Wetherell in reference to the vigour and raciness of his intellect: but described him as an invariably circuitous reasoner, *baffling an opponent beyond belief.*

What O'Connell said of Peel's preparing a great many parts of his speeches, gave me the idea, from the manner, that he entertained a *personal* jealousy of him.

## 8: ADD.MS 44819, f. 5

Wednesday, July 15. [1834].
Dined at Sir E. Kerrison's. Mr. Peach told me a curious story: he heard it from the Duke of Wellington. A person was travelling in the

autumn of 1830 over Pennenden Heath in Kent. A public meeting was in progress at the time: and he saw Cobbett addressing the assembled crowd, and heard him distinctly advising them to burn, burn, burn, as the only effectual method of raising wages.

He rode on to the next inn, and took the landlord back with him to the heath to be a witness with him of the proceedings. He came up to London and brought the landlord with him. He obtained an interview with the Duke of Wellington who resolved to pursue so atrocious a person to *extremities*: but in the morning when (if I remember right) he was to have returned to the Duke with this landlord, he (Mr. Peach could not remember which) was found dead in his bed. No suspicion of violence arose.

## 9: ADD.MS 44819, f. 5

July 21. [1834].
Sir H. Willoughby told the Bishop of Exeter and myself, privately, he had heard from Lord Howick the circumstance, somewhat astounding, that the Privy Seal had been just offered to Lord Grey!

## 10: ADD.MS 44819, ff. 5—7

July 29. [1834].
Dined at the Carlton—House dinner. Sir R. Peel, Lord G. Somerset, Baring, Scarlett, etc. Lincoln got up the party. Sir R. Peel was in good spirits and very agreeable—he delivered very unfavourable opinions of Lambert, Ronayne, O'Dwyer—thought much better of O'Connor, King Fergus as he is now called since the Union debate. Ill also of O'Reilly. He thought Walker the cleverest of the Irish set (after O'Connell and Sheil?) as I have heard him before describe Warburton to be among the English—meaning I presume the most farsighted and dangerous. By the bye a meaner authority (an M.P. for Knaresborough) told me yesterday there were but four Radicals in the House of Commons: neither O'Connell, Hume, nor Roebuck were of the number, but Warburton was! This I conceive to be a shrewd opinion, at least inasmuch as it went to penetrate that disguise of apparent moderation which veils Warburton's political conduct: let a man watch him, and

observe his tenacity in following an object, the acuteness of scent with which he perceives from afar anything calculated to advance his purposes: let a man watch him and say, when does he omit to avail himself of ever so small an opportunity to help on the movement? Except in reference to currency and the funds.

I fancy Sir R. Peel was pleased with Lord Ripon's speech this evening. He spoke very kindly to me of my attempt last night, which he thought in good taste. My fate is peculiar; it so often happens to me that men go beyond any degree of kindness which equity would entitle me to expect in the relations of life, and so rarely that they fall short. Thus it is necessary to keep in mind the disposition to forgive, even without the opportunity of calling it into active exercise.

Sir J. Graham *staid away* from the division last night. On Lord Chandos's motion, I came down stairs almost the first, and found him wrapped in his cloak in the Members' Waiting Room. Stanley on that evening was in the House till an hour from the division, and I believe immediately after it.

Sir R. Peel thought the best point about O'Connell was the apparently affectionate relation between him and his sons. It was said Maurice smelt of whisky. Perceval told me, O'Gorman Mahon's father was in prison for (I think) sheepstealing—O'Connell's grandfather a common labourer: I record this, because his conversation the other day conveyed a different impression.

Mr. Daly told me Sir Herbert Taylor who has the ear of the King was disposed to act with Stanley and Graham, who thought it impossible to coalesce upon the late juncture; and that therefore it was no practicable overtures were made.

In the autumn of 1833, Lord Arbuthnott told me that before the introduction of the Reform Bill a meeting of Tories was held at which it was discussed whether the introduction of the Bill should be opposed by division: and that the old Tory party refused to divide against it in that stage.

## 11: ADD.MS 44819, f. 7

August 1. 1834.
Lincoln told me Peel had told him he would have taken the Government on the retirement of Lord Grey had it been offered him independently.

That he would have applied to Stanley but would not have cared much whether he joined or no.

## 12: ADD.MS 44819, f. 7

October 1834.

P. M. Stewart told me that the main cause of the war of *The Times* against Brougham, was the transfer of favour from that print to the *Chronicle*, in which Le Marchant, Brougham's secretary, had lately been writing—as had also Drummond. He had heard A. Baring was concerned in the *Herald*.[1]

In the winter of 1833, Donald Home told me that when the Tories quitted office in 1830, they left some £300,000 of accumulated secret service money: that the Whigs had spent this upon the elections; that £5,000 (I think) had come down to Captain Elliot in Roxburghshire and they knew the mail which brought it.

## 13: ADD.MS 44819, ff. 7–8

December 20. 1834.

Arrived in Town early and had my interview with Sir R. Peel. He received me very kindly: and it was to be expected that under the circumstances his expressions should be warmer than would otherwise have been the case. He assured me that his letter[2] was one of the first he wrote (he arrived I think on the 9th and wrote the 13th Saturday)— that he did so without communication with any one and simply from his own opinion and feelings towards me.

He offered me my choice of the Admiralty and Treasury Boards: recommending, however, the latter: and he gave as the reason that I should be there in confidential communication with him, and that my relation to him would there afford me much general insight into the concerns of government. Lord Granville Somerset told me afterwards he meant me to do some of his work for him: and of course I am glad if he thought he had seen in me any indications of diligence.

---

[1] Stewart visited Fasque where WEG was staying, 18–27 October.
[2] ADD.MS 44275, f. 1.

He added there was another person very anxious to go to the Treasury if I preferred the Admiralty: for I had shewn some surprise or hesitation, I conceive: partly because T. G.[1] had told me I was fixed at the Admiralty already, and partly from having in my mind the remembrance of my brother John—regarding whom, however, I was afterwards satisfied of the propriety of my course while on the other hand the sentiments expressed by Sir R. Peel were quite such as to preclude my taking any other course than that which he recommended. Said he, 'I wish you, however, notwithstanding *his* anxiety to come to the Treasury, for I intend to go upon the principle of putting everybody to that for which I deem them best fitted. I know you will be glad to hear that your friend Lord Lincoln is one of your colleagues, for I know he is a friend of yours.' I felt and expressed my pleasure. People call Lord Lincoln my friend and he acts as such: but it is well for me to remind myself of the difference of rank between us.

More passed upon my introducing the subject of re-election—much would I have given to be able to tell him what I felt on that of dissolution which I understood to be near at hand: not as presuming to compete with him in opinion, but from the burdensome and painfully oppressive feeling on the subject which I could not help entertaining. But I need not say more. He wished me 'Good morning' with great kindness and bid me believe that it would be a pleasure to him to number me among his followers. O God! that I were better worth the having.

*December 26. 1834.*

## 14: ADD.MS 44819, f. 9

January 17. 1835. (Little thinking of the sad, sad rumours which another fortnight produced.)

Dined at Lord Lyndhurst's. He said, 'The malt tax will be an awkward question. Never defend yourself before a popular assemblage, except with and by retorting the attack: the hearers, in the pleasure which the assault gives them, will forget the previous charge.' Sir W. Horne was there: alone (I believe) among a mass of Conservatives. I have before known cases of persons situated in some degree as he is and planted in the middle of a Tory dinner-party: Sir C. Burrell at the Speaker's: Horatio Ross at Sir R. Peel's. I sat by Sir William. He was

---

[1] Probably Thomas Gladstone, WEG's elder brother.

very communicative and free. He said he was £12,000 minus for his public career. His late defeat cost him between 2 and 3,000. He never stipulated for any exemption from any of the duties of a judge. He considered himself vilely used: 'I acquit', he said, 'the Ministry as a body, but one individual, he's a scoundrel and a rascal'—I do not doubt in my own mind that he alluded to Lord Brougham.

Furthermore he acquainted me that there was a great disposition to have got rid of D. W. Harvey by providing a place for him: in one person especially but not I understood exclusively. The one was, Brougham—as he all but told me. Denman and he had to consider the matter: and the result was, that it was deemed out of the question: and the intention of the one individual, which had already begun to act, was intercepted. (N. B. Denman had been his counsel.)

*January 20. 1835.*

## 15: ADD.MS 44819, ff. 9–11

Monday, January 26. [1835].
When the afternoon was well advanced, as I sat in the boardroom at the Treasury, I was summoned to Sir R. Peel. In a few minutes I found him alone: having paid him several visits on matters of public business, I presumed this to be a call of the same description.

He said to me, 'I am about to make a great sacrifice of my own personal feelings and convenience'—I half interrupted him with an expression of regret, having as yet but a blind inkling of the nature of his meaning—'but at the same [time] to give you the strongest mark of my confidence and regard, which I hope will be gratifying to you. I am going to propose to you, Gladstone, nothing less—for you know Wortley has failed in obtaining a seat—than that you should undertake to be the organ of the Colonial Department in the House of Commons, as Under Secretary for the Colonies: and I give you my word that I do not know six offices in the State which are at this moment of greater importance, when you regard the present state of affairs referring to it. You know there perhaps never was such an opening for a young man.' I listened with very mixed feelings: in which gratification of a high order undoubtedly preponderated, for with my sentiments towards him, those which he was moved to utter could not but penetrate deep: but I had also a strong emotion of shame in reflecting inwardly, how much better and abler I had appeared even to him to be, than I really was. Versatile and intricate is the craft of the human soul: and it is one of the curses and consequences of the common vice of hypocrisy in conduct, of which I have far more than a common share, that when you are reaping benefit and praise from having exhibited a fair show in the eyes of men, you *absolutely cannot* cure the evil by disclosure, for all that can be said is then set down to the score of humility and heightens the favourable misapprehension. However, I expressed as well as I could and very ill a deep sense of his kindness, unfeigned I hoped and durable: a great reluctance to give in to the natural bias and instinctive dictate of selflove which teaches us at once to assume our competency for whatever may come within our reach, as well as for much that does not: but I added that I would throw myself upon his judgment and not shrink from any responsibility which he might think proper to lay upon me. He replied that was the right and manly view to take of the case. I expressed my regret at the dissipation of the hope excited in my mind by a paragraph in the newspapers, that they might have Sandon. He said he offered it him, with a statement that he heartily wished he had much higher office to place at his disposal, but he well knew that he (Sandon) would be altogether above estimating it by its nominal rank and would look at its substantial importance. Sandon took three or four days to consider of it, and at length declined as thinking it incompatible with his position at Liverpool, though most friendly in his own sentiments. I expressed great admiration of his course and sentiments there at the election.

He expressed regret at removing me from a place where by frequent communication he would have been enabled to do so much for me: and both selfish motives, and the little experience I had had of his suavity and effectiveness in business, caused me at once and heartily to reciprocate this regret: of course I had hoped much from that source.

He stated that it had been Lord Aberdeen's particular wish that I should be appointed: that Lord Aberdeen said, 'I do not know that I have ever spoken to Mr. Gladstone in my life, but I should much wish to have him, unless you have some great political object to attain by disposing of the office differently.' 'I replied', said Sir R. Peel, 'that no political object could be considered so legitimate or weighty, as giving him a man who would satisfactorily represent his feelings and wishes.'

I said I was not without fear that my connection with the West Indies might create a difficulty: but he said quite the reverse, it would give confidence to the West Indian body, and those who looked to the religious and moral condition of the black population would not be averse to it. Here indeed was a new responsibility brought upon me. Alas! that any creature's hopes of their improvement should hang by such a thread.

More passed on both sides—all he said was in a character which would have tallied with the very reverse of what he was once reported to be. His manner was not only friendly: it was, as from an older man to a young man—unless his cheerful spirits and my selflove deceived me, what may be termed affectionate: and above all when I came away he said what I take it is not the usual salutation of a statesman to his follower—'Well, *God* bless you, wherever you are.' *That* word was emphatically sounded, that word of high, sacred, and sustaining import; may it be his support in his lofty station and labours: his guiding light: his everlasting reward. And may the same God who has hitherto wonderfully disposed events for my temporal prosperity, make me available according to my measure for the promotion of His holy will.

I next went and saw Lord Aberdeen, who received me with extremely encouraging kindness: but I have recorded enough to stimulate my exertions if not to inflate an empty *and* causeless pride.

*February 7. 1835.*

## 16: ADD.MS 44819, ff. 11–12

February 4 or 5. [1835].[1]

C. J. Canning called for me at the Colonial Office in the forenoon and again in the evening. He found me upon his latter attempt, and told me Peel had offered him the vacant Lordship of the Treasury, through his mother. They were he said very much gratified with the manner in which it had been done though the offer was declined, upon the ground as stated (I venture on memory alone thus much) in the reply, that though he did not anticipate any discrepancy in political sentiments to separate him from the present Government yet he should prefer in some sense deserving an official station by parliamentary conduct, and should first establish by pledges his political character in the eyes of the public so as not to have it assumed that it had been determined simply by the proffer of an office and his avidity to seize it.

Peel's letter was written at some length, very friendly, without any

---

[1] The correct date is 3 February.

statesmanlike reserve or sensitive attention to nicety of style. In the last paragraph it spoke with an amiable embarrassment of Mr. Canning: stating that his 'respect, regard, and admiration' (I think) even if apparently interrupted by circumstances continued fresh and vivid, and that those very circumstances made him more desirous of thus publicly testifying his real sentiments.

We had much and interesting conversation on Canning's political position: his views appeared to me perfectly just. While convictions had evidently and avowedly grown in his mind in unison with the Conservative policy of the day, and while he was prepared to act upon them as an independent Member of Parliament, he obviously felt a delicacy in coming forward upon a hustings as the avowed adherent of Ministers: remembering the relation in which some of them stood towards his illustrious father, who would not feel that his feelings may well require not only political concurrence with the present Government but full and palpable proof of that concurrence in the eyes of the world, by coincidence of acts and tendencies, before it be solemnly sealed by an official connexion? On the other hand he is totally alienated from the apostate Canningites. I regretted his refusal, however, on public and on personal grounds: rejoiced at the offer: mentioned my own feelings relative to Mr. Canning, but I did not mention the stand I made upon them in July 1832.                                          *February 11. 1835.*[1]


## 17: ADD.MS 44819, ff. 13–14

February 17. [1835].
Met Croker for the first time at Mr. Hay's. Lord Vesey was also there and kept up the ball with him. The former still adheres to all his dark prognostications. I confess my mind recognises a preponderating probability in most of them, and the most material, but while the struggle is making, I feel it my duty to resist that decisive depressing preponderance, which hinders us from girding up the loins. I thus in my small way. His mind appears to be most varied, fertile, and acute: but with somewhat of inaccuracy and caprice. The tone of the party was not sanguine even as to the Speakership. Croker would have it a small

---

[1] MS: 1832. The 2 was altered in pencil to 5, probably by WEG.

majority on the Speakership would show the Government to be doomed. True I think: but Lord Vesey said no vote now was formidable but a vote of want of confidence—and that the present House would not give. They may, however, find a *mezzo termino* that will *do*. Croker thought that the Opposition would work harmoniously together till they had attained their end. Can it be doubted? However, it was. One thing in Lord Vesey I liked particularly: he had the manliness to take great blame to their party for maintaining so large an expenditure without retrenchment through many years after the war. There was little or no response: but nothing approaching to denial. And when Croker afterwards spoke with some strength of feeling, of those whose votes in blindness given helped on the Reform in its earlier stages, I could not help thinking with concurrence in the reproach, that it ought also to be shared by those, whose resistance to *practical* improvements or hesitation and timidity in adopting them did entitle them at all events to participate to some extent in the blame.

Croker gave an account of Lord Melbourne's writing to the King before Lord Spencer's death of the prospective difficulties of Government likely to be consequent on that event. The King he said not being so much shocked as they thought he ought to have been, they told him no more of their difficulties. But Lord Melbourne went to Brighton with a string of men to propose Lord J. Russell as Leader. 'Surely, my Lord, he will not do'—'But then Mr. Abercrombie will, Sir'—and, that Littleton was he believed proposed to be Chancellor of the Exchequer. I confess I still greatly prefer the account I had heard earlier. That Lord Melbourne proposed Rice as Chancellor of the Exchequer and Lord John Russell as Leader. Croker said, he was interrogated on men and measures and broke down on both.

It seemed the unanimous opinion that Lord Brougham by violent and uncompromising opposition to the present Government, would again and at once vault to the head of his party.

He [Croker] had an admirable story of Lord Palmerston. He was engaged to dine with him at seven—whiled the time away with Peel at Harrow so that he came in at eight—found Lord Binning waiting and growling: he had been there an hour: and a quarter of an hour after he arrived, said Lord Binning, he heard horses at the door—'Oh it is Palmerston come in from his ride'—he went to the window—no it was Palmerston going out upon that quest!—he made his appeareance at length. This story was told minutely but (it seemed) not accurately.

45

Lord Mahon who may be trusted remarked to me that defect in the mind of this very able man to which I have adverted.

*February 17. [1835].*

## 18: ADD.MS 44819, f. 14

Friday, February 20. [1835].
Today we had a conversation at the Colonial Office on the events of last night. Hay and Stephen seemed to feel in the same manner as I did, i.e. chagrined. My feeling is, that a defeat on the Speakership is *a fortiori* a defeat upon many other questions if properly managed. But I had hoped that more sense of decency was left among certain individuals of the Whig party. They showed tact—in disclaiming untenable charges—but even this fact is astounding, that without definite or specific charge they could prevail on 316 men to reject the admired Speaker of 18 (?) years and the chosen of the first reformed Parliament. Lord Aberdeen had understood they meant to bring forward a moderate amendment upon the Address, i.e. condemnatory of Ministers but not in violent language. This course and this only he dreaded. He disliked the impression through the country, but otherwise thought not much of the defeat. He considered the King's Speech which is to be of a novel character, as one of our weapons and hopes—I might say more. I understood that the Ministers will endure every defeat, and bring forward their measures in spite of all, but his dread was mutilation of the measures and bringing them into such a shape that it would disgrace Ministers to proceed with them. This they will not bear. The idea of stopping the Supplies he deemed almost ludicrous. I am *far* from agreeing with him.

*February 21. [1835].*

## 19: ADD.MS 44819, ff. 14–15

Monday, February 23. [1835].
I had a conversation with Mr. Taylor about Lord Stanley. He said Lord Stanley threw him overboard—and Stephen also. That Stephen wrote his (opening) West Indian speech. That he thought Lord Stanley was surrounded by parasites and flatterers—and that whenever he came

into contact with a man that could cope with him at all in point of talent, he got rid of him. Allowances must be made on both sides.

Thursday, February 26.
Sir M. S.[1] told me confidentially that Col. G—y[2] and C. W—d[3] doubted much whether they would vote for the amendment to the Address. This was afterwards borne out by Lord H.'s[4] speech. Sir James Graham's speech was more liberal *towards* the Ministry than Lord Stanley's had been, and did not seem to indicate such a sensitiveness. Sir Robert Peel's courage, temper, and tact never appeared more conspicuously to my mind than when after so mortifying a defeat he got up and addressed to his minority a repetition of Lord John Russell's advice.                                     *Friday, February 27. [1835].*

## 20: ADD.MS 44819, ff. 15–17

Wednesday, April 8. [1835].
At half past twelve I had a conversation with Lord Aberdeen whom I met, I suppose for the last time, in the capacity of his *bona fide* under Secretary. I regret to dissolve my official connection with a man, whose serious and earnest benevolence, and practical competency for affairs have impressed me much, perhaps the more deeply from their contrast with his phlegmatic exterior manner.

Peel was gone to the King to resign. Nothing confidently anticipated of the future. The King courageous and determined: but it seemed to me that the Ministers had never so much as entertained the thought of dissolution as an alternative under any contingency. I lament that their *one* resource was so early spent, namely the dissolution. What would have been the effect of his appeal to the people, could he have brought to bear upon it the credit and confidence which his splendid behaviour has gained for him everywhere except within the walls of the House of Commons?

Equally remote from their views and deliberations appeared to have been that other alternative which the ready wit of their friends had

---

[1] Possibly Sir Michael Shaw Stewart.
[2] Possibly Charles Grey.
[3] Charles Wood.
[4] Probably Lord Howick.

devised for them, namely the continuing to hold office, combating the appropriation clause in the Commons and throwing it out in the Lords. This indeed would exhibit the Government in a critical and dangerous point of view to the country, and might produce very great excitement.

Lord Aberdeen thought there were many possibilities of saving the constitution, if the House of Peers would lie by and reserve itself—but he seemed also very much alive to the probability of their repeating the game of the Reform Bill; namely to their adopting measures conceived in the spirit of Radicalism at the moment when they find they cannot stand supported by the property and intelligence of the country, and procuring for themselves a factitious strength, and an evil popularity, by inflaming through some appeal to their cupidity, that portion of the people whose feelings must ever be accessible by such methods. If they adopted their Reform Bill apparently not uninfluenced by some such motives, when Stanley, Graham, and their friends were in the Government (Stanley not I believe in the Cabinet) why should they hesitate now when that section has been replaced by Hobhouse, Ellice, and Lord Duncannon? Lord Aberdeen thought some union might be formed by Peel with the moderate men of the other side: that they might consent still to hold the principle of alienation suspended and in the abstract: that Peel never would compromise: that if he were Premier the union might be satisfactory. I am not sanguine enough to anticipate on their parts any such conduct. Nothing could be higher or warmer than Lord Aberdeen's estimate of his leader's character and conduct.

Sir E. Kerrison told me that the King was very sturdy last night and in answer to some remark that the Ministers had resigned said it was a d—d lie! He seemed to have some confidence in the idea that the King would take in Stanley and Graham and on that ground dissolve and[1]

In the evening at Lord Salisbury's I was introduced to the Duke of Cumberland who was pleased to express himself favourably of my speech. He is fond of conversation, and the common reputation which he bears of including in his conversation many oaths, appears to be but too true. Yet he said that he had made a point of sending his son to George the Fourth's funeral, thinking it an excellent advantage for a boy to receive the impression, which such a scene was calculated to convey. And (it appears) he burst into an uncontrollable flood of

---

[1] This sentence was left unfinished.

weeping, as the coffin was placed in the vault and disappeared from his eyes.

The Duke made many acute remarks, and was I should say most remarkably unaffected and kind—'My dear Sir' and thumps on the shoulder after a ten minutes' acquaintance. These are fine social qualities for a Prince, though of course not the most important. He spoke broadly and freely—much on the disappearance of the Bishops' wigs, which he said had done more harm to the Church than anything else! *(April 8)*.

Two things I hear of Sir R. Peel relative to his religious feelings. (a—Lord Ashley) that he says he finds more support and refreshment to his mind in reading the works of our best divines than from any other source.

(b—Walter R. Farquhar and Mrs. Walter) that his brother wrote to him begging him to have no Sunday dinners or Cabinets. He wrote back complying, absolutely for the first—generally for the second, i.e. in case of necessity—was pleased with the request, and hoped he should continue to have an interest in his prayers. This is very delightful.

## 21: ADD.MS 44819, ff. 17–19

April 13. [1835].
Lord Aberdeen acquainted me that Graham speaking for himself and Lord Stanley declared their identification in principles and views with Peel the day before, April 12—saw that an attempt would be made on the Corporation question to separate them—believed that they might certainly meet and agree upon a basis if each would agree the one to go as high the other as low as could be done with honour and consistency —declared the new Cabinet would be one of Jacobins and infidels—and lamented that he had made two mistakes for which he did not know how he could ever atone—voting for the Roman Catholic claims—and for the Reform Bill. And a perfect readiness to combine in Administration was indicated. All this apparently intended to go to Peel.

Sir R. Peel made a very nice speech on Lincoln's proposing and our drinking his health. The following is a slight and bad sketch. 'I really can hardly call you gentlemen alone, I would rather address you as my warm attached friends in whom I have the fullest confidence, and with whom it has afforded me the utmost satisfaction to be associated during the struggle which has just been brought to a close. I can safely say that there has not been among us any particle of mutual suspicion or distrust, not one single case if I may so express myself of disobedience, except one which has just occurred, namely that of my noble friend, who has persisted in proposing my health although I pressed him to refrain. I am sure that every one of us has been actuated throughout by public motives alone, and it is most gratifying to me to have been united with such a body of men in such a cause. As for myself, I have had very great labour but no uneasiness: I look back on what has been done with the utmost pleasure, and I shall continue so to regard it to my latest hour. In undertaking the Government from the first I have never expected to succeed: still it was my conviction that good might be done, and I trust that good has been effected. I believe we have shown that even if a Conservative Government be not strong enough to carry on the public affairs of this country, at least we are so strong as that we ought to be able to prevent any other Government from doing any serious mischief to its institutions. We meet now as we met at the beginning of the session, then perhaps in somewhat finer dresses, but not, I am sure, with kindlier feelings towards each other, and again I say that I refer to the course of the contest now concluded with the very highest gratification at having been confided in and supported by such a body of gentlemen as I now see before me.'

Today Lord Aberdeen talked to me, very kindly, on the paper[1] which I wrote and gave him yesterday, relative to West Indian education. He could not concur in all my opinions—and was so far glad that we had not been called upon to act upon the question. He did not feel absolutely certain that we must have gone further than I proposed, but was not prepared to stand upon those conditions which I regarded as essentially necessary. I on my part expressed the extreme relief I had experienced personally in the midst of this storm at finding that it would rescue me from the possibility of a difference which would have been extremely painful.

Lord Aberdeen does not concur in all my views about the Church, but I could not do otherwise than admire the sober and practical character of his opinions: 'The great object', said he, 'you must allow to be, to save these poor people from the devil, and to send them to

---

[1] ADD.MS. 44724, ff. 4–39.

heaven.' He, however, could not *comprehend* the Socinians. He approved strongly, I found, of the part of my paper on which I was most afraid of appearing too speculative, namely the connection of Church and education principles with the foundations of government.

*April 15. [1835].*

## 22: ADD.MS 44819, ff. 19–20

At the Archbishop of Canterbury's last month (March) I learned the following interesting anecdotes.

1. M.G.[1] told me that when Mr. W. took leave of the King, His Majesty said he hoped in God soon to see him back again. With this coincides an account Sir E. Kerrison gave me, of strong language used by him a night or two before the resignation.

2. Mr. Ward told me that a lady of rank asked Sir R. Peel whether he ever commenced any official business without prayer? that his reply to her was, he would not say that each individual matter was prefaced with prayer, but he certainly never commenced a day without praying for the divine aid in his business as he well knew nothing could be done without it. The lady herself was Mr. Ward's informant.

3. Mr. Ward likewise informed me that when Sir R. Peel was passing through Paris on his way to or from Rome, a number of English people went to call on him; it was Sunday: they were apprised he was at church: when would he be back? It was uncertain, as he would stay the Sacrament.

These anecdotes were in return for one which I had given Mr. Ward, to the following effect, as I have heard it. That when Sir Robert assumed office, one of his brothers (Mr. E. or L. Peel) wrote to him and apologising for his freedom begged of him that he would hold no Councils and give no dinners on Sunday. That Sir Robert answered thanking him for his letter: promising absolutely as to dinners, and as to Councils that nothing but necessity should cause him to violate the rule, which he approved: and finally desiring to have an interest in his prayers.

This is very interesting and deeply important. And indeed the rare selfcommand, the quick and farsighted tact, the delicacy and purity of principle and temper by which the speeches of this great man have been

---

[1] Perhaps James Milnes Gaskell.

distinguished in a period of extraordinary stress and trial, bear the marks, it may be fairly said, of a Providential governance.

In conformity with these accounts, Ashley acquainted me he had learned that Sir Robert Peel expressed the deepest interest in the perusal of our best divines, and said he found them the greatest resource and refreshment of his mind.                                        *April [1835]*.

## 23: ADD.MS 44819, f. 20

July 25. [1835].
Some time ago being alone with Sir E. Kerrison in the Sinecures Committee Room, I conversed with him on the subject of that dissolution of Parliament whose premature arrival was so disastrous an event: and of which I have ever believed that it was not the dictate of Sir R. Peel's individual judgment. He agreed in lamenting it. And I learned from what he said, though not in the way of direct understanding, that the Duke set our candidates in motion all over the country before Sir Robert's return: accordingly, active measures, and of course expense, had so generally commenced, and so much impatience for the dissolution had been excited, and the anticipations had been permitted for so long a time to continue and to spread, that a pressure on the subject apparently was felt such as to preclude the possibility of the requisite delay, without risking altogether the strength and success of the effort to be made by the favourable effect upon the general spirit of the party.

## 24: ADD.MS 44819, f. 21

August 5. [1835].
At a meeting at his house on Monday [3 August], Sir Robert Peel expressed distinctly his conviction that the course taken on the introduction of the Reform Bill in 1831 was a *very bad* one. (Seven nights' debate and no division.)

At a meeting previously he spoke of the Corporation Bill: and said there were some matters in politics where a principle was to be maintained at all hazards: there were others which were matters of expediency. This was evidently enunciating a conviction: and it convinced me the more of what I have never in my own mind doubted, namely that he will stand, and stand to the last, upon that which he takes up as matter of principle.

## 25: ADD.MS 44724, ff. 164–175

Private. Recollections of the last hours of my mother.
Fasque. Wednesday, September 23. 1835.
The following account is intended as my contribution towards a record of the circumstances attendant on the removal from this mortal life of the tenderest and best of mothers.

Returning home on Monday the 7th from London, I saw her in her bed after the funeral of my Uncle Robert which took place in the forenoon of that day. She was suffering very considerably, but in a manner not unusual with her, and which we had long learned to contemplate with less emotion, than it would cause when it was unaccustomed. Circumstances, however, of interest to myself had been partially made known to her, and she did not fail to indicate that they were in her mind. For several days we all saw her as usual at intervals. On Thursday the 10th she appeared better, and spoke to me of the matter to which I have above alluded, as well as others. She then felt easier and was disposed to have conversed on it at length: but seeing that she was weak, and then fully anticipating that in three or four days more I might enjoy, in full communication with her, what has upon all occasions been the greatest relief to my own mind, I begged of her to defer the subject until she was well, saying only a few words intended to set her quite at ease. It was deferred: but until the time and place, where they neither marry nor are given in marriage.

On Saturday afternoon the 12th, I was with her for a considerable time, and read to her, at her wish, the Epistle to the Philippians from the commencement of the second chapter, and I remember then to have observed, though without melancholy forebodings, that she appreciated the Scripture with less manifestation of her artless and lively feelings of delight in it, than was usually, the case: an indication, as it cannot but now be considered, that the depressing power of the disease, which had been discovered to be erysipelas, was already upon her. Later in the afternoon, her wandering was apparent. Tom and Louisa had arrived on Friday: and she said to me that the time was a good one, while Louisa ('this dear creature' was her expression) was in the house, for her to go with my father to Strathpeffer: on account of the wart and the erysipelas, on her back, which she connected together, but evidently by no clear idea nor any method intelligible to herself. She also said to her beloved husband when he spoke of bathing her back, 'You're

53

always bothering me', and this I well knew could not be referred to a selfpossessed or lucid state of her understanding. At night she asked many times for me to tell me of a supposed discovery of misconduct on the part of a person in the house. Dr. Guthrie[1] when he came determined that her children ought not to go and see her, while the fever alone caused her so much excitement.

On Sunday night he told Tom and myself that the case *might become* dangerous if the erysipelas took a turn towards the head, which it had not done: and that at all events we must expect the fever to last for (I think) ten days.

During the next few days the dear invalid was believed to be improved in her bodily health. On Wednesday Tom was allowed to see her, and on coming from her he said he had been a good deal shocked with her appearance. On Thursday I went into the room. The sight of her cut me to the heart: not only nor so much from the hot and sallow complexion of her face with the parched state of the skin, as from an apparent general prostration of her powers greater than I had seen, even in the worst of her illness last Spring in London.

She did not speak of recovery, nor respond to what I said upon the subject. She said she wished to speak of the fulfilment of dear Anne's wishes about her place of final interment: and her being placed between her parents: evidently with a view to her own dissolution: she inquired whether ground could be had in the cemetery at Liverpool, apparently with a wish, though it was not distinctly embodied in terms, that it should if practicable be procured: and she lamented that no tablet had been erected to her daughter's memory. I made a remark on the very powerful character of the verse[2] which I had understood from her, it was Anne's wish to have inscribed, without addition, upon her tomb: and it *now* strikes me much, that she made no reply: as, in general,

---

[1] Thursday, September 10. Dr. Guthrie first sent for? on that afternoon we spoke of several matters.

Dr. Guthrie was sent for on Tuesday night, according to T.G. [WEG]

[2] Romans, viii, 11. 'But if the spirit of him that raised up Jesus from the dead dwell in you, he that raised up Christ from the dead shall also quicken your mortal bodies by his Spirit that dwelleth in you.'

My observation was upon the connection in the verse between the hope, and the ground of our hope, which latter was placed so high by the Apostle, and upon the choice of *such* a verse as characteristic of the very powerful understanding which made it. [WEG]

even the feeblest observation upon Scripture sufficed to elicit a response from a heart attuned to it like hers. On parting I said to her I hoped she would soon be able to see me again as well as all her children, and more frequently. Her only answer was, throwing out the hand listlessly upon the bed at the same time, 'I am so much exhausted'—there was no echo of the hope, and knowing the habitual tenor of her feelings, this appalled me much. Especially as she had said she thought herself injudiciously treated in being secluded from her children during the preceding days. But my painful impressions were removed when I heard Dr. Guthrie say in the afternoon that he could then pronounce a more decidedly favourable opinion of the case than on any previous day, the erysipelas having shown an inclination to yield.

On Friday morning however, the 18th, Dr. Hunter arrived and disclosed to us a new cause of anxiety in the debility arising from her exhausted state. I did not see him upon the subject and generally we felt no serious uneasiness till the evening. He then showed in his countenance and manner great and oppressive anxiety. After dinner he announced a coldness in the feet, between seven and eight. But this was subdued by the blankets alone: and about nine the pulse had abated. It had generally ranged from 85–90 in the day to 90–100 in the evening. He under these circumstances said however that he should consider the case one of extreme danger, even though not precluding the hope of her being carried through by the vigour of her constitution, unless there was a decidedly favourable change in its character before midday on Saturday.[1]

At half past two in the morning John and I went to rest with an unfavourable account of increased rapidity in the pulse: but at six we were awakened by Helen with greatly improved intelligence. Wine, which Dr. Hunter had administered under the necessity of the case on

---

[1] About midday on Friday my father and Helen were in my room. My father said that as Hunter's only apprehension had reference to the vigour of the constitution and its power of enduring the regular course of the fever, he who knew that constitution so well, felt perfectly at rest. Helen took rather a more serious view of the doctor's opinion, but I believe without the idea of a fatal result as in the least degree probable. The thought of writing to Robertson never entered any of our minds, I believe. John was out shooting, and I joined him. Her strength subsequently appears to have justified my father's anticipations as it was the repetition of the assaults of the disease which finally snatched her from us. [WEG]

his previous view at two, had produced beneficial effects: the pulse was lower and the strength greater. At these periods we had no communication with her, in order to avoid excitement.

We met on Saturday morning with the fond hope that the condition named by Dr. Hunter had been fulfilled, and that the danger from debility was passing and that no other was to be apprehended. But about midday Dr. Guthrie arrived. Upon an examination of her person which had been deferred till he came, in order to avoid unnecessary fatigue, it was found that the erysipelas had spread again, and the cold feet of last evening were referred to the first stage of the new accession of fever. Dr. Hunter, who had made up his mind to go, resolved to remain for the night, to our great comfort. We now felt it to be a case of fearful danger, though far from being without hope.

There was no unfavourable change in the afternoon and we retired to rest in the evening, less desponding.

On Sunday morning the 20th at five, Dr. Hunter awoke me by Helen's desire, and I John, to say that the pulse had risen to 130, the face was flushed, and an early approach of death was to be expected. We all, with the exception of my father whom we allowed to rest a little longer, gathered round her bedside, unaware that we were likely rather to injure her, by causing a bewildered astonishment as to the occasion of our presence. Whey was given her and a little wine. Tom asked her whether she had any wish or sentiment to express. She answered in the negative: but presently asked for me, and when I went up to her said, 'You all give me the idea that this is my last hour, but I have no such notion—I have no such notion.' She also said, 'You would not think it presumptuous—to fix a data' (meaning a time)—she was unable to finish the sentence and evinced a great weakness and difficulty in speaking though she recognised us all perfectly. She was asked if she had anything to say to Robertson, who had only been summoned by Saturday's post, and her reply was simply on catching the name 'Dear fellow'. It appeared soon that she was better informed than we were of the strength of her constitution.[1]

My father soon came in and she used various kind expressions regard-

---

[1] One of her expressions about this time, and a very characteristic one, was 'This is my Waterloo day'. Her articulation was faint and thick, and this as well as much more of what she said was with difficulty to be distinctly made out. [WEG]

ing the 'dear man'. One was, not in my hearing, 'that all was right between that dear man and her'. At nine there was a new and great accession of fever. Dr. Hunter was called and said the rapidity of declension was much increased. The pulse was fluttering and intermittent. At this time, we afterwards learned, he did not expect her to live over three or four hours—and such I believe was the apprehension on the minds of her children—I can speak for myself. When Dr. Guthrie came at half past nine he agreed with Dr. Hunter. Wine was administered more freely under the necessity of the case, and the pulse immediately reduced. She continued to improve till Dr. Hunter went between one and two, and he then considered she might live till the next morning.

The rally produced further mitigation in the symptoms through the afternoon and evening, and the erysipelas assumed a favourable aspect, but a hardness in the bowels continued and increased, and was attended with considerable distension, so that it became the great foundation of alarm: pulse, strength, countenance, and the appearance of the erysipelas being all improved. Spirits of turpentine were given with great relief to the bowels.

In the course of this day she had said she knew she had not an hour to live—and exclaimed,[1] 'Oh I am weary to be off, weary to be off'. To an offer from John to read prayer by her she said, she was unequal to it, or would be delighted. I said, 'Mother, the peace of God is with you; you are in good hands'. 'Yes' she said, raising hers, 'merciful hands'. And at another time, 'Oh what a glorious—'. But there was an evident incapacity, both in the organs of speech to act for any length of time, and in the mind to deal with any complex combination of ideas. I once or twice attempted to say more on the subject of her sufferings, well knowing, that the poorest attempt to remind her of her consolations would be a delight to her spirit, if her strength was sufficient to enable her to comprehend it. But throughout this closing period of her life, and during that portion of it, the last, in which the intellect was collected and clear, it was still feeble: the beautiful, affectionate, and pious instincts of her mind displayed themselves, in perfect congruity and propriety, but the vigour was gone which would have enabled her to evince more instructively in what way it was that death was to her disarmed of its

---

[1] She also said I believe on Sunday that she had not a desire to live remaining. [WEG]

terrors, and that she was ready, without a moment's trepidation or reluctance, to go forth and meet the bridegroom.

My brothers and I agreed to divide the night: during the whole of which she held up wonderfully. I sat by her from 2.15 to 5.15. In this period there was a good deal of occasional pain which she seemed to bear with perfect willingness, raising up her hands to heaven with short and scarcely audible ejaculations of prayer. The suffering resulted from the action of the medicine upon the bowels, which had been administered with a view to relieving the distension, now the most formidable of all the symptoms. The pulse was good and kept under 100. She was at no period in the crisis more selfpossessed. This was evinced by her anxiety for the comfort and ease of others, even in the minute particular of their rest. All who knew her know that this sentiment in all its forms was one of the most marked features in her character. John told me that she had repeatedly requested him to go to bed. And she said to me while I sat there, 'My beloved William, my beloved son, are you there still? go to your bed.' And again she said, 'My precious, why do not you go to rest?' Such were the epithets, which she was accustomed to bestow upon her children, while she esteemed herself vile. But she is now a plant blossoming for ever in the garden of the Lord, beyond the reach of cold and storm.

We remained during the day (Monday, September 21) in painful but not yet unhopeful suspense. In the afternoon the appearance of the symptoms generally was favourable. A suffusion of the eye which the doctor had observed the night before had not increased. The pulse had sunk at one time to 80, without losing its tone. In short, the first attack of erysipelas—the general debility—the second attack of erysipelas— and the distension of the bowels threatening distinct disease there— all these several obstacles appeared to have been successively surmounted. I resumed my watch at eleven to sit by her bedside till two, when the rest went to bed, with hopes raised higher than they had yet been. At ten a general listlessness had made Guthrie apprehend the passage of the erysipelas to the head, but this symptom had been greatly abated when I went there and the others to rest.

But those hopes were soon disturbed with pain, and then utterly dissipated. From eleven to twelve the pain was on the increase. Instead of its being occasional and convulsive, it became nearly continuous: the moanings scarcely intermitted, and were often loud. The fingers and hands twitched more, and as it seemed more unconsciously than they had yet done in my sight. She was sensible during this period and knew me. She said to me at one time, 'My dear, this is become an awful case: I am in the depths of despair.' I said some few words in answer to these, which she did not seem to receive: there were frequent mutterings of prayer, with pain. In one very pleasing reverie she evidently dwelt on her daughter in heaven. 'Oh my first—dearest— beloved'—then came the single word 'precious'—and a little after 'she was blessed'. I soon entertained a gloomy apprehension, which speedily formed itself into a conviction that, as the doctor said when I asked him, these pains could not be considered as only the effort of nature for relief, or the conflict between the medicine and the immediate obstacles it was intended to remove. A new and unfavourable, alas! as it proved, fatal change, was manifestly matured during this my melancholy watch—the treatment was changed, it was not now the time for cordials but an opiate was administered, with external fomentation, and suffering was very considerably allayed while her dear mind and her existence were thus removed a step farther from us. I called John rather before two and remained up till half past five when Tom came down. Dr. Guthrie felt himself in perfect possession of her case so that the idea of sending to Aberdeen for further advice if he should wish it was abandoned. Between one and two she called her waiting maid and said, 'Mary Anne, do not let me out of your sight, but protect me while I am here.'[1] Once to Guthrie 'Foolish man'—as if meaning to add, for prolonging a hopeless struggle: and again 'Foolish fellows'. These were at rather a later period, when I believe that for the purposes of distinct conception, or perception, the beloved sufferer had ceased to live.

In the morning it appeared to be a question of hours only, not of what the event might be, for the will of her Heavenly Father now seemed intelligibly announced. We dispatched our letters by the post in the most desponding terms. And at 4.15 I wrote to Robertson, expected at four in the next morning, that he must not expect to find her alive.

We were then all called into her room, just as the last named letter had been dispatched. An almost immediate departure was anticipated. The pulse had not yet failed, the extremities were quite warm, but the flush which had formerly suffused her brow and face, like a light rosy cloud beneath the skin, had become concentrated and deeply purple:

---

[1] I do not know of any palpable recognition of any person later than this of Mary Anne her maid. [WEG]

and the fatal death-rattle was in her throat, and marked and oppressed each successive respiration.

Since Sunday at five a.m. she had been in the jaws of the grave: yet brief as was the space between her then state and death, the descent into the dark valley was divided into many distinct stages, and chequered with great variety of feelings. For eight more hours yet was she to remain in her prison house. We were all in the room nearly all that time: going by turns to dine. Dr. Guthrie never went down stairs. After dinner the pulse gave way: its strength diminished, and it became intermittent, reaching in its rapid action the rate of 160. The livid hue appeared under the nails. The flesh sank upon the features, which were marked in their outlines with unnatural precision. Twice, before nine o'clock, I saw her ineffectually attempt to open the eyelids. Up to that time there were not unfrequent and strong convulsive movements. From that time they ceased, but the fearful rattle grew louder and louder as the load of obstruction accumulated. It seemed, however, that she was now quite unconscious, and nothing remained but the strong muscular effort of animal nature, resolved to *live*. Life clung with great tenacity in every fibre. The pulse I think it was which made the doctor warn us at about a quarter before twelve, that she would do little more than pass midnight. And then every remaining power was mustered and exerted in each respiration, and each labour seemed as great as if it must be the last. The chest, then the head, wrought upwards and downwards. But the muscular movement descended from its climax, and subsided into perfect, childlike, gentleness and peace. A few breaths of decreasing force, at increasing intervals—my dear father who asked anxiously if she were gone came forward—then three slight movements of the head as if meant to second the chest which had ceased to act—and all was over: we wept for her who perhaps at that very moment was employing her young immortality in bringing truths and consolation to our minds from Him who is the source of both. Tender, affectionate, unwearied in love and devotion as she was, she is perhaps nearer us than ever.

She was not during her illness in a state of mental vigour to warrant its being proposed to her to receive the Sacrament. Though she was deprived of this joy, and we of this palpable manifestation of her faith, we cannot feel it a cause for permanent regret while we know that in her daily life she had realised that communion with her Lord, which the ordinance is intended to convey and assure.

Sin was the object of her hatred—and she can now sin no more. Sin is the cause of all the sorrow in the world: she can now no more add to the sin nor to the sorrow which is its fruit alone. She departed in seraphic peace, like the gentleness of her own disposition, like the serenity of her everlasting home. She was eminent in the discharge of every duty: she sorrowed for sin: she trusted in the atonement of Christ. But this was not all: these elementary sentiments of religion were matured in her by the power of God, and she was made partaker of the nature and very life of her Redeemer, and her will conformed to his. Therefore being, like Him, perfected through suffering, she had no new thing to learn, no fresh character to assume, upon translation to the world of spirits: her mind and affections had received already and for ever their mould and their bias, and she has but carried the one vital principle of love which cannot be bound in death, from a thick and clouded atmosphere to one of perfect purity and freedom. Two only have been taken from our family: and both are angels in heaven.

> Her grudging ghost did strive
> With the frail flesh: at last it flitted is
> Whither the souls of men do fly, that live for bliss.
>
> *Faery Queen*, i. 19

(I have altered the last line for the sake of the truth of description in what precedes. October 3).

And this is connected with a very important truth. δῆλον δ'ὡς καρτεροῦσι πολλὴν κακοπάθειαν οἱ πολλοὶ τῶν ἀνθρώπων γλιχόμενοι τοῦ ζῆν, ὡς ἐνούσης τινὸς εὐημερίας ἐν αὐτῷ καὶ γλυκύτητος φυσικῆς.[1] Aristotle, *Politics*, 3. 4. Because the sweetness of mere life is one of the strongest and most permanent and palpable grounds for thankfulness to the Giver of Life.

(*October 7*).

## 26: ADD.MS 44777, ff. 23–28

Private. Drayton Manor. January 18. 1836.
The Earl of Harrowby and I were the only strangers. There was a good

---

[1] 'It is clear that the mass of mankind cling to life at the cost of enduring much suffering, which shows that life contains some measure of well-being and of sweetness in its essential nature.' (Translation by H. Rackham, Loeb edition)

deal of conversation after dinner on public matters between Lord Harrowby and our host. The cast of mind of the latter is in no degree I should say less liberal than that of the former: but the reverse, more so. Once the conversation bordered on theology: and here Lord Harrowby struck me as the more ready and familiar. I cannot record anything continuous, but commit to paper several opinions and expressions of Sir R. Peel, which bore upon interesting and practical questions.

That Fox was not a man of settled, reasoned, political principle. Lord Harrowby added that he was thrown into opposition and Whiggism by the insult of Lord North. That his own doctrines both as originally declared, and as resumed when finally in office, were of a highly toned spirit of government.

That Brougham was the most *powerful* man he had ever known in the House of Commons: that no one had ever fallen so fast and so far.

That the political difficulties of England might be susceptible of cure and were not appalling: but that the state of Ireland was to all appearance hopeless. That the great difficulty lay in procuring the ordinary administration of justice. That the very institution of juries supposed a common interest of the juror and the State. A condition not fulfilled in the present instance. That it was quite unfit for the present state of society in Ireland. Lord Harrowby thought that a strong Conservative Government might still quell agitation. And Sir R. Peel said Stanley had told him, that the Whig Government were on the point of succeeding in putting a stop to the resistance to payment of tithe when Lord Althorp, alarmed at the expence already incurred, wrote to stop its collection by the military.

That we should probably live to see the independence of Poland established. That the late speech of the Emperor of Russia was no less than infatuated. That nothing could be more injurious than the French declaration by amendment to the Address: that no such sentiments ought to be uttered by a legislature unless prepared to support them by force.

He spoke of the possible approach of the war of principles: and of the rallying of the dissatisfied as against despotism under the constitutional banners—and he used these memorable words, or such as these—'Every body blames Canning for that speech he made, but it was the simple truth.' Thus recognising in the clearest way the line between prediction and invitation, which have been in this instance so unjustly confounded.

He thought that the proposal of an Irish Poor Law would be well received next session: did not express hostility to it: had predicted the evil consequences which would follow from the speech of Nicholas.

*January 18.*

They also spoke of lawyers. 'You have got the two best', said Lord Harrowby, 'Follett and Pemberton.' Sir Robert replied that they were not to be named in the same day, and went on to speak in very high and warm terms of Follett's merits as an advocate and a speaker.

Wednesday, January 20.
We have now a large circle at dinner, and Sir Robert consequently does not lead conversation nor is there any one else who aspires to that task. But all the gentlemen in the house met about midday in his room: the Earl of Harrowby, Sir Henry Hardinge, Mr. Goulburn, Mr. Herries, Lord Granville Somerset, and two of the Mr. Peels—to discuss the coming session and the propriety of an amendment. It was a course discontinued for twenty or thirty years—the only grounds were, Irish Church and House of Lords. Stanley might not go with them on the first: the effect of a beating on the second would be to place the House of Lords in a position of great delicacy before the country.

Sir Robert read a letter from Croker, which did not recommend an amendment. It spoke of the final doom of the country as *sealed*: but expressed the utmost anxiety that that catastrophe might not be in the slightest degree accelerated by any violent or precipitate step of the Conservative party. He likewise said how unfortunate it was that the Conservative gentlemen in [the] House of Commons could not be impressed with the fact that they are not contending for the interests of a party. With some idiosyncrasies, it was an excellent letter in point of temper and moderation.

It seemed to be felt by all that a volunteered amendment was undesirable but that a coerced one was probable. To explain, however, to the party the intentions entertained with reference to an amendment, Sir R. Peel said that he thought a large meeting necessary, much as he disapproved of them.

Although during the Corporation Bill Stanley was in concert with Sir R. Peel, no communication has passed between them since the session, directly or indirectly. There seemed some disposition to draw sinister inferences from his dining repeatedly with his old colleagues. I mention this as a proof how little *confidence* properly so called is at this moment reposed in his individual *steadiness*: his honour is unsuspected. But *il Maestro* said, 'He is much more with the Ministers, than with us.' He said Ripon and Graham were both with us: the Duke of Richmond almost as much with the Ministers, and all but relapsing into their ranks.

From the time Graham came to Town it was observed Stanley's tone last year was perceptibly improved.

The Duke of Wellington and others arrived later in the day: it was pleasing to see the deference with which he was received as he entered the library: at the sound of his name every body rose: he is addressed by all with a respectful manner. He met Peel most cordially: and seized both Lady Peel's hands. I now recollect that it was with *glee* Sir R. Peel said to me on Monday, 'I am glad to say you will meet the Duke here', which had reference I doubt not partly to the anticipated pleasure of seeing him, partly to the dissipation of unworthy suspicions. He reports that Government are still labouring at a Church measure without appropriation. *January 20.*

The Duke of Wellington appears to speak little: and never for speaking's sake, but only to convey an idea commonly worth conveying. He receives remarks made to him very frequently with no more than 'Ha': a convenient suspensive expression, which acknowledges the arrival of the observation, and no more.

Of the two full days which he spent here he hunted on Thursday: shot on Friday: and today travelled to Strathfieldsay, more I believe than 100 miles, to entertain a party of friends to dinner. With this bodily exertion he mixes at 66 or 67, a constant attention to business. Sir R. Peel mentioned to me tonight a very remarkable example of his perhaps excessive precision. Whenever he signs a draft on Coutts's, he addresses to them at the same time a note apprising them that he has done so. This perfect facility of transition from one class of occupations to their opposites, and their habitual intermixture without any apparent encroachments on either side, is I think a very remarkable evidence of selfcommand, and a mental power of singular utility.

Sir Robert is also I conceive a thrifty dealer with his time, but in a man of his age this is less beyond expectation.

Today he received a notice from Mr. Spencer Perceval and Mr. Sitwell, that they wished to call on him this evening or tomorrow after church. He proposed this evening, and dinner. They came accordingly, and saw him entering the library. For a party of seven, we were a re-markable combination. A late and probably future Prime Minister, chief of the statesmen of the English Empire: the young heir of a con-spicuous ducal crown: his blooming wife, a creature of ethereal grace, and of a thousand gifts, on whom I can never look without feeling, such is the being to embody whose representation the ideal man might long strive in vain, so bright, so gentle, so refined, bearing so few outward marks of the curse that is in the race of Adam: the more matronly lady who seems to combine the fondness and fragility of youth with a mother's practised character: and now add one, who never can write sincerely of himself, without seeming insincere: and to these approach two men, one the son of a Prime Minister, but both with minds apparen-tly gathered inwards upon themselves, and girt up as it were for the purpose set before them at the sacrifice of every wordly tie and enjoyment and desire: seeming to say we are among you but not of you, depart from us that lie in the valley of the shadow of death.

Such are the suggestions of the *prima voglia*: but may we and they be saved together from Satan and ourselves.

After they departed in the evening Sir Robert said they had brought and left him a paper, declared themselves commissioned from God, that is intermediately through inspired ministers of an increasing sect: they spoke of national sins and retribution, the speedy coming of the great day, and the awful responsibilities of those that refuse to hear.

He told them he would deal seriously with them, impressed upon them the duty and necessity of verifying the powers they claimed, and pro-posed to them as a test that in their separate congregations in London and Manchester, without concert, one person of each, believed to be inspired, should be set to expound a particular text, and to prophesy on a particular subject: their concurrence would constitute a *prima facie* evidence in their favour. But he said he found it impossible to tie them down in any way to the subject of *proof*. *January 23.*

Sir Robert mentioned that they had expressed a horror of that licen-tiousness in religion, which is now so prevalent: spoke strongly of the unity of the Church and of the shame of that spectacle in a family where some are seen of one sect some of another. He bid farewell to Perceval in the evening with great warmth and kindness.

On Sunday, after Lady Peel had perused the printed address of Mr. Perceval she gave it to me saying she had been very much interested in it: I found cause to appreciate the justice of that sentiment, agreeing generally in the principles *au fond* and only regretting that their application seemed to be spoiled by partial and morbid views; yet still there is much to learn from the solemn appeal of a single minded servant of God independently of those peculiarities of the time with which he I think overloads his argument. They are great indeed and fearful, but I think their action is more diversified, and retarded, by the counter-workings of good principle, than he seems to allow.

I left Drayton with regret Monday, January 25. 1836.

## 27: ADD.MS 44819, ff. 21-22

February 6. [1836].
Called on Lady Canning, and met the Duchess-Countess there. Her conversation was very Conservative: but I did not watch it narrowly, as I was ignorant of her person and learnt her name after she had left the room: having talked very freely in her presence to Lady Canning, as usual. I admire her (Lady Canning's) acute and statesmanlike understanding: from her almost alone have I heard that comprehensive statement of the abuses of the half-century of Tory governments, and indeed of the whole period since 1688: that men forget how these abuses were intimately connected with the greatest political benefits. The Revolution wrought in this country a substitution of patronage for prerogative as the chief *mechanical* stay of regal government. The abuses with which the country has since been vexed, have flowed out of that substitution. Were they therefore to be retained? Certainly not: and accordingly they were in course of diminution since the first accession of Mr. Pitt [to] office: a course of increasing efficacy, for the three years preceding the Reform Bill. But he alone will truly estimate those abuses, and wisely regulate the *manner* and *time* of their removal, who sedulously bears in mind that even these were upon the whole a comparative advantage: otherwise, forgetting that they replaced something worse, how likely are we to replace them again by something worse. For we are apt to deem the evil which is ἐμποδών[1] to be the only evil.

She has always taken the very strongest view of the extreme inexpedi-

---

[1] Literally 'before the feet', 'in one's way'; as we should say 'under one's nose'.

ency of the unfortunate dissolution in December 1834 as having ruined Sir R. Peel's government: and believes, as I have ever done, that a short manifestation of his policy in the previous Parliament would have sent him and his friends to the hustings with such an increase of repute and popularity as would have secured to him a thoroughly favourable result of the general election a *little* later, perhaps six weeks or two months.                                                         *February 12.* [*1836*].

## 28: ADD.MS 44819, f. 22

In sorting old papers today I found one[1] written in November 1830, called the Cabinet as it is and as it should be, in which I find (with shame) four notes of admiration i.e. astonishment placed after the name of the Duke's Foreign Secretary. This is mainly referable to my own precipitancy and prejudice—but it reminds me that a public man may be too modest, if not for himself, yet for his country, and that such is perhaps the case with Lord Aberdeen, whose statesmanlike mind, calmness of temper, warmth of benevolence, high principle, and capacity for business, must always render him a most valuable accession to a British Cabinet: and I think that should Sir R. Peel again take office, from this colleague he will never part, unless it be by the absolute resolution of Lord Aberdeen himself.          *February 12.* [*1836*].

## 29: ADD.MS 44819, f. 2

N.B. As to opinions of character in this book[2]—they are opinions of a censorious and fastidious man—they are opinions of a party man—and they have reference to party men. Another period and different circumstances may enable me to measure the amount of reservation with which on this score of defectiveness alone, they ought to be received: I write these few lines to remind myself hereafter that I was not ignorant

---

[1] This paper contained by anticipation nearly those persons who afterwards formed Lord Grey's administration, the composition of which indeed it was not difficult to foresee. [WEG] [This paper has not been found among the Gladstone Papers at the B.M.]

[2] ADD.MS 44819.

of the probability of distortion in my views at the moment when they were taken.                                                  *April 26. 1836.*

## 30: ADD.MS 44819, ff. 22–23

In a conversation today with Sir Stratford Canning he told me that Lord Stanley had shown him letters of Mr. Canning's at the period when the Revolutionary War had just begun or was about to begin, explaining to Lord Skelmersdale, then Mr. Bootle, who was abroad, the tendencies of the Minister and the country, and indicating the progress of his own mind towards the political creed which he adopted with his mature and manly years, and contemporaneously with the awful development of principles which then gave a new character and decision to party distinctions. He observed that Canning was evidently the man of principles in politics: a position in which I concurred: that Lord Londonderry was *without* principles: of this sentiment I could not fairly judge. He thought Lord Londonderry was a man of decided talent, and of remarkable generosity and highmindedness: that he moved along with a great party, and that his good personal qualities supplied in great measure the want of definite political ideas; which was the sense he meant to give to the term principles.                      *April 26. [1836]*.

Of Buxton I should say not that his mind is without weight or force, but that it is a force arising mainly from weight, and that his intellectual movements are loose and lumbering. He has strong and benevolent instincts which are, I believe (and I rejoice to believe) at the bottom of all his conduct, and really his motives: but there is an indistinctness in his particular perceptions, or some other defect, which takes away clearness from his purposes and communicates inconsistency to his expressions, and he does not, I verily think, know his own mind with reference to the details and specific forms of his proceedings from day to day. His propositions are perpetually changing: if he lays down limits for himself it seems to be that he may presently overstep them: yet not deliberately, but because he sees a present advantage, and forgets his rule or his pledge: and being in like subject matter liberal to others he is lax to himself. So that in his parliamentary conduct[1] he is devious from

---

[1] Labouchere very well remarked to me, that his power of speaking was much beyond his power of thinking and judging; and that it was very considerable.                                                  *July 19. 1838.*

want of feeling, and he requires to be watched as carefully as if he were a man of duplicity which I do not believe him to be.

*April 26. [1836].*

## 31: ADD.MS 44819, ff. 24-25

June 8. [1836].
Wordsworth since he has been in town has breakfasted twice and dined once with me. Intercourse with him is upon the whole extremely pleasing: I was sorry to hear Sidney Smith say he did not see very much in him nor greatly admired his poems. He even adverted to the London sonnet as ridiculous—Sheil thought this of the line

Dear God! the very houses seem asleep:
I ventured to call his attention to that which followed as carrying out the idea

And all that mighty heart is lying still.
Of which I may say, *omne tulit punctum.*[1]
Wordsworth came in to breakfast the other day [30 May] before his time—I asked him to excuse me while I had my servants to prayers: but he expressed a *hearty* wish to be present which was delightful. He has laboured long: if for himself, yet more for men, and over all I trust for God: will he ever be the bearer of evil thoughts to any mind? Glory is gathering round his later years on earth, and his later works especially indicate the spiritual ripening of his noble soul.

I have but few of his opinions; but these are some—he was charmed with Trench's poems—liked Alford—thought Shelley had the greatest native powers in poetry of all the men of this age—in reading 'Die Braut von Korinth' translated, was more horrified than enchained, or rather, altogether the first—wondered how any one would translate it or the 'Faust', but spoke as not knowing the original—thought little of Murillo as to the mind of painting, said he could not have painted Paul Veronese's 'Marriage of Cana'—considered that elderly age in great measure disqualified him, by its rigid fixity of habits, from judging of the works of young poets—I must say that he was here even over liberal in selfdepreciation. He defended the smoke of the steamboat as more poetical than otherwise to the eye (see Sonnets)[2]—thought

---

[1] *Omne tulit punctum qui miscuit utile dulci* (Horace, *Ars Poetica*, 343). 'The way to win applause is to be instructive as well as agreeable.'
[2] Blank in MS.

Coleridge admired Ossian only in youth—and himself admired the spirit which Macpherson *professes* to embody.

Serjeant Talfourd dined here to meet him yesterday. He is vehement against Byron: saw in Shelley the lowest form of irreligion, but a latter progress towards better things: named the discrepancy between his creed and his imagination as the marring idea of his works, in which description I could not concur—spoke of the *entire* revolution in his own poetical tasks.

We were agreed that a man's personal character ought to be the basis of his politics, their law and canon: he quoted his sonnet on his contested election, from which I ventured to differ as regards its assuming nutriment for the heart to be inherent in politics. He described to me his views: that the Reform Act had as it were brought out too prominently a particular muscle of the national frame: the strength of the towns: that the cure was to be found in a large further enfranchisement, I fancy of the country chiefly: that you would thus extend the base of your pyramid and so give it strength: but he wished the old institutions of the country preserved, and thought this the way to preserve them. He thought the political franchise upon the whole a good to the mass— regard being had to the state of human nature: against me: it seemed to me the due limit was found in the necessity for the prevention of abuse, and that political franchise, periodical duty *agrément* annexed, was not, relatively, good.

This was yesterday. Today I met Sheil at Mr. Bingham Baring's. His expositions of opinion were most extraordinary, taken altogether. They fell thus—that he wished to pay tithe to his clergyman, and never meant to withhold *ultimate* payment—but at last he demurred to answer questions on this head. He said Peel ran after events and caught them by the tail—that the idea of an unsettlement of property in Ireland after repeal was chimerical—he said, why do you not pay the priests: but declined then to say whether he would agree to it. Soon after with singular incongruity he declared that the following measures would pacify Ireland, complaining that Governments allowed them to agitate instead of taking four or five aside and asking what they would think necessary.

1. Municipal institutions (ma)[1] when the temporary ferment had subsided.

---

[1] 'Ma' is the Italian for 'but'. It is frequently used by WEG to express doubt or dissent (*ex. inf.* Professor M. R. D. Foot).

2. Redistribution in the Church, and adequate provision.
3. Surplus alienable—but perhaps a compromise on this.
4. Payment of the Roman Catholic clergy—which would make it their interest to maintain tranquillity.

He said he now wrote to the Archbishop, at an election, to send him all the priests of the county to the hustings, and they all came, with the farmers behind them, mounted, as *black colonels*. That Maynooth instruction at present was as bad as it could be. That his party held at their disposal all the patronage of Ireland, down to the tidewaiters— judges, magistrates and all; though O'Connell had got nothing personally. That our conceding the Irish measures would break up their party—that the Roman Catholics were not really radical—then, that our alliance would be fatal to them—that middlepartymen in Ireland ought to be treated as the lukewarm Christians in Scripture—that you must either have a hot Tory or a hot reformer—'Up with the black banner and no quarter'—then I think a prudential compunction stung him and he protested several times he had only been speaking in metaphors. The Duke of Bedford's subscription to the O'Connell fund he considered as that of Lord John Russell—Catholic Emancipation he said was not the cause of their present power in Ireland, but the Reform Bill—that the Protestants had decidedly and overwhelmingly the *property* of the country, but that reform had taken power from property, and given it to *numbers*.

The impression of him left on my mind was, that his character had the same defect as Brougham's though differently seated, and differently compensated or disguised: want of a radical perception of truth, of its unity, integrity, and combination, and of ultimate purposes. He has a very brilliant mind.

## 32: ADD.MS 44777, f. 29

June 24. 1836.
This morning I breakfasted with Mr. Rogers: Mr. Wordsworth only was there. Rogers produced an American poem—the death of Bozzaris—which Wordsworth proposed I should read to them: of course I declined—so even did Rogers—but Wordsworth read it through, in good taste, and doing it justice.

Rogers said that in 1827 Lord Lansdowne lost reputation by his allowing Lord Goderich to become leader in the Lords under Canning: but said the cause was this: that Lord Lansdowne had imbibed an apprehension that the Duke of Newcastle was to be sent to Ireland by Mr. Canning, with whom he felt that as Home Minister he could not act. He described Lord Lansdowne as regular in private life: much averse to business: strictly just, though short of being generous.

All seemed to agree in fearing greatly the results of the remission of the newspaper Stamp Duty.

[*Blank in MS*] said he had two Satanic friends—Lord S. and B. of E.[1]

## 33: ADD.MS 44777, ff. 31–35

Haddo. October 27. 1836.

A man's political creed is naturally confirmed by discovering in the personal characters of those under whom he acts, the principles which command his reverence or the tempers and affections which are the worthy objects of love.

It is impossible not to be struck with the equity and gentleness which mark the mind and language of my host Lord Aberdeen. There is a vein of sarcasm but tempered and subdued by these the more prevailing elements of the composition. Mr. Forbes spoke of Charles Grant with more mildness I thought than I had ever seen in a man holding very decided opinions on public affairs: yet his sentence was too severe for the ejected Minister whom Grant has followed in office. He would not hear of a suspicion as regarded his integrity: that is the consistency of his actions with his selfpersuasions: but he admitted—for it was an admission—that pecuniary difficulties might have had a share in vitiating the mental processes and producing selfdelusion.

In the evening he conversed upon politics—and with much freedom. He said, 'In the Irish Church question we stand upon a principle. Not so in that of the Corporations. There our opposition rests upon temporary circumstances: and it cannot very long be continued. There must be some compromise. It is impossible to make an absolute refusal of municipal institutions to Ireland after having given them to England and Scotland.' This was the substance. It remains, however, to inquire whether there be not a principle involved in continuing the resistance

---

[1] Perhaps Lord Stanley and Henry Phillpotts, Bishop of Exeter.

so long as the circumstances by which it is maintained and justified endure. He thought the political character of these new corporations would be rather an inconvenience, than an evil of overwhelming magnitude.

He seemed to doubt Stanley's *junction* with Peel: to draw a broad line between him and Graham: he reported well of the Duke of Richmond: who lately expressed his hope in *public* that Brodie would soon represent the Elgin burghs: and declares that Sir J. G. Craig shall have no political influence whatever as his agent: but he has not the character of entire singleness. Again I give the substance.

When the Duke of Wellington made his celebrated and most unjustly handled antireform declaration in 1830, he said to Lord Aberdeen on sitting down, 'Have I said too much?' Lord Aberdeen's answer was, 'You will hear of it again.' He volunteered to add, that the Duke probably had in view to reassure the minds, and attract the support, of those who had opposed him since the Roman Catholic relief.

October 28.
We are today joined by our Lord Lieutenant.[1] A political conversation in the evening. Our host reprobating the wish entertained by some at the time of Peel's resignation that he should have dissolved again: and further considering that it was impossible for him to have protracted the struggle any longer: I led the conversation to the previous dissolution, lamenting it but only in the person of 'on'. He expressed himself pretty fully on the subject: first to the effect that a Government could not have been *made* in the first reformed Parliament: but to this view he did not seem tenaciously to adhere. That the dissolution was inevitable in December 1834 he considered undoubtedly a great misfortune: could there have been delay, we should have gone to the country with 1. a factious spirit on the other side displayed, 2. the real character of the Ministry unfolded, 3. substantive public measures throwing into the shade what was he thought *the* great misfortune of all at the time, namely the illtimed and premature dismissal of the Melbourne Government: which would certainly without Althorp have crumbled in pieces of itself (*io altrimenti*,[2] the Radicals I believe would have kept it in) after meeting Parliament: or a Church question would have given an

---

[1] John, 8th Viscount Arbuthnott.
[2] 'I thought otherwise'.

appropriate cause for dismissal. That said Lord Aberdeen is undoubtedly the nail to be driven: that is the question which, if any one, will bring us home after all. Frequent dissolutions in the long run, more ruinous than any other cause to the Conservative party: it cannot bear the expense. Such was the early policy of Charles the First, and how fatal.

I ventured to insinuate some way a doubt, whether this evil was inevitable: having always been in my own mind fully persuaded, that a fair exhibition of the positions of the contending parties in the existing Parliament might have been made within the course of a few weeks with every probability of its producing those effects on the *public* mind which have since been wrought without having an occasion afforded for their telling throughout the country by a General Election: whereas the immediate dissolution was certain ruin. It was against a good axiom too of Machiavelli: good though expressing only a part of the truth: not to hazard the whole of our fortunes upon a part of our means.

The statements of Lord Aberdeen were in substance these. It was thought that the majority would be so great against the Government— probably two or three to one—that an effect would be produced in the country more prejudicial from the *votes* of the House, than advantageous from the light of discussion and of party movements thrown upon the general subject. That the Duke was studious to keep the question open for Peel's decision: but still the party had generally commenced active measures and expenses: every body *assumed* that there must be an *immediate* dissolution, though without reasoning it: so that when Peel came home, the question was to a certain extent virtually prejudged: the mind of the party was fixedly set towards it. Our Lord Lieutenant thought there was much weight in the first of these considerations. But is it so heavy in the balance of probabilities as were the risks, approaching so nearly to certainty, of an immediate election, with the people in the dark, and the battle fought upon the dregs of the Reform question?

I mentioned Lady Canning's deep regret at the course which was pursued. Lord Aberdeen rejoined that Lord Lauderdale warned him against it on his way up to London. I might have added a conversation with the Duke of Hamilton, though not a friend, at Clumber, immediately after my election.

Upon the whole I could not positively collect from the general tenor of what passed, that Peel consented to the dissolution against his own opinion: or that he would certainly have done otherwise had he been on the spot in the first instance: as I have sometimes been led to think. On the other hand the conversation was far from *negativing* the latter supposition. Haddo. *October 28. 1836.*

I should have added both the Lords A. were strongly of opinion that the main support of the Lords was in the greatness of the minority opposing Government in the lower House: and that without it they could not persevere.


Today my host expressed an opinion that Stanley had by hot language needlessly embroiled the Canadian question: and had on the other hand done wrong in granting the Committee.

Mr. Forbes reported to me his having said, that he never knew the Duke express regret for the course he has pursued at any time, on any measure or question, in public life.

Lord Aberdeen thought J. Stephen a man of almost the greatest abilities he had ever known. I said what a pity, and shame, that he cannot rise. He said he did not see why if in the position of Peel or the Duke, he should not make Stephen being *such* a man, Secretary of State: although there were great difficulties. Or why he should not be put to do anything, that man might do. He had entire confidence in his integrity (*anche io*[1])—considered him Conservative.

He gave a fair opinion of R. W. H[ay] as an useful public servant in his office, from his acquired habits of business and knowledge of affairs.

*October 29. 1836*


## 34: ADD.MS 44819, ff. 26-30

1837.

I visited Sir Robert Peel on the 4th of March 1837 about the Canada question and again by appointment on the 6th with Lord Aberdeen. On the former day he said, is there any one else to invite? I suggested Lord Stanley. He said, perhaps he might be inclined to take a separate view. But in the interval he had apparently thought otherwise. For on Monday he read to Lord Aberdeen and myself a letter from Stanley, written with the utmost frankness and in a tone of political intimacy ('my dear

---

[1] 'Me too'.

Sir Robert') saying that an engagement as chairman of a committee at the House would prevent his meeting us. The business of the day was discussed in conversation and it was agreed to be quite impossible to support the resolution on the Legislative Council in its existing terms, without at least a protest. Peel made the following remark: 'You have got another Ireland growing up in every colony you possess.' There is too much of melancholy truth in this. O for the blending and harmonising power of the Church!                                        *March 17.*

Yesterday I had the following communication with Ashley on the subject of my speech delivered the night before. It was in the Carlton Club: he seated himself opposite (but close) to me. I spoke of the division: and regretted that he had been unable to speak. He said: 'Now I will tell you what, Gladstone: you made an able speech, but you disappointed me. I expected that you would have taken up the question on higher grounds but you did not, and I was much grieved at it.' I expressed in the first place my great obligation to him for this true friendly conduct: and I begged him to particularise wherein lay those defects which had given him pain. He replied: 'This measure cuts up by the roots all our national homage to God, which is the meaning of a Church Establishment. If it be passed we separate ourselves as a nation from Him. It is true you spoke about the principle of a national Church, and alluded to the spiritual destitution of the country, but you did it in the same cold manner as ——:[1] what could be more flat and void of feeling than his description of that destitution? Now you have many gifts and advantages, and you may become a considerable man in this country and one of God's most efficient instruments: and I am sure you had it in your heart to say more than you did in last night's debate, and so I said when conversing on the subject with several others as we walked home, but you did not give that high tone to your speech which I had expected from you: I am sure you will excuse my saying it.

'Then as to your quotation from Polybius I must say I thought it altogether misapplied: the mention of the heathen gods as producing the same result with the revealed Gospel! I will tell you the remark my wife made upon it, and I thought it a very sensible one: she said, "Why if that religion could have produced such effects, they will naturally ask, where was the need of Christianity?" It is true that Polybius writes as

---

[1] Blank in MS.

you quoted him, but his statement is not true, and if you examine the Roman character you will find it fraudulent, selfish and hardhearted, and their policy towards other nations the most grasping and oppressive on the face of the earth.'

I have here condensed what he said: for I could not faithfully portray and I was unwilling to caricature by an attempt at detail that warm and noble eloquence of feeling with which he spoke of those highest and deepest truths which are at the bottom of his whole life and conduct. And I proceed to my own reply.

'As regards the Polybius', I said, 'I am confident it was merely the want of a fuller explanation which has caused your present impressions and that upon your own principles, with which I concur, I could show that I was not fundamentally wrong. My meaning was this. On looking at the Roman institutions I find they had a principle of vigour and of permanence which belonged to no other in those times: and that the phenomena presented by them require the assignment of a gigantic cause which alone is adequate. Then I find the man who of all writers of the period most united philosophy with practical habits, discover that cause in the extraordinary degree to which that religion though false was brought home to the mass of the people and interwoven with all public concerns. I grant you that the Romans were fraudulent, selfish, and hardhearted: but I say compare the individual character of the Roman with that of the Athenian or other ancients in general and you will find him less fraudulent, less selfish, and less hardhearted than they. (I meant in early times.) Now I say this is fairly ascribable to the influence of their religion which blind, false, and degraded as it was, had nevertheless this efficacy, that it tended to impress his mind with the idea of a power beyond himself, and to carry his desires beyond himself, concentrating them upon the glory of the State—this I do not call a right principle, but it is better than the principle of mere selfworship: and thus we show not only like Bishop Warburton and others that the principle of religion was found by lawgivers to be the only one capable of binding together social institutions, but that in the case where those institutions were of the most effective structure, we find coexisting with that fact an extraordinary degree of attention to religion. There comes the *argumento fortiori* for the influence and use of revealed truth. I admit my reference to it was brief and obscure.'

'Yes your quotation was looked upon as the end of your speech and immediately after it they began to talk.'

'But I felt I had been unconscionably long. And further: I feel this: it is comparatively easy to speak in the House of Commons on matters merely secular: but as you ascend higher into the region of principles, the work of expressing what you feel in the face of a popular assembly becomes incomparably more delicate and difficult.

'So much for Polybius: and now my dear Ashley for the remainder of what you have said: I concur in every sentiment: I bow entirely to your animadversion: I did desire, and intend, to state your own very words that the plan went "to rob God of His honour and the poor of their right"—but it was with this as with many of my best intentions and desires—I am striving to learn how to speak, but I have not yet acquired the effective use of memory in the face of such an audience nor my selfpossession so as to express with any fullness what I feel and the words wholly escaped me: in every speech I have ever made, and more in proportion as the subject was a lofty one, I have painfully had to feel how entirely I have failed of realising even my own conception of the subject, and much less the subject as it really is. I therefore only hope that this fault may hereafter be less weighty. I admit its existence to the full.

'But pray tell me whether you had any affirmative objections to the speech: whether you thought that in what I *did* say there was anything of untruth or of unworthy compromise?'

He assured me nothing of the kind. 'Then I trust you are satisfied with my avowal of the want which I cannot too much lament.' He expressed himself quite so. Mr. Goulburn came up while we were speaking about Polybius: praised that part of the speech which described the vacillation of Ministers, and objected to the citation. I thanked both very heartily: and admitting the want of elucidation said I thought the groundwork of the idea in my mind came from St. Augustine *De Civitate Dei*, at least that it was that book would *permit* me to think and say.

Mr. Goulburn went away. Ashley and I sat writing for a little. When I had concluded, I rose and to attract his attention said 'Good day': I shook him warmly by the hand as the simplest way of offering my thanks to this true and highminded friend and he replied 'God bless you'. May blessing be upon him. Now what a character is this—he would not join in the tones of compliment and congratulation without showing me how sadly I had fallen short of my duty. Of what value is such a friend! I felt with him in all that he said: and yet had he not said it, that feeling would have fallen asleep in my mind, I should have indolently acquiesced in the less courageous sentiments of others, and should have lost the advantage of remembering hereafter the previous deficiency, and of being thereby incited to use every effort for the purpose of supplying it. Would that such were the acknowledged law of friendship and its universal practice!

He spoke of himself in depreciating terms: of his having omitted to acquire the power and practice of speaking and of its being now too late. I entirely demurred to this low estimate: I have never heard him speak, except with talent, clearness, and general effect. He spoke of retiring from Parliament—I replied God forbid—unless you go thence to some still more extensive sphere of usefulness— I had in my mind, whether wrongly or not, the desirableness of his appointment to some important government abroad. Some effort must be made for religion in our colonies.

I might have said much more of our conference but I was anxious to make it really a narrative not a dissertation.                    *March 17.*

The same day I had a very pleasing conversation with Mr. Shirley and found we thought together upon public matters—that our sole and sufficient encouragement, and hope, and consolation amid the circumstances of the day is the knowledge that there is a scheme of government larger than the scope of any political combinations, which comprehends them all, and in which both their general effect and all their minutest particulars, are subordinated by a Divine power to a supreme law of wisdom and goodness. Without this belief the turmoil of political life would be intolerable: by it, not only is it alleviated, but ennobled.                                                           *March 17.*

The same evening I had an interesting conversation with Mr. G——V——. We began about colonies: I spoke of the desirableness of framing colonial administration as a scheme of education, intended to terminate when the growing state should become adult. Thence of prospective legislation in general—and from that we narrowed our range again to the Irish Municipal Bill. *His* desire was that it should be treated as a temporary question: and the concession as one to be withheld only until the special facilities for agitation in Ireland were removed by securing the property of the Church and by the establishment of a Poor Law. I had the same view but hoped above all things that we should hold and act upon the question, which was of more importance than anything else. I understood him to agree. Personally he now felt disinclined to vote but did so at Stanley's request.

He told me that some time ago he went to Peel, expressed these feelings, and with them the hope that he would place the question explicitly on this ground, or at least leave room for the inference that he was not opposed to the grant of municipal institutions to Ireland for ever—acquainting him at the same time that there were men, such as Morley and Wilmot for example, who felt this to be an insuperable stumbling-block—he for his part thought it would prove the one serious obstacle to an effective Government in the hands of Sir R. Peel.

That in reply Peel at first demurred: did not see any possibility of compromise: and at last said, as I understood, that he could not carry the question: apparently having in mind the Bill of 1829—and the prognostications of Hobhouse in his speech on Lord Francis Egerton's instruction—to the effect that he (Peel) would come in and carry it. So that V—— left him as I understood without seeing his way in any degree to a conclusion. Sir Robert Peel threw out the following hint— had it never struck him (Mr. V——) that a majority of the Lords would probably have refused to extinguish any of the existing Protestant corporations but that this compromise had been laid as a basis upon which there should be a similar action in both Houses?

From this V—— inferred that the Lords were, even if by anticipation, the cause of our adopting the course of last year and the present. I thought otherwise: and mentioned Lord Aberdeen's opinion in conversation—Lord Wharncliffe's in print—and what I had heard of the Duke of Wellington's which would no doubt have carried the body.

He told me that he had been Stanley's instrument in organising the 'section'—that at their meetings the question of English Municipal Reform had been chosen as that which should distinguish them from the followers of Peel—but that they happily arranged to leave the declaration of their feelings to Stanley alone instead of each man's issuing or not as he pleased an individual manifesto. The feeling of repugnance to identification with the then Government on account of the English municipalities question, was now he thought reproduced in some minds with reference to the Irish one.

He told me that Stanley voted for the amendment to the Address in 1836 rather against his own opinion which was in favour of a protest with explanations, for the sake of cooperating with the Conservative body in whose feelings as to the substance he entirely sympathised. Shaw came to Stanley on that day to announce what had been decided at the Conservative meeting after the Speech. Previously to that time Stanley had not been in communication with the Conservative party. Of this I was aware at least up to near the end of January when I was at Drayton.

V—— of course regarded Stanley and Peel as now for some time past firmly united.

On four questions out of five in my opinion Stanley will, *where there is a difference*, be disposed to take the stronger line.      *March 17. 1837.*

## 35: ADD.MS 44819, ff. 30–31

Tuesday. April 11. 1837.

At night during the division I had a conversation with Sir H. Hardinge in the lobby. He was, like myself, full of admiration of the speech we had just heard by Sir Robert Peel. Not merely of its boldness as a manifesto, the quality which will be most generally attractive: but of the combination with that boldness of the exquisite tact and skill with which he had extricated himself and his party by the terms of that speech from the difficulties that might have flowed out of a perseverance in the course of last year, if unexplained. He had shown them that this question of which the intrinsic merits are less important than its extrinsic relations, and determinable by them. Sir H. Hardinge observed that this Corporation question might have become, in a degree, to a future Conservative Government, what the Appropriation Clause has been to the present Administration, a heavy load, contracted through conduct in a previous state, impossible to shake off. Not that our course on the Corporation Bill was analogous to that of the Government on the Irish Church in itself: but that it might have appeared so—and would probably and plausibly have been argued to be so—unless this explanation had been given before the Ministerial offices became vacant. He seemed to anticipate that the Lords would postpone the Bill until they could see the Ministerial Church plan. He did not expect that the Government intended an Irish Church Bill this year: but having given the pledge (in the King's Speech) they ought to be bound by it.

The division of 55 was highly satisfactory. As I came out of the lobby (rather bored, however, with the prospect of a trip to Rossshire in three hours by the Dundee steamer) Stanley touched me and said, *Bon voyage*, evidently in great spirits: and the same in the passage coming out to my brother and me. He said I suppose it is sure. I said, it should be so but the Scotch are very apt to look at the powers that be. He rejoined in a tone very audible, 'But they are very far sighted, and I think they will be inclined to look a little at the powers that *may be.*' *April 13.*


## 36: ADD.MS 44819, f. 31

Thursday June 8. [1837].
Lord FitzGerald spoke at dinner of the Bishop of Exeter's having declared (in his place I believe), that he would never again believe a Roman Catholic Archbishop on his oath. Lord Harrowby said, 'He was quite right: but not in saying so.' *June 14.*

I heard from Sir R. Peel in 1835 immediately after his resignation that Lord Grey was against the abstract resolution, on the Irish Church. Yesterday this was confirmed to me by the Archbishop of York who told me—that Lord Grey told him, at the time, that it was folly to attempt to legislate upon such a resolution: that he did not believe there was a surplus: that Church purposes remained unsatisfied, viz. the building of churches and glebehouses and the augmentation of small livings—after these perhaps Protestant schools: that he did not believe there were funds to satisfy these purposes: and that he would consent to no diversion until they had been one and all fully met.

Why did he not speak as well as say this? The Corporation Bill unsealed his lips for an opposite purpose. *June 14.*


## 37: ADD.MS 44727, ff. 176–177

Of Mr. Gladstone.
Born December 11. 1764.
Early 1777 apprenticed to Mr. Ogilvy at his ropewalk for three years.
1780 At the expiration of the term, went to assist his father in the shop, which furnished flour and groceries both to ships and in retail. Would

if need even carry a sack of flour into a cart at the door. About 1783 made a partner. In this capacity saved £500.

1784 First voyage to the Baltic to buy corn—loaded two ships, and returned to Leith.

1785 Second voyage to the Baltic for the same purpose—returned in one of the ships to Liverpool, not by arrangement with his friends—arrived about the New Year. Saw Mr. Corrie: who visited Leith in the summer to make himself better acquainted—and proposed a partnership for fourteen years.

1787 Partnership commenced on the first of May. He found fifteen hundred pounds: five saved by himself, five lent by his father and five more by Allan Stewart (and Co.?) at five per cent. Corrie furnished the same—and B. the third partner £1,000.

Visited London in February or March to attend Mark Lane and became acquainted with the corn trade. There became acquainted with Sir Claude Scott who expressed a wish to take him into partnership—but the parties to the existing agreement would not consent.

178— Visited America to purchase corn with unlimited confidence from Sir Claude Scott—found a scarcity and very high prices on arrival—some dozen ships chartered and on their way to him for cargoes. Thrown entirely on his own resources—travelled south from New York, making the best arrangements practicable: loaded the ships with lumber and other commodities: one only with flour: upon the whole only about £1,500 were lost by the enterprise and it confirmed Sir Claude Scott's confidence and friendship for him.

Visited Rotterdam. Fasque: *September 1837.*


## 38: ADD.MS 44819, f. 2

November 20. 1837.

With great delight I learnt yesterday from Sir A. Grant (what it is odd enough that the West Indians present in the House at the time were not apprised of) that Stanley had a deputation of them at the Colonial Office after the division on Buxton's motion—placed himself entirely in their hands—stated to them the impossibility of carrying the twelve years' apprenticeship—and offered to resign his office as incompetent to redeem his pledge: at the same time saying that they might do well under all the circumstances to release him from it—which they did, and it was under their allowance that he acted.

## 39: ADD.MS 44819, f. 32

November 28. 1837.
This day I had for the first time an interview with the Duke of Wellington on business. Its immediate object was the Cape of Good Hope. His reception of me was plain but kind. He came to the door of his room, 'Will you come in? how do you do, I am glad to see you.' We spoke a little of the Cape—he said with regard to the war—and with sufficient modesty—that he was pretty well aware of the operations that had taken place in it having been at the Cape and being in some degree able to judge of those matters. He said 'I suppose it is there as every where else: as we had it last night about Ireland in the House of Lords: they won't use the law: as it is in Canada: as it is in the West Indies: they excite insurrection everywhere (I, however, put in an apology for them in the West Indies); they *want to play the part of opposition*: they are not a Government for they don't maintain the law.' He appointed me to return to him tomorrow.

## 40: ADD.MS 44777, ff. 36–39

1837.
On Wednesday December 6 a meeting of Conservative Members was held at Sir R. Peel's where Lord Stanley appeared—the first subjects of discussion were the Spottiswoode subscription and the Controverted Elections Bill. When they had been disposed of Sir Robert Peel stated that there was a question remaining which he felt absolutely bound to notice—that of the pensions inquiry. He regarded it alike as a breach of faith equitably pledged and as a blow to the principle of monarchy. He detailed the circumstances of the settlement on the accession of Lord Grey's Government, including the fact that Lord Althorp made resistance to the inquiry a vital question: he stated that of course it was to be expected that some gentlemen might hesitate to accompany him in an unpopular vote, but without presuming to dictate to or advise them for his own part he felt that he must under what ever circum-

stances divide the House upon this question which he regarded as essentially one of principle and not expediency, stating markedly the distinction which he conceived to subsist between these classes.

Lord Stanley then said that standing in circumstances somewhat different from those of Sir R. Peel he might be allowed to state a few words. 'It is probably known', he proceeded in some such words as these, 'to the present meeting that in former times differences of opinion have subsisted between Sir R. Peel and myself on subjects of great political importance: but it should also be known that with regard to every public question now pending—with regard to the quarter from which danger to our institutions is to be apprehended—and to the manner in which that danger is to be met—there subsists between us the most uniform and unqualified concurrence.' He proceeded to speak with spirit and feeling of the immediate subject matter.

(December 15. 1837. But I have repeated this several times in the interval.)

The same night in the House of Commons I had a phrenological conversation with Wakley, during a part of the debate on Colonel Verner's motion.[1] He is free in strictures on the men of his own party and looks for more reciprocity than I was disposed to give.

'What folly, Mr. Gladstone, in your party to bring forward these questions such as Perceval and Verner have taken up.'

No reply.

'It makes the Government quite saucy—they are quite up again.'

I said, 'At all events two Irish Colonels do not constitute "our party".'

'No', he replied, 'that is true. You don't get into these scrapes Mr. Gladstone—you may be very well satisfied—you've a good organ of caution.'

I turned the conversation to Sir R. Peel's head.

'It is out of sight the best head in the House: before I came into Parliament I had never seen Peel and had a mean opinion of him: directly I got here I saw that I had been wrong. The powers of his intellect are prodigious: though they are rather restricted in their development by his organs of caution and secretiveness which are immense. His benevolence and veneration are small: I think he cannot

---

[1] This debate took place on 5 December.

be ardent in his friendships, and must be very reserved. He has a power of comprehending a subject entire and in detail at once, far beyond that of any other man here—though I have seen as fine heads elsewhere.

'O'Connell has better perceptive powers but his head in general is very inferior—he shows a great deal of quickness and talent on parts of a subject—but then he is *done*.

'Inglis has little veneration—a very large organ of obstinacy—but he is a good man: conscientiousness is well developed.

'Estcourt has an enormous organ of obstinacy. I'll be bound he has all his own way at home.

'Warburton has a large veneration: but with it a large causality. Such combined induce the worship of God but in His works, not direct.

'When we sat together on General Darling's committee in 1835, directly that he had entered the room I saw, that he was innocent of the cruelty imputed to him—he is not deficient in benevolence.'

Upon the whole he seemed instead of taking his phrenology as a help to his experience to make the former the absolute standard of judgment and almost to overlook the latter.

I pointed out to him Milnes and Acland and he promised to regard their heads with attention.

The latter had his hat on. 'Ah', said he, 'he is a good natured fellow but there's not much in him.' At that moment he happened to take his hat off. 'Oh', said he, 'I see I was wrong, he has a good head.'

*Friday December 15. 1837.*

## 41: ADD.MS 44777, ff. 40–51

Saturday, December 9. 1837.
Today Sir R. Peel entertained Lords Stanley and Sandon, Sir G. Clerk, Sir G. Murray, Sir S. Canning, Gally Knight, Hope Johnstone, Milnes, and myself. The conversation principally sustained by the two first, was *most* interesting and I never heard Peel speak with such continued freedom.

Of Talleyrand he said that he had declared he never lived in private with the heroes of the French Revolution in its later stages, but kept the society of gentlemen. Mirabeau was by far its greatest orator. He spoke well of Barnave, less of Vergniaud.

Peel did not think him a man of great intellect properly so called:

but a *roué* thoroughly experienced in the ways of the world, and having a peculiar gift of escaping from difficulties. The memoirs Talleyrand had written they thought of no value—he was accustomed to read them to his company, and it was an essential condition of the value of such compositions that they should be shown to no one during the writer's life. This was Stanley's remark. Peel added they should be written within two days of the events recorded—and no corrections subsequently made.

(It was further observed of Talleyrand that he was always studying point and was generally without eloquence or emotion—his speeches were epigrammatic but in very many cases, said Peel, would hardly bear repetition.)

He [Peel] observed that at this time a man with the first information might write the most interesting book that any period of history could supply: recording simply as facts the impressions entertained and propagated with their variations from day to day.

Lord Stanley said that ten years ago he had begun to record the divisions in the House of Commons, with remarks re the debates—but flung away his book when he had advanced through three or four pages only, finding it impracticable to maintain in this way the action of a double life.

Peel then told us that on the day before he brought forward the Roman Catholic question in the House of Commons, the Duke, Lord Lyndhurst, and he, were with the King for five hours, going over the Bill. The King strangely took a new objection—suggested to him he supposed by the Duke of Cumberland. It was for the Oath of Supremacy that he stood out, though without the proposed alteration the Bill would have been quite nugatory. 'What', he said, 'alter the Oath which has subsisted from James I!' Both stood out—the King gave them the farewell kiss; they returned to town in the evening having quitted him at five, virtually out of office. But late that night Peel had a note from the Duke saying the King found his difficulties so great that he was obliged to recall them.

Peel did not think the King had a strong genuine antipathy to the Bill—but that he wished to make as good a case as possible having resisted it to the last—and he conducted the fight with great ability.

Stanley said that when he parted from Huskisson as his undersecretary in 1828 at the commencement of the year, Huskisson said to

87

him, 'Depend upon it if I don't find that I possess in the Government I am now joining the influence I think I ought to have, I shall quit it in less than four months.'

Sir S. Canning said Huskisson predicted that the country would be covered with railroads, at the time when the Liverpool and Manchester was first introduced.

The resistance of the Archbishop of Cologne both Peel and Stanley appeared to consider as '*the* event of the day'—so Peel termed it.

'Which side would you take, Lord Stanley?' quoth Milnes—'I assure you I have not an idea.'

(The King's—said I to him, aside.)

'Very little doubt which side I should take', said Stanley—but he did not specify which in words. Milnes described the Archbishop as a man of meek but firm piety without temporal objects.

Peel said, 'That does not at all satisfy me—he may be I think a man ready to advance the interests of his Church through a democratic and anti Prussian party.'

The Pope will support him said Milnes: and the great mistake now is that we do not recognise in the Pope the great Conservative power of Europe wherever his influence extends.

'Conservative disposition perhaps', said Stanley, 'but Conservative power I doubt.'

'What *we* want in Ireland', rejoined the unconquerable Milnes, 'is to rivet the Papal power, which always goes to support the Crown. The Pope is supporting Dr. O'Finan against Archbishop Machale.'

'If the Pope comes into collision with Dr. Machale in Ireland', said Stanley, 'I'll back Dr. Machale. As to mildness, there is no milder man to all appearance than Dr. Murray the Roman Catholic Archbishop of Dublin—but let any occasion arise on which he can support the Pope against the King, and he will do it to the uttermost.'

'The King of Prussia in fact is trying to *do* what we have failed in the attempt to do in Ireland or in Canada: and the difficulty is to keep the Roman Catholic Church quiet where a Protestant religion is either ascendant or coordinately established'—said Peel. 'The Government of Prussia is extremely tolerant and this opposition to it therefore is to be suspected. Hitherto peace has been kept by compromise—the Bishops have winked at the division of the children according to the sex and religion of the parents.'

'And this Archbishop', said Stanley, 'would not wink.'

(Sandon added, that Protestantism was the great support of the Crown as against the Church.

This is capable of being stated in a very different form!)

'I almost never heard', he likewise said—and Peel assented to it all—'a commencing speech so pleasing and so full of promise as that of young Acland.' He thought it in great measure unpremeditated.

'Wholly so', I said—'I have it from himself.'

'He spoke', resumed Lord Stanley, 'with so much character, and so much like a gentleman, in possession of his subject, readily turning his mind to it, and having abundance of easy and good language to express what he felt.'

'I am inclined to think', said Peel, 'that the less preparation a young man makes for his first speech, the better. Mr Fox when informed of some brilliant first speech, said he was sorry to hear of it. That of course is an extreme statement of the case—but there is much truth in it.'

Stanley said he complained of Pemberton for coming forward so little—he thought him so nice and so able a speaker—though nowhere near Follett.

Peel considered him gentlemanly but still feeble—he spoke of the luminous mind as Follett: his perfect safeness, never making a false step: Sandon said, he never rose to a very *high* eloquence but concurred in all that had been said—and added he never uttered anything that one could wish unsaid.

Stanley declared he could hardly name the man to whom he would rather listen—in all his parliamentary life—unless perhaps Canning. He likewise observed his perfect selfpossession. The other night on the Spottiswoode question, he (Follett) in the middle of another part of his speech, upon an interruption, turned coolly to him in the interval, and said, 'If you don't mind giving it up, I wish you would give me that newspaper with O'Connell's speech in it'—to which he (quite in character) instantly agreed.

They spoke of the Canadian question: Peel observed on the responsibility Ministers were here undergoing—especially in connexion with the present removals of their Governors—acts independent of Parliament, while they failed to act upon the support Parliament had given them. The Canada question both he and Stanley considered as the great present embarrassment of the Ministry.

They spoke of Italy. Of Ferrara, as very striking and poetical in its desolation: the grass of its wide streets: and its castle. (Thus far the same night.)

Wednesday, December 13.
Sir R. Peel and Sandon both observed that Ravenna appeared much older than Rome. Milnes gave Hazlitt's explanation: referring it to the vagueness and indefiniteness of the idea of art found in the former more than the latter and thus carrying the idea of remoter antiquity. Ma.

Talleyrand, Peel said, appeared to rate Berryer very high indeed, and perhaps next to Mirabeau. Stanley seemed to have a somewhat similar impression.

'Whatever party is in', said Peel, 'the Ministers who sit in the House of Lords will be very different men from those in the House of Commons: will live exclusively among gentlemen, will dine out every day, and pass their time in abusing the House of Commons.'

Five-sixths I think of the conversation was from the lips of Peel and Stanley.

Clerk told me afterwards that he had seen Peel and that he was much pleased with Stanley's unreserve at the party, and at his feeling himself apparently so much at home among the men with whom he acts.

I had a conversation with him (Sunday evening) upon the Church question in Scotland. He agreed with me that Charles I was the best friend of the Kirk as the source of its administrative efficiency: that the severities of Charles II's reign belonged to the *State*: that the establishment of Presbyterianism at the Revolution was a very great blow to the principal of national Churches: that the Dissenters of Scotland (of course not including the Episcopalians) were more bitter in their temper and more outrageous in their demands than those of England: and he expressed no surprise when I communicated to him what Mr. Miller had said to me, that in his belief the bulk of the Scottish clergy were desirous, if they could have it, of a moderate episcopacy.                                          *December 13. 1837.*

## 42: ADD.MS 44777, ff. 52-53

December 14. 1837.
I sat with Mr. Rogers an hour and a half at night.

He thinks that Wordsworth has a higher order of poetical talent than any other man of the day—but has never done himself justice, riding his theory of poetry to an extreme.

When the Duke of Wellington went out he met him, by expectation if not by appointment, at Mr. Arbuthnot's in company with Mrs. Arbuthnot alone: and the Duke, knowing him he said to be in constant communication with Lord Grey said emphatically and with great emotion, 'They want me to place myself at the head of a faction—but I won't. When I differ I will state my difference from the present Government: but I will go down into my county and do what I can to keep order there.'

He thought Mr. Canning—as well as Peel—associated with inferior men. Lord Dudley was hardly his friend: and Lord Haddington rather his butt.

Wordsworth and Southey are not on the most unreserved footing in their communications: the latter is more intimate with Taylor.

'Women will always be true and faithful to you if you make known your preference of their sex.'                    *December 15. 1837.*

December 15. 1837.
Lord Aberdeen after dinner said he had mentioned to the Duke of Wellington Brougham's observation, 'that his despatches would live when they—the politicians of the day—were all forgotten'. The Duke replied, 'By —— it's true: and when I look at them, I can't think how the —— I could have written them.'

Lord Aberdeen thinks the ancients had not painting, in our sense.

Lord Ashburnham maintained, that painting and sculpture never are in a really flourishing state together. Ma?        *December 15. 1837.*

## 43: ADD.MS 44819, ff. 32-33

January 20. 1838.
On Tuesday [16 January] I was at Sir R. Peel's privately about Canada: two or three were present. The chief said that Sir F. Burdett

was very warm in his Toryism at Drayton Manor. He said of him, evidently with regard not to his honour or character but to his understanding, that he was 'a poor, a miserable creature'.

Today there was a meeting on Canada at Sir R. Peel's. There were present:

Peers—Duke of Wellington, Lord Aberdeen, Lord Haddington, Lord Ripon, Lords FitzGerald, Wharncliffe, Ellenborough.

Sir R. Peel, Lord Stanley, Hardinge, Lord G. Somerset, Mr. Wynn, Sir S. Canning, Lord Eliot, Fremantle, Lord Lowther, Holmes, Lord F. Egerton, Sir W. Follett, Sir F. Pollock, Pemberton—and myself.

Lord Ellenborough thought the Bill went beyond the necessity of the case and should be rejected: he also thought the Government could not and would not take the right measures in the present emergency, and that it would be desirable by the rejection of the Bill to throw them out.

Peel said, he did not object to throwing out the Government provided it were done by us on our own principles: but that to throw them out on Radical principles would be most unwise: he spoke strongly and I thought hardly with sufficient *ménagement* for a friend: but I am not able to judge.

He agreed that less might have been done, but was not willing to take the responsibility of refusing what the Government asked. He thought that this rebellion had given a most convenient opportunity for settling the question of the Canadian Constitution which had long been a thorny one and inaccessible: that if we postponed the settlement by giving the Assembly another trial, the revolt would be forgotten and in colder blood the necessary power might be refused.

He thought that when once you went into a measure of a despotic character, it was well to err if at all on the side of sufficiency: Lord Ripon strongly concurred.

The Duke sat with his hand to his ear, turning from one towards another round the circle as they took up the conversation in succession, and said nothing till directly and pressingly called upon by Peel: a simple but striking example of the selfforgetfulness of a great man.

Nothing could be more harmonious. Where any variation of opinion was stated, it was given subject to the general wish of the meeting. And no one except Lord Ellenborough seemed really to dissent from Peel's proposition to accept and modify the Bill.

With regard to omitting in the preamble those words which allude to summoning the quasi-representatives, he thought the case against them so strong, that he was almost afraid of the Government's giving way at once on the bare proposal of his amendment.

*January 20. 1838.*

## 44: ADD.MS 44819, ff. 33–34

January 26. 1838.

I was myself present at about eight hours of discussion in Peel's house upon the Canadian question and Bill,[1] and there was one meeting held to which I was not summoned.

The Conservative amendments were all adopted in the thoroughly straightforward view of looking simply at the Bill, and not at the Government and the position of parties. Peel used these emphatic words: 'Depend on it, our course is the direct one: don't do anything that is wrong for the sake of putting them out: don't avoid any thing that is right for the sake of keeping them in.'

The following amendments were finally fixed upon.

1. The omission of the words in the preamble.  ⎫Sir R. Peel
2. Of the clause empowering the Crown to repeal the Act.⎬mover
3. To call Lord Durham's councillors (clause 2) by some other name than legislative. Mover Sir E. Sugden.
4. To except from his power of altering laws all Imperial Acts, and all Colonial Acts altering Imperial Acts. Mover, Sir W. Follett.
5. To reserve the power of the Crown to disallow, etc. This was entirely met by the alterations introduced in the *pro forma* commitment of the Bill yesterday.

Every one of these points has now been carried without limitation or exception. For the Opposition party this is, in familiar language, a feather in its cap. The whole has been carefully, thoroughly, and effectually done. Nothing since I have been in Parliament—not even the defeat of the Church Rate measure last year—has been of a kind to tell so strikingly as regards appearances upon the comparative credit of the two parties.

[1] 20, 22 and 25 January.

## 45: ADD.MS 44819, f. 34

February 17. 1838.
Molesworth's motion against the Government under the name of Lord Glenelg may prove a trick—or a farce—or the cause of the overthrow of the Government.

The feeling of our friends appears to be, so far as I yet know, that it is hardly possible to avoid voting for it. I speak both of leaders—as Lords Ellenborough, FitzGerald, Wharncliffe; and of more private persons.

And Bonham told me yesterday that Peel said to him on Friday night he was convinced the time was now arrived when it had become desirable to eject the Ministry.

It is clearly I think a case for great consideration, between the general principles of our party policy and the desirableness of adhering to them—that is to a defensive course—on the one hand—and the pressure on the other of the constitutional principle of executive responsibility, which must one would say become a mere name if the case of Canada remains unnoticed, as it involves the conduct of the Government, except in one or two speeches in each House of Parliament.                                                          *February 17.*

## 46: ADD.MS 44819, ff. 34–37

February 28. 1838.
On Monday [26 February] Ashley told me that he had spoken to Peel the Saturday evening before at the Palace respecting Molesworth's motion and that he then expressed an invincible repugnance,

1. to fighting under Radical colours;
2. to countenance a personal attack on Lord Glenelg.

Sometime before Mahon told me he had suggested a vote of censure on Ministers—and that our leader answered it would do very well if we could carry it.

And Bonham told me about ten days ago that Peel had told him he thought the time was now come when it was upon the whole desirable to eject the Government.

Last night Peel asked me in the House what I had thought about

Molesworth's motion and desired me to go to his house today at one, not mentioning the meeting to other parties.

I found there with him Sugden, Follett, Pollock, and Mahon. All present read in succession three letters which Peel produced, one from Stanley of the 19th, one from the Duke of Wellington, and one from Graham, of later dates.[1] Upon these a conversation of two hours, very deeply interesting, ensued.

Stanley's letter was in answer to one of Peel's which he did not produce—probably it was not copied?

He went through the various alternatives open to us, rejecting each in succession until he arrived at one which Peel's letter I fancy had intimated—namely to move an amendment on Molesworth's motion conveying our own disapprobation of the Canadian policy of the Government. To this upon the whole he decidedly inclined; preferring it to a general vote of censure because he thought we should lose by the confusion of an universal debate and he was anxious to avoid an Irish discussion. He came, however, to this decision with very great regret: sensible of the advantages heretofore attending our defensive policy, and its tendency to draw to us moderate men from amidst our opponents: but thinking it impossible to vote against Molesworth or stay away, as well as very undesirable to vote with him. He stated I may add that the amendment would probably be so worded as that Molesworth and the small section acting with him would in all likelihood vote with us.

The Duke's note referred it to Peel to decide what course to pursue: stated with great sagacity the difficulties of our position: inquired how, with all the spare troops locked up in Canada for some time to come, and with the additional embarrassments that the American Government by pressing the boundary and other questions might produce, and with O'Connell ready to agitate for Repeal i.e. against rents in Ireland, we were to throw the present Ministers into his arms and to hope to be able to govern Ireland under such conditions? He did not see his way, he concluded, as to any part of the course proposed, Peel thought he inclined to 'the previous question'.

Graham's letter was written on perusal of the Duke's, and concurred with it in spirit to a considerable extent. He upon the whole recommended the previous question, observing that if the Government

---

[1] C. S. Parker, *Sir Robert Peel*, ii, 361–364; ADD. MS 40318, ff. 116–120.

refused to avail themselves of it we might with more justice on being forced to an opinion vote for Molesworth. He thought we could not vote for him in the *first instance*. Peel after a considerable discussion backwards and forwards tending to bring out the points of the case went through the list of the alternatives before us: which appeared to be:

1. To stay away—upon almost every occasion a wretched course: he would not entertain it for a moment—he at all events would meet the difficulty.

2. To move the previous question—a course ill understood: much damaged by having been so unsuccessful with the Government on Monday night: and tending from all he could understand to break up the party for a length of time, which he deemed a misfortune of the highest order, since its union enabled it to sustain the House of Lords and neutralise all legislative mischiefs. He had written accordingly to the Duke of Wellington: and he evidently had no idea of this course.

3. To move the adjournment of the House—or (he believed) also to move the Orders of the Day—would have this advantage as compared with the former—that when it was rejected, it would leave the main question open to amendment. But it seemed to be the sense of all, that the Government though they would not dare a counter-resolution, could not be satisfied with less than a direct negative, and the question therefore arose, whether they would not join Molesworth against us on any of these three motions, and thus beating us, leave us after all in the midst of the entire difficulty of the original question.

   Besides that the party could not be so carried.

4. To *oppose* Molesworth's motion outright was deemed incompatible with the state of feeling amongst ourselves.

5. To support him was objectionable besides other grounds, on the same as the last named alternative: men among our friends, few but respectable, would rise and declare their determination not to join in any personal attack nor to follow a leader in this censure of Government who was founding that censure on principles diametrically opposite to ours—and who had but very lately exulted in the prospect of the defeat of our troops.

6. It remained to move an amendment. There said Peel you must be prepared for the consequence of that amendment. He thought that

in the present state of the House we should probably carry it. Follett thought so too. Peel contemplated the whole subject with great apprehension. He did not think a Conservative Government formed in consequence of a hostile movement could permanently stand—and he saw no escape from the dilemma. He was prepared to grapple with it: but he saw in it ruin, for years at least, to the Conservative cause. If the Government were beaten, they must resign. If they resigned it was impossible for those who drove them out to refuse the call of the Queen. Considering the present Conservative force and *Conservative attendance* he could not look forward with any sanguine anticipation. Our position was much altered for the worse by what the Duke has said respecting troops. He doubted from the Duke's note what course he might individually pursue in the event of a change of Administration. The eagerness of Brougham, and of Molesworth and those who thought with him, should be a warning to us that the measure they held out was probably most detrimental to our cause. By a defensive policy we had gained much. Had the wishes of the young men, had the talk of the Carlton Club, been the rule of our actions, he doubted whether we should have reached our present position. Those who were loudest, and keenest for strong measures would afford least of real assistance when the period of pressure came in carrying on a Government. They looked no further than to the satisfaction of an immediate desire. He would have wished to hold off, and let the internal jealousies of the body on the other side work for good, and operate the removal of the present Administration. He intended to defer making up his own mind finally until the latest possible moment.[1] And at all events he would not be the mover of the amendment.

He looked also to the other alternative—that of our being beaten on it. In that case, he seemed to think with nearly all of us, our hands would be free to take almost any course upon the original motion. After proposing our own views in an amendment, we might decline any vote at all.

Sugden suggested that many might not be satisfied even with an amendment and would at all hazards vote for the motion. Then said Peel if any considerable body acted so, he could not longer consent to hold his present situation, and would immediately request

---

[1] MS: movement.

that another person might take it—he at all events would absolutely withdraw.

He knew that there were complaints of his withholding his opinion on this motion—but what motive could he have for withholding it ? It was necessary for the general interests of the party to keep its movements quiet until they came to be authentically declared—but to him personally it could be no pleasure to reserve his opinions.

All seemed convinced that our friends would be satisfied with an amendment.

7. It was further agreed that the amendment should, if made, not touch the general but the Canadian policy. We could not touch in that policy the military question. The Duke of Wellington's opinion would be repeated against us a thousand times. We must attack the hesitation and feebleness of the despatches from home—and the unfaithful use by Lord Gosford of his executive powers.

There remains one topic curious, as showing I think a latent and unconscious inclination in Peel's mind to grapple with the Government and come to issue upon their Ministerial existence with all his powers. Mahon suggested, when Peel expressed his apprehensions as to the stability of any Government that might be formed—that we might so frame our amendment as to embody in a very palpable form our Conservative principles and thus prevent any Radicals from voting with us: the result would be, a majority for the Government. *Peel did not at all adopt this idea*: and yet it seemed to meet the difficulties suggested in his own previous reasoning. Sugden made some general objections about Peel's lowering his own position if he did not come forward with the greatest possible support—and Peel threw out as the terms of an amendment something extremely general—'that this House upon a review of the Canadian policy considers so and so'—which form would be most likely to include the Radicals. Following Mahon I said, 'You might censure them, for example, on account of not going by resolution—last year to the repeal of the Act of 1831 instead of merely to the payment of arrears'—but Peel replied, 'You must not do what will touch Ripon, Graham, and Stanley.' Now this would not have done so, for Stanley advised this very course last year in his speech on the resolutions. I was struck by this answer, apparently very inconclusive, from *him*—and by the previous indisposition to work upon Mahon's hint—as if Peel were really anxious in spite of himself, or without his own consciousness, to *try a fall* with the Government.

It was finally agreed (in my absence) to send for the Duke to town: and that notice of any amendment should be given on Friday.

For my part I see, 1. a crisis not of our seeking nor making: 2. a constitutional obligation of no common stringency to censure weak and paltering conduct on the part of the Canadian executive: 3. on party grounds an obvious inexpediency and many dangers: 4. those hopes that belong to men who follow with resolution the call of a higher duty. *February 28.*

## 47: ADD.MS 44819, ff. 37–38

March 5. [1838].
On Saturday night [3 March] at Bridgwater House I understood from Mahon that the Duke came up on Thursday night and had a long conversation with him on the case: he sat long with Peel on Friday, but nothing was arranged as to the terms of any amendment.

By conversation with Fremantle I find he entertains the same impression as I do about Peel's own private inclinations, i.e. that they rather point towards coming to issue with the Government.

In my morbid state, I could not say which way I would have the division go did it lie in my power: partly from that state: partly because on the one hand the conduct in question so loudly calls for censure: because on the other I dread offending weak brethren, i.e. consolidating in a party adverse to the Constitution men who are in intent its friends, though I believe in error as to their means.

*March 5.*

Sir R. Peel today very luminously and powerfully explained his views on the question of tomorrow.

Lord Stanley has made some change I think in his opinions since he wrote. Today he was most anxious that the amendment should be worded *for the very purpose* of precluding Radical support.

Peel would neither look to the right nor the left, but would have it a full expression of our own sentiments.

Graham was studious that it should not be so worded as to repel any one for the repulsion's sake.

Lord Chandos was desirous that it should be so framed as that the Radicals might join us.

The substance as given by Peel was not quite in Lord Stanley's sense, but nearly.

There was not a dissentient voice upon the propriety of moving an amendment as the most honourable course. *March 5.*

## 48: ADD.MS 44819, f. 38

April 14. [1838].
Easter Eve. On Wednesday [11 April] I dined with Sir Alexander Grant. Croker spoke of the rupture with Mr. Canning as the great misfortune of the Tory party. In that all seemed to concur. He then said to Sir H. Hardinge and Mr. Sturges Bourne, 'Well, we had nothing to do with producing it.' George Dawson sat by him and felt the allusion whether it was intentional or not: he responded to it courageously and said, 'I must say, for myself, that I am *heartily ashamed* of what took place at that time.' *April 14.*

## 49: ADD.MS 44819, f. 38

April 22. [1838].
Sir James Graham joined me when coming out of St. James's church and walked with me for an hour and a half. He spoke very freely and I rejoiced in an opportunity of making pretty nearly a clean breast on the Church questions most immediately impending, to one of the leaders of my party. We conversed first on the Irish Church resolutions: then on cathedrals, clerical education, learning, preaching: then on the Commission, the Convocation, Synods, and of a Church Government, and of a new development of Church powers: with something on the distinctive character of the Church as maintained in England, and her identity before and after the Reformation. In the last point, and the contrast with the Church of Scotland where though the faith was reformed the institution was destroyed, I think he concurred. He did not seem alarmed at the idea of restoring Church Government: and this it was which gave me the liveliest pleasure. He entered into her idea as a divine institution, and thus her as it were indefeasible right and necessity of government. On the question of cathedrals I thought him candid and accessible.

He had learned that the Scotch Church deputation were extremely pleased with these sayings of the Duke of Wellington: that whatever people might say of Canada, or Spain, that was all very well, but the real question was Church or no Church. That the Roman Catholic Church was bad enough but the voluntary system far worse. That Churches without endowments, were no better than so many mosques.

*April 26. 1838.*

## 50: ADD.MS 44819, ff. 38–39

April 25. [1838].

A long sitting and conversation with Mr. Rogers after the Milnes marriage breakfast. He spoke unfavourably of Bulwer: well of Milnes's verses: said his father wished them not to be published: because such authorship and its repute would clash with the parliamentary career of his son. Mr. Rogers thought a great author would undoubtedly stand better in Parliament from being such: but that otherwise the additament of authorship, unless on germane subjects, would be an hindrance.

He quoted Middleton, that a man should strive 'to do what deserves to be written, to write what deserves to be read, and to leave the world the better and the happier for his having lived in it'. He commended the English of the passage—which I have probably destroyed.

He quoted Swift of women—that in a woman love produces desire, in a man the reverse. He has a good and tender opinion of them: but went nearly the length of Maurice (when mentioned to him) that they had not that specific faculty of understanding, which lies beneath the reason.

He thought Bulwer was not sought in society—met him only at two places. Peel was odd, in the contrast of a familiar first address with slackness of manner afterwards—the Duke of Wellington took the greatest interest in the poor around him at Strathfieldsay—had all of eloquence except the words—pointed to the grate and said, it is not in meat or in drink that the poor suffer here, it is in *that*. Condemned Milnes, his preface especially, on the score of affectation. Thought the great beauty of style was, to be a *mere* medium of thought, not severally and substantively the object of perception. Fox's father said of him he was glad he was going to be married for then he would be one night in bed. Pitt was without some human propensities—with them could not have done his work.

*April 26. 1838.*

## 51: ADD.MS 44819, f. 39

Mr. Rogers quoted[1] saying of Brougham that he was not so much a master of the language as mastered by it. I doubt very much the truth of this. Brougham's management of his sentences, as I remember the late Lady Canning's observing to me, is surely most wonderful. He never loses the thread, and yet he habitually twists it into a thousand varieties of intricate form.

He said when Stanley came out in public life, and at the age of thirty, he was by far the cleverest young man of the day: and at sixty he would be the same—still by far the cleverest young man of the day.

The Duke of Cambridge told me when dining last month at the Archbishop of York's that his brother the King of Hanover was a thoroughly well intentioned man towards his subjects, as he was fully persuaded: but very liable to be misunderstood. *April 28. 1838.*

## 52: ADD.MS 44819, ff. 39–40

May 19. [1838].
A confidential meeting today at Sir R. Peel's on Irish matters, with reference to Lord John's declarations of yesterday in the House. It was felt by every one present (except Mr. Litton who yielded to the majority) that the opportunity of settling the tithe question ought not to be lost. Many, however, thought that we ought not to grant twenty-five per cent of deduction, but Peel said he would feel a difficulty in diminishing this amount and Sugden spoke to the same effect. The point was reserved: and no more determined than to entertain the proposal.

We were unanimous in the opinion that, at considerable political disadvantage as appears probable, we must allow popular corporations to Ireland the tithe being settled and a bona fide rating established under the Poor Bill. Peel led the way in giving expression to these sentiments but they were evidently those of the Members present, comprising the leading persons of our side except Lord Stanley, with others in all near thirty. *May 19. 1838.*

---

[1] Blank in MS.

## 53: ADD.MS 44777, ff. 54–59[1]

In the debate on Sir Eardley Wilmot's motion [22 May] I was anxious not to speak at all, or if at all, late, so as to catch whatever animadversions might be made on my speech of March 30. I would, however, from not feeling satisfied of the state of the House at the close of Bulwer's speech have risen to prolong the debate, but that Mr. Goulburn ten minutes before had requested me not to think of it, and in a manner which indicated I thought, and which afterwards I found was the case, that he spoke not from himself alone. Lord Stanley had suggested it to him.

Now the responsibility of the blunder evinced by the division undoubtedly lies with the Government as they were leaders and we followers. But Grey told me today that he remained silent in obedience to orders: and further that Stanley had just been over the way and told the Government they might depend on nearly every one from our side, whereas one third voted against them.

However, immediately after the division, feeling that the only course of justice to all parties, especially to the negro, would be to rescind immediately, I spoke to Mr. Irving and to Mr. Ellice to that effect: the latter called Rice and he did not seem to differ: he went and spoke to Lord John: but Lord John immediately after made the feeble and unstatesmanlike announcement that *if* a Bill were now introduced he would resist it to the uttermost.

From more and more reflection feeling more and more convinced of the fatal impolicy of such a course I wrote strongly on Wednesday the 23rd to Sir George Grey to that effect and my note went on to Lord John. It stated especially the necessary misapprehension which would arise in the mind of the negro if such a vote went out uncontradicted by the next packet. The West Indians also pressed the Government in a similar sense, but Stanley told me at Sir R. Peel's Lord John had just told him they had determined nothing beyond this: in case of a Bill, to rescind the resolution: and otherwise, to consider it as abandoned. Stanley had replied, 'Take what line of opposition you please, we shall support you: but the stronger the better.'

Finding, however, from communication with all parties during the

---

[1] WEG later added the title 'Apprenticeship' (i.e. negro apprenticeship) to this memorandum.

day and in the evening at Lady Salisbury's that but one opinion existed, and that in conformity with the impressions I had entertained and which Ellice told me he had first proposed to Lord John, I wrote another stronger note to Sir George Grey, representing it as nothing short of *infatuation* to allow the vote of Tuesday to go without a contradiction: and even hinting that my feeling was so strong I could not pledge myself not to become the mover in default of any fitter party: and I was indeed only deterred by the conviction that the ricketty men of the Government side who were with difficulty brought to support them would infallibly leave me. My father saw Lord John in the course of today, Thursday, and asked if he would support the motion supposing it made by an individual Member? Lord John said for himself he would. But he laid little stress on the division, considered it of no very great importance, and said he could not depend on either side of the House in support of a motion to rescind.

At three I saw Grey by his desire and most earnestly urged the arguments that this resolution must be to all intents and purposes a law in the eye of the negro, that he *must* misunderstand it, that the explanations of Governors and magistrates would be in vain, that the law could only be maintained under those circumstances by increased coercion and punishments, that the ground gained in establishment of a friendly understanding would thus be wholly lost, and that the maintenance of the apprenticeship law *here* next session would be rendered I thought both in a moral sense unjust, and in a parliamentary one impracticable.

He adhered to what I think the wild dream of believing that the resolution might be explained away to the negroes, feared that a motion to rescind might be lost, yet foresaw accumulated difficulties, evidently, for next year, as the result of the negative and temporising course.

All that I could now do was to ask our *whippers in* whether they anticipated worse voting from our side: and finding that they did not, to lay this before Grey and E. Stanley, that they might know it and that so the Government might not lay the blame of a highly culpable inaction on any doubt of the staunchness of the Conservative party: then further to lay it before Stanley and Peel that they might be aware Lord John had laid the ground of his intentions partly in a supposed disposition on our side of the House to flinch: and lastly to see Ellice and press upon him the necessity of immediate and decisive action.

Peel's short declaration to this effect produced an immediate result. Lord John who had just before said he did not deem it necessary for Government to take any measures rose again and stated that if Sir Eardley Wilmot did not give his answer tomorrow he would reserve to himself the power of then declaring what line the Government might take independently of his movements.

And in the course of the evening Grey told me that the Government intended now at all events to move resolutions setting forth what had occurred and declaring the necessity of maintaining the term of apprenticeship, and the rights of the negroes under the existing laws; and of carefully providing for their enjoyment of entire freedom after August 1840. This they are to propose on Monday or Tuesday: and they have a steamer to be held in readiness to carry out the intelligence.

Peel had shown me a little before his sketch which was in the main a preamble as in the Government plan, reciting what had been done and then proceeding to declare the determination of the House with regard to the future. This he had shown to Ellice, and Ellice had no doubt given it to the Government, who were glad enough to adopt it, Peel's but not from Peel immediately.

Thus thank God this important matter seems again to be laid in a right train: and the incredible weakness of the Government has been stimulated into the requisite exertions ere yet the critical time had altogether escaped. *May 24. 1838.*

Lord Stanley, as I learn from Sir James Graham, oversets the account given to me of the miscalculation which led to the second of our divisions. He stopped at the Treasury bench on his way into the House, and did *not* at all encourage the idea that nearly the whole of our side would vote with Government. It appears on the contrary that Rice was the person who examined the House, and recommended dividing, in opposition to More O'Ferrall, whom E. J. Stanley had left to look after the House. Lord Stanley merely sent the message to me through Mr. Goulburn, not to speak: thinking the Government ought to carry on the debate. *June 5. 1838.*

## 54: ADD.MS 44819, f. 40

On June 12 we had an interesting meeting at Sir R. Peel's on the Scotch Church Extension. There were present: Lord Aberdeen, Sir

Robert Peel, Lord Stanley, Sir James Graham, Hope Johnstone, Clerk, Pringle, Colquhoun, Sinclair, Ashley, and myself. The question raised was whether the recent vote of the General Assembly on the Auchterarder case had not rendered it in a prudential view proper to postpone the motion for endowment, on account of the large powers of independence which it seemed to claim.

In my view it made little difference as I am ready to vote for the endowment only in fulfilment of a contract to which I was not a party.

Ashley was friendly to endowment but much staggered by these Popish pretensions.

Lord Aberdeen thought by appealing they had acknowledged the authority of the House of Lords in the matter, and did not condemn their claims: they merely understood themselves to be vindicating the guaranteed rights of their Church.

Colquhoun regarded the point as a nice question of law, whether they had a right to make the *call* a real condition instead of a nominal one, or as involved in this: and thought the decision of the Lords would be conclusive.

Stanley and Graham seemed to regard the claim as one essentially tending to the separation of Church and State.

Peel did not think that by appealing they had admitted the supremacy of the appellate jurisdiction, and did not give a decided opinion on the claim.

The general inclination was against an immediate motion for endowment. But the collateral question is one more important still. Its true position seems to be this. The governing body seem to feel that the real title to the ministry does not depend on Presbyterial ordination. For if it did, why an absolute veto, not motive nor subject to appeal, in the people? They have not the divine commission by succession. They grasp at the best image of it, in the sanction of the majority of communicants: better than that of a ministry if fictitious—better than that of a patron or of a civil court. I cannot but sympathise with them: although it is their false principle which consistently leads them out into this conduct, yet they are probably acting in conformity with their own (bad) ecclesiastical constitution. The question they may fairly raise is this: whether popular consent at the very *least* be not essentially embodied in the discipline of that Church which was incorporated with the constitution by the Act of Union? But the results are yet in impalpable obscurity—they may be immense.     *June 13.* [*1838*].

## 55: ADD.MS 44819, ff. 40-41

June 13. [1838].

Sir R. Peel dined at Mr. Dugdale's. After dinner he spoke of Wilber-force: believed him to be an excellent man independently of the book, or would not have been favourably impressed by the record of his living in society, and then going home and describing as lost in sin those with whom he had been enjoying himself. (Upon the other hand, however, he would have exposed himself to the opposite reproach had he been more secluded, of morosely withdrawing himself from the range of human sympathies.)

He remembered him as an admirable speaker: agreed that the *results* of his life were very great (and the man must be in part measured by them).

I spoke to him of Stephen as a man of extraordinary powers—yes, said he, but a bad adviser, is he not? This is I fear a just description.

He disapproved of taking people to task by articles in the papers for votes against their party.                                         (*June 22*)

We had a meeting today on Irish Corporations where Sir R. Peel explained himself with admirable clearness and force; showed the pains he had taken by repeated meetings to ascertain the sense of the party in both Houses: stated the necessity he felt of abiding by the course to which he had pledged himself: a bona fide ten pound franchise: that there were two conditions of our assent: one the precedency of the committee on the Tithe Bill: the other the acceptance of certain amendments: that neither were fulfilled. He evidently felt the conduct of our seceders on this question.

It is pleasing to see that we are acting on a higher ground than in 1835. The amendments were equally (if I remember right) refused in the House of Commons upon the English Municipal Bill—but we, I fear inconsistently, did not divide against the third reading.

One of the few exaggerated sentiments I ever remember to have heard Sir R. Peel express was on the first production of this Irish Municipal Bill: he then spoke of it as a question of first rate magnitude and importance. I do not think it takes this rank even now when many circumstances have combined to give it an additional factitious weight.

*June 22.* [*1838*].

## 56: ADD.MS 44819, ff. 41-42

July 17. [1838].

I had a letter from Sir R. Peel, forwarding one of the Rev. Mr. Ryder's of Rathcormac, in which was given an extract from a note lately addressed by me to him. The purport of the extract was that I regretted the 25 per cent proposal—thought 20 the highest deduction compatible with equity—and believed there was a prevalent feeling of that kind among those who voted for the 25 as against 30. This says Sir R. Peel Mr. Ryder has pretty generally circulated.

Here is rather a difficult question raised. I think the 25 per cent *unjust.* I voted against the thirty, thinking the 25 a smaller injustice. At first sight it appears strange that one should not be at liberty to excuse one's self for an apparent participation in injustice to a person affected by it.

Yet I incline to believe that I was wrong in not guarding my letter as one not to be communicated. There remained no reasonable hope of substituting twenty for twenty-five: and therefore it was not a wise course to spread dissatisfaction with the Bill as it stood. But I ought to have foreseen that Mr. Ryder being much concerned might make this use of my letter, and therefore to have guarded it. Had there been a fair probability of amending the provision, the case might have been difficult.                                                                    *July 19.*

July 18.

I complimented the Speaker yesterday on the time he had saved by putting an end to discussions upon the presentation of petitions. He replied that there was a more important advantage: that those discussions very greatly increased the influence of popular feeling on the deliberations of the House: and that by stopping them he thought a wall was erected against such influence—not as strong as might be wished, probably some day it might be broken down, but he had done his best to raise it. His maxim was to shut out as far as might be all extrinsic pressure, and then to do freely what was right within doors.

*July 19. [1838].*

## 57: ADD.MS 44819, f. 42

July 25. [1838].

We had a meeting today at the Primate's on the question of accepting Lord John Russell's plan respecting the arrears, open as it is to the twofold objection first that it recognises the violation of the law and encourages its repetition by the absolute surrender of the claim against the tithe payer; secondly that it extinguishes without option legal rights upon an inadequate composition.

There were present—the Archbishop of Canterbury, the Primate, Archdeacon Stopford, the Earls of Haddington and Aberdeen: Lords Lyndhurst and FitzGerald. Of the Commons, Peel, Graham, Stanley, Sugden, Inglis, Estcourt, Goulburn, Fremantle, Captain Jones, and myself.

Lord Lyndhurst and Sugden were the only two who seemed to be eager for acceptance: singular that the great lawyers of the party should have been the men least alive to the above objections.

The Primate and Archdeacon Stopford would not be responsible for the assent of the clergy and their willingness to receive the measure: but they thought it upon the whole for their interest.

Peel asked for the opinion of every one round in succession. The general tone of the replies was, reluctant acceptance. Graham saw in the 25 per cent a waiver of principle—and was content that this too should pass as a part of the same arrangement.

Lord Haddington regarded the concession with the greatest repugnance and could hardly say yes to it.

Stanley agreed, but he never had had, and hoped never to have again, such a struggle to bring his mind to assent to a vote. He took this fair distinction—that as a member of the Government he never would have consented to forgo the claims of the law—but the Executive having already surrendered them, and thus rendered the arrears infinitely more difficult to recover, he had to consider what were the best terms that could be made for them upon their diminished value.

Fremantle wished we could get a fixed composition of 50 per cent, instead of the probable sum of £260,000 to meet the probable claim for £500,000 or £600,000. Peel thought it better not to define the percentage—for obvious reasons.

The Archbishop of Canterbury thought it for the benefit of the clergy to accept: but did not give an opinion on the propriety of waiving the principle involved—he said it was not the first time, and (I thought) that the mischief was consequently diminished. But query this position ?

I could not escape, and said I would individually prefer retaining the prospect which had seemed to be regarded at former meetings as the alternative on the rejection of Peel's propositions: namely letting the arrears question stand over for settlement next session, to the grievous principles here involved: but that adverting to what the Primate and Archdeacon had said, I would not act apart from the rest.

*July 25.* [*1838*].

## 58: ADD.MS 44819, ff. 43-44

March 1. 1839.
Bunsen to breakfast.

Stern said Italy was possessed by two demons, superstition and irreligion. The opponents of the superstition are very bad.

The family principle is destroyed in the upper and middle ranks.

The religious system is at war with the intellectual life—the intellectual speculations are consequently very gross and material: rank and blank atheism—and materialism.

Horrible disclosures of Bishop Ricci—a moral man but a low believer—as to the state of monasteries but especially of nunneries: and published by De Pottu in his Memoirs—he had had a visitation of them.

Petition of Baden clergy in 1837 to Chamber: signed most generally by those above 50 and 60, against compulsory celibacy.

Prussia is improving in moral and intellectual life from affliction endured in the Revolution—not so Spain and Italy. (But query the French priesthood ?) French priesthood extremely low in learning. Trevern the best Bishop they had at the time, he wrote against Faber— and he had much the worst of it.

Number of communicants high under Napoleon and Louis XVIII —fell under Charles X—and now rises. Cause, influence of the Jesuits, and reaction.

Protestantism requires the basis of a national life.

In Prussia the chapters elect—the King has a *veto*.

Drosti was proposed to the chapter—which had no determinate inclination.

In France there is nothing between Voltaire and superstition—the priests have *petits séminaires* so the priest is a priest from a boy upwards and has no contact *avec le siècle*: which would be destructive.

In Prussia no Jesuit may dwell: and the priest must pass through the National Schools and universities and their examinations as a preliminary to his theological education: and such alone can hold benefices.

In Silesia candidates for the priesthood are not enough for the cures, by 25 per cent: though the King has founded 40 bursaries to encourage them within the last few years: through the dread of the celibacy.

In Baden only four of the cures are supplied, such is the want.

Canonico Iocio has a very respectable position among the Italian clergy: but he introduced Bunsen to his mistress: saying *Io non posso aver moglie, ma, ho figli*[1]—no mother with grown daughters would allow a priest to be *ami de la maison*. The women would not confess to married priests, would not confide in their silence.

Laws of the Frisians in the Middle Ages that priests should have each his concubine, and Bishops two, *ne turbent aliorum mulieres*.[2]

King of Prussia could not help the five priests who petitioned him: the people would not like the abolition of compulsory celibacy.

Schlegel and Holberg enlightened the Roman Catholics to whom they went over: they had no others like them.

Astounded at Wiseman's declarations concerning *toleration*, and *education*, in Rome.

Thinks rationalism will be fought down in Germany by the principle of faith. The greatest men are believers: and the most popular lecturers.

Germany acts on the principle in religion, on which England in politics—everything must be spoken out.

The great battle on the Continent is now that between the Jesuits and the Governments for the education of the people.

In Rome the Jesuits pick out all boys of talent for the priesthood: of higher talent for their own Order. But they repress mental activity and investigation: and they *drill* a man rather than educate him.

---

[1] 'I cannot have a wife, but—I have sons.'
[2] 'So as not to upset other men's wives'.

## 59: ADD.MS 44819, f. 44

March 19. [1839].
Yesterday A. Kinnaird told me the Duke of Sussex at Lord Durham's had been strongly condemning my book and by way of an odd contrast just after as I was standing in conversation with George Sinclair, O'Connell—with evident purpose—came up and began to thank me for a most valuable work, for the doctrine of the authority of the Church and infallibility in essentials—a great approximation to the Church of Rome (in answer to Sinclair)—an excellent sign in one who if he lived etc.—it did not go far enough for Dr. Machale, but Dr. Murray was delighted with it—he termed it an honest book—as to the charges against Romanism I was misinformed.

I merely said, I was very glad to approximate to any one on the ground of *truth*, i.e. rejoiced when truth immediately wrought out, in whatever degree, its own legitimate result of unity.　　　*March 19.*

This day I had a long conversation with Bunsen on Church and collateral matters. On the Eucharist, baptism of infants, Nicene Creed, he frightened me: either his line, admirable as he is, is not quite safe, or which is more probable, the narrowness of my view prevents my accurately comprehending its securities.

He gave me a very interesting account of his own biography: of the King of Prussia: of the religious reaction there: of such sermons as were preached, utter and universal desolation: *Church* still prostrate: individuals can now do little, and less as the tendencies of the age are developed: they must witness to their convictions.　　　*19 [March].*

## 60: ADD.MS 44819, f. 45

March 23. [1839].
Count Montalembert came to me and sat long, for the purpose of ingenuously and kindly impugning certain statements in my book, viz.

1. That the peculiar tendency of the policy of Romanism before Reformation went to limit in the mass of men intellectual exercise upon religion.
2. That the doctrine of Purgatory adjourned until after death, more or less, the idea and practise of the practical work of religion.

3. That the Roman Catholic Church restricts the reading of the Scriptures by the Christian people.

He spoke of the evils: I contended we had a balance of good—and that the idea of duty in individuals was more developed here than in pure Roman Catholic countries.

## 61: ADD.MS 44819, ff. 45–46

April 19. [1839].
At Sir Stratford Canning's on the 6th of April there was an agreeable dinner party—though made up of political persons: and I had the privilege of a good deal of conversation with Lord Stanley—his mind grasps large and little with equally activity, ease, and power: though I suppose it has not travelled into certain ranges of subjects.

He told me when he came into the Colonial Office he found Stephen in the habit of reporting on colonial laws in such form as that his reports might at once go out to the colonies, with the alteration of a few words, at the commencement and close, in the character of despatches. He altered this practice: on the principle that the legal duty of the professional man reporting to his chief on all the possible bearings of an Act, might introduce matter unfit, and exclude matter fit, for the despatch which that chief writes in his political capacity. Lord Ripon very goodnaturedly admitted that he had signed very many of Stephen's productions but alleged that he cut out the epithets which formed a considerable proportion of the whole.

I think Stanley is looking to the Colonial Office in the event of a change.

He laid down a principle respecting Governors, to this effect: before the public, you must always support them, until you dismiss them: reserving the privilege of writing private admonitions.

Sir Robert Peel told us the really sad story that the other day when the Queen was riding through the arch at the head of Constitution Hill (very recently) some person from among the crowd called out to her (in allusion to the recent affair of Lady Flora Hastings at the Palace) 'Mrs. Melbourne, why don't you turn off the doctor?'

Yesterday Sir R. Peel spoke to me at 4.30 in the House about the debate and wished that I should speak after Sheil, if Graham who was to speak about 8 or 9 could bring him up. He showed me likewise several points with regard to the committee which he thought might be urged. This is very kind in him as a mark of confidence: and assures me that if as I suspect he considers my book as likely to bring me into some embarrassment individually yet he is willing to let me still act under him and fight my own battles in that matter as best with God's help I may: which is thoroughly fair.

It imposes, however, a great responsibility—I was not presumptuous enough to dream of following Sheil: not that his speech is formidable, but the impression it leaves on the House is. I meant to provoke him. A mean man may fire at a tiger, but it requires a strong and bold one to stand his charge: and the longer I live the more I feel my own (intrinsically) utter *powerlessness* in the House of Commons. But my principle is this: not to shrink from any such responsibility when laid upon me by a competent person. Sheil, however, did not speak, so I am reserved and may fulfill my own idea, please God, tonight.

*April 19. 1839.*

## 62: ADD.MS 44819, ff. 46–47

Lord Stanley told me at Sir S. Canning's that when Lord Spencer was Minister in the House of Commons he felt the pressure of the anxieties attending that position so acutely (and yet he appeared a very phlegmatic impassible person) that he thanked God he did not on waking in the morning find loaded pistols by his bedside or he believed he should be tempted in the halfstupefaction of that peculiar moment to blow his brains out.                    *May 8. [1839]*.

Yesterday speculation was hungry and unfed. From the negative state in which we were left, we may understand thus much: that the change in the Administration is, as might be expected, highly distasteful to the Queen. The utmost that could be probably detected was, that the Duke of Wellington had been with Her Majesty late in the day. Alas! poor Majesty! we have reached the day when thine once awful name carries no magic: and personal freedom is less entire in the case of the Sovereign than in that of the meanest unconvicted subject. And if thou hast, as they say, dined apart in thy chamber, and wept freely yesterday, those tears will not be the last nor the bitterest.

Many of our club-hunters were in high spirits: for my own part, this change neither lowers nor raises my pulse. We stand in an awful crisis of the destinies of the Empire: a crisis distinctly and long foreseen: a crisis contemplated by me with accurately balanced fears and hopes, but with no doubt as to the main guiding lines of duty: nothing new or strange has *yet* happened, whatever may be hidden by the curtain of the future.

It is to me matter of great interest to have known something at least of the private history of the late motion on the Jamaica Government Bill, in Sir R. Peel's mind. The notice for the introduction of the Bill stood originally for the twenty-sixth of March. On the 25th he asked me in the House if I had thought on the question. He said something like this: 'Do you not think it would be an advantageous arrangement for the proprietary body of Jamaica, if the Assembly were to be suspended for a few years, with an assurance that reasonable provisions should be made in the mean time to secure labour?' I answered to the effect that I did not regard the question as a planter's question: but as one of constitutional principle: viewing it in that light, I understood that the coming measure was to be defended on the ground that the Jamaica legislature had demanded the repeal of the Prisons Act as a condition of proceeding to business: that this allegation was without foundation in fact, and therefore I did not see that they had case enough to justify their taking so extreme a step. Sir Robert Peel seemed surprised at my saying they had not made this demand and appeared to think Burge had told him they would insist upon that condition, and that the demand was practically if not literally made in the papers before us. (Goulburn had also been under the impression that the demand was actually made.) I turned, I think, on the moment to the papers, and Sir Robert Peel seemed to take what I said as if he would reflect upon it.

I have recorded this while it was clear in my mind, because considering the large consequences which the matter has already produced, it is matter of great interest and importance to know, that the first bias of our leader's mind was as far as it existed at all *against* the Assembly, and that (as I think is the fair inference) not a party motive but the force of the facts absolutely though gradually drove him to the course which in the end he adopted.

Again when we had a small meeting at Sir Robert Peel's house on the day when the Bill was introduced (in the forenoon) he heard the opinions of those present, but entirely reserved his own judgment until the case of the Government had been stated.

In denying then the charge of a party plot we do not merely bandy allegations but we have facts to rest upon.

I was amused with observing yesterday the differences of countenance and manner in the ex-Ministers whom I met on my ride. Ellice (their friend) would not look at me at all: (he had expressed to me on Monday night a great anxiety that the debate should be closed without further adjournment, I suppose in order to prevent the Stroud letter from doing more mischief). Charles Wood looked but askance and with the hat over the brow: Grey shouted 'Wish you joy': Lord Howick gave a remarkably civil and smiling nod: and Morpeth a hand salute with all his might as we crossed in riding. *May 8.* [*1839*].


## 63: ADD.MS 44819, f. 48

On Monday night after the division Peel said just as it was known and about to be announced, 'Jamaica was a good horse to start.' He seemed much pleased.

The events of the intervening days have been strange indeed: these things seem specially to require note:

1. That when the negotiations began Peel (as I learn through James and he I take for granted from Sir H[enry] H[ardinge]) spoke of its being necessary to make some changes in 'the Household'—reserving the details: to this the Queen is understood to have consented.

2. On Thursday afternoon the point was reopened with reference to the *Ladies*, of whom the Queen declared that she would part with none: first to Peel—then to Peel and the Duke—she took the night to consider of it and in the morning wrote to the above effect. Peel answered by letter that he must in such case decline proceeding further. His claim was only with regard to those who had been immediately connected with his political opponents.

3. Lord Melbourne summoned his Cabinet, it appears, on Thursday night, upon understanding that Peel had demanded the removal of *all* the Ladies of the Household: and did not *see* the papers until Friday, when I hear he expressed great astonishment and he was thought to look wretched at the ball last night. I did not see him. Morpeth and one or two more whom I saw appeared to consider themselves really in again.

Today in the Park with George Hope I saw Hume and we went up to him. Hope said to him jocularly, 'Well I thought the Queen had sent for you, Mr. Hume'—'No', he said, apparently before he knew the words were out of his mouth, 'that has not come yet.'

Tonight at ten Peel has a meeting of eight at Lord Aberdeen's from which one would infer something is reopened.     *May 11. [1839].*

(Morpeth asked me at the Queen's ball if I was to have gone to Ireland? and kindly added, I think if you had I should not have grudged leaving them: of course I told him I knew nothing. August 23. 1841.)

## 64: ADD.MS 44819, f. 48

January 16. 1840.
Goulburn told me the leaders were mainly influenced to Buller's motion by the feeling out of doors among their supporters. The majority expected to range between two and ten. 317 fast votes on each side.
*January 18. [1840].*

## 65: ADD.MS 44819, ff. 48–49

March 18. 1840.
Yesterday I had a long conversation with James Hope. He came to tell me, with great generosity, that he would always respond to any call, according to the best of his power, which I might make on him, for the behalf of the common cause. He had given up all views of advancement in his profession—he had about £400 a year, and this which includes his fellowship was quite sufficient for his wants: his time would be devoted to Church objects, in the intermediate region: he considered himself as having the first tonsure.

We then discussed the questions: whether there was a point, actual although very difficult to be exactly discerned, at which the service of the State became lifeless or polluted: at which a man who sought employment for the service of the Church, must institute his search in some other quarter—especially, in holy orders: whether the case of a refluent Christianity, which is in course of expulsion from our institutions and public life, be not very different from that of an aggressive

Christianity, which is in course of occupying and pervading them—
inasmuch as personal influence may in the first case fairly be regarded
as the thin end of the wedge which may introduce the religion, but
which in the second case, of the retrogressive movement, cannot retain
or reinstate its hold—in the first it has a natural and Providential
instrumentality, in the latter none: whether when a country once
thoroughly impregnated with the religious life has expelled the
animating spirit, it can ever be reconquered except by the directly
ordained means, namely the agency of the Church: whether at least
an individual whose original covenant has been with the sacred
ministry, and who has altered its form under the impression that from
peculiar circumstances the Church required more service in another
quarter and might not receive it, would not, upon the unfavourable
termination of such an experiment, remain bound by his first plighted
faith. All this was spoken with personal application—*in the strictest
confidence*—and in contemplation of a contingency which may not be
but which even if less probable yet must be included in the calculations
of a man who does not wish to be overreached and taken unawares by
the progress of events.

Hope urged strongly the principle 'let every man abide in the
calling'—I thought even over strongly. My belief is that he foregoes
the ministry from deeming himself unworthy.

Today a meeting at Peel's on the China question, considered in the
view of censure on the conduct of the Administration—and a motion
will accordingly be made objecting to the attempts to force the
Chinese to modify their old relations with us: and to the leaving the
Superintendent without military force.

It was decided not to move simultaneously in the Lords—particularly, because the Radicals would, if there were a double motion, act
not on the merits but for the Ministry. Otherwise, it seemed to be
thought we should carry a motion. The Duke of Wellington said,
'God! if it is carried, they will go': that they were as near as possible
to resignation on the last defeat, and would not stand it again. Peel
said he understood four Ministers were then strongly for resigning.

The Duke also said, our footing in China could not be reestablished,
unless after some considerable naval and military demonstration: now
that matters had gone so far.

He appeared pale and shaken but spoke loud and a good deal, much

to the point and with considerable gesticulation. The mind's life I
never saw more vigorous.                                    *March 18. [1840].*

## 66: ADD.MS 44777, ff. 60-62

Tuesday, March 24. 1840.
Sir R. Peel, Lord Aberdeen, Lord Ellenborough, Sir James Graham,
Sandon, Clerk, Fremantle, and myself, met at Sir R. Peel's house, to
consider the terms of the motion to be made respecting China.

Lord Ellenborough had drawn a long and able series: Graham a
short censure in two clauses: Sir R. Peel had also drawn one but rather
expressing an affirmation of the propriety of the threatened war, which
he readily withdrew and with the modifications of successive hints he
worked out amidst the conversation what seems to me a wise resolution:
dealing with the question retrospectively and not prospectively—and
of the retrospective question, handling not the part which lies between
England and China, but between the Administration and Parliament.

The retrospective question between England and China is of itself
manifold and might raise differences of opinion. To the prospective.
Sir R. Peel said he could well conceive some persons of opinion that we
had no cause for war with China. There was a great harmony of
opinion among those present: indeed it must be hard to give any but
one answer to the question whether Lord Palmerston has a justifying
case with the papers before us.

After this question was disposed of there was something said of
warmth and precipitancy in the Archbishop of Canterbury and Bishop
of London on the previous evening, in condemning utterly and at once
the Clergy Reserves Bill just sent home. Graham I think blamed, and
adverted to Lord Ellenborough as having risen in a timely manner to
check the discussion: but Graham did not speak of the merits of the Bill.
Sir Robert Peel expressed great disapproval and apprehension of the
principle of the Bill—and seemed to have in his eye its ready application
to Ireland.

Yesterday evening Catherine and I dined at the Archbishop of York's
where Queen Adelaide and the Duke and Duchess of Cambridge were
to be before the Ancient Music.

Duke of Cambridge was sonorous as ever, 'the cheerful roaring
lion' according to the Bishop of London who quoted the Creation to

me aside. He asked me if I was writing any thing now, and said pointing to Catherine, 'I suppose she does not give you any time'—I said, 'No Sir I am too busy reading the China papers': *sic me servavit Apollo*.[1] The Duke of Wellington was speaking about Lord Wellesley's age and said he would be (I think) eighty on the 30th of June—'30th', said the Duke of Cambridge, 'why, it should have been the *eighteenth*—it should have been the *eighteenth*, Duke'—'Ha!' replied the Duke of Wellington— there is really so much that is characteristic of him in the use of this little monosyllable: although it seems to approximate to the burlesque shake of the head in the *Critic*. But it is a frequent thing with him and it shows I think the manly independence and simplicity of mind which will not debit some crude phrase or other in reply to a compliment— which is above feeling the need of 'something to say'—which repays civility with the brevity, almost abruptness, of military courtesy—the safe sagacious understanding which will not be betrayed into the premature or inconsiderate expression of an opinion on any subject.

Lord Howe expressed pleasure at the Queen's beginning to tinge her dinner parties a little less faintly with Conservatives. Feared it was true Lord Melbourne had urged her to invite Sir Robert Peel and that she had been reluctant. Greatly approved of our going to Eton to examine and wished he were in our place.

The plain aspect and disagreeable voice of the Queen Dowager are quite overcome by a positive grace of manner, as well as by her gentle and sweet demeanour to every one. She was very kind to Catherine and made her sit down. At the concert of course she took the centre seat: but ceded it to Prince Albert when he came in.      (*March 26. 1840.*)

## 67: ADD.MS 44819, ff. 49–51

June 9. [1840].
I conversed on the morning of this day with the Bishop of Nova Scotia (Inglis) on the clergy reserves and on colonial government. He advocates the maintaining with a high hand the perpetuity of British connection, the general ascendancy of the party attached to it, and

---

[1] Horace, *Satires*, i. 9, last line. A famous tag. Horace was button-holed by a bore and could not escape until one of the bore's creditors appeared and hauled him off to court. The poet's patron saint, so to speak, had rescued him.

most of all, of a British *will* in the government of the colonies, to form and controul the colonial will. I expressed to him my differing from his views: in language substantially to this effect or to the effect of a comment on this text. 'Consider first the Reform Bill and the immense changes which this period has introduced into the principles and practice of home government. Secondly the composition of society in the colonies. Thirdly the want of concurrence with us among the loyal party in the most essential of all our principles: namely that of State religion—which actually deprives us of a basis whereon[1] to build. All these things considered I arrive at the following conclusions. It is our true wisdom to see and know our circumstances with their *potentialities* —these are the materials with which a man is to work. I think them to be as follows: we cannot mould colonial destinies against colonial will (in this class of colonies, formed of true settlers): we cannot save loyal Houses of Assembly from the consequences of their own erroneous desires: we cannot maintain the friends of British connection if they are greatly exceeded in numbers or weight or activity, or in the sum of these, by their enemies: we can possibly hold up our heads above water at home against the enemies of true British principles—we can even possibly lend, and will to the utmost of our power cheerfully lend, you some aid in maintaining the contest in the colony: but the issue of the contest must mainly and ultimately depend much more upon yourselves than upon us. Of course these are matters to be handled with reserve: and only so far developed as may suffice to rouse the energies of those on whose activity we must considerably rely.'

In the evening I saw the Bishop of Exeter and had a shorter but as far as it went similar conversation. He said, 'I think both Peel and the Duke of Wellington are made to help downwards this country in its gradual declension: made for its ruin, the first by his feebleness, and the second by his obstinacy.' I said, 'There is a manifest and peculiar adaptation in Peel's mind to this age, in which he lives and its exigencies and to the position he holds as a public man. What the ultimate and general effect of his policy may be is a question too subtle and remote for me strongly to presume upon.' He said, 'I think him a strictly honourable man, a man of high principle' to which I of course could easily and cordially assent.

Peel has been very uneasy about the fate of the Canada Union Bill in

---

[1] MS: wherein.

the House of Lords where we have understood the Duke of Wellington means to oppose it. I attended him at his house yesterday forenoon: where were Stanley, Graham, and Goulburn, on this subject. In the evening he came in much relieved and satisfied from the division—and said to me, 'This is a very important night and has great bearings on the fate of the Bill'—meaning that it would be very difficult for the Duke to throw it out after such a division as 156:6.

Tonight I have conversed a good deal with Sir Francis Head and with Lord Seaton on the union: and a fortnight ago I had a very long conversation on Canadian matters with the latter. He disapproves of the union: says it will bring an unmanageable assembly, and accelerate the separation. I agree. Yet I am much inclined to doubt whether, unless led by the Duke of Wellington—or even if then—he will record his vote against it. He would have continued the present Government in Lower Canada for a time until men's minds were mollified, which he thinks might have been done by measures on which all are agreed and by lenient administration.

Sir Francis Head looks at matters keenly but solely from his own point of view. He says why did not the one party or the other take up Lieutenant Drew ?—I say we as Opposition cannot compel the Crown to behave well to its own servants, even where we may think the case pretty clear. He says, why not thank the people of Upper Canada for what they did ? I apprehend great anomalies and inconveniences would arise from the introduction of such a practice. He says you must not adopt the will of the people as your principle: if I had done so when I went to Upper Canada I should have failed. I said, 'You successfully evoked the will of the people against a disloyal Assembly: and that loyal will so evoked demands the union.' He replied that they were worried or cajoled into it: that two years ago when cool they were against it: that the Queen's message, the Governor, the Ministry, led them into it. I say, we *cannot* lead the destinies of Canada for good against the errors of our friends. It is matter I believe of sheer impossibility. If the Assembly will follow the Ministers, how can you expect us, who are unable to overthrow the Ministers, to resist both ?

*June 13. [1840].*

## 68: ADD.MS 44819, ff. 51–52

June 14 [1840]. Meeting at Sir R. Peel's on Clergy Reserves.

When the leader has no particular course to advise, nor any particular course to deprecate, he generally invites all those whom he summons to declare their opinions before he says anything: but if there be any one line of action which he wishes to prevent, then without giving out his own positive opinion, he generally opens the proceedings by strongly stating the objections to that particular line. Today he was much afraid of an adverse decision on the Canada Clergy Reserves Bill and was therefore most desirous to avoid dividing against it: the reason of his fear being that such an occurrence would break the whole force and effect of the favourable votes on Irish registration which we have had and still expect to have.

I do not think he had thought much on the merits of this question, distracted as his attention is by a thousand others; or on the principles of a safe settlement respecting it.

Stanley (who had passed on to the House of Commons) thought that we should secure by Imperial Act the portions intended to be given to or rather retained by the Established Churches of England and Scotland and remit the residue to the absolute disposal of the Canadian legislature. This I think an excellent idea: but I would combine with it the further principle: that residue must only be such as is surrendered by those who are empowered to act for and represent the claims arising under the Act of 1791: and said so.

The principle which Stanley has thus shadowed out and which Peel I think approved has dwelt in my mind for many years past with a growing belief that it is the right guide for our colonial policy in matter of religion: namely to restrict the action, the influence, the example, of the home Government, as respects religion within the colonies, to those principles which are acted upon in the mother country, and with reference to anything which is beyond them, to make it purely permissive.

Follett thought the judges by their opinion intended to admit the claim of all Protestant bodies having anything like a regular ministry.

Graham was very desirous of a total sale of the lands and of drawing the proceeds into investments on this side the water, in the public funds.

After this subject I was asked what was to be done about the

Ecclesiastical Duties and Revenues Bill: and mentioned that some members had agreed on an address to Her Majesty praying her to direct the bishops and visitors to lay before her such plans as they might deem best adapted to promote the objects designated in the original commission.

'Praying Her Majesty to whip the Archbishop of Canterbury and the Bishop of London', said Peel with a laugh. *June 16.*

## 69: ADD.MS 44819, f. 52

June 19. [1840].
Curiosity led me to look at the reports in *The Mirror of Parliament* of conversational discussions in committee: to state these accurately is I should think a work so difficult as to be nearly impracticable: and it is hardly worth great pains. I find myself seriously and disagreeably misrepresented, but without surprise, for I do believe it unavoidable. In 1838 on the Irish Education vote I defended the Commissioners against a *specific* charge, that of having given too small salaries to masters whereas they have in fact greatly deviated from Lord Stanley's letter by enlarging gratuities in special cases into a general system of salary on whatever scale: and I said the value of a joint education was so great that as long as there was any hope of giving effect to the original idea I would suspend condemnation although I saw much that was objectionable in the working of the system. My recollection is pretty fresh on the subject as it is one which I have thought and felt much. But this is changed into a general defence of the Commissioners and a general defence of the schools with a declaration that under all circumstances they are decidedly the best adapted for Ireland: and Rice is made to follow with an expression of satisfaction at my having given this generally and decidedly unfavourable opinion. Of course this kind of misstatement may be in a hundred places which it is not worth while to hunt: but I thought it well to record on paper my first observation of it.

We divided last night 289:296 on Lord Morpeth's amendment to Stanley's first clause. This defeat is a great triumph. The Government instead of attacking the Bill outright, as they had threatened, have only moved an amendment upon a particular point: and have carried no more than this, that with reference to the existing lists there shall be revision only and not reinvestigation, no rehearing of the original case upon which the voter got his place on the register. The best confirmation of my view is to be found in O'Connell's notice that he will move an instruction to the committee when next the order for it comes on.                                                        *June 20. [1840].*

## 70: ADD.MS 44819, f. 52

June 20. [1840].
On Saturday from 12 to 3 I was at Sir R. Peel's: most of the time was spent in discussing Clergy Reserves. The Archbishop was present and read his proposition. Peel was for delay until the commencement of next session in order to have communication with the organs of the Church of Scotland. *He* seemed much more than Stanley to make a point of leaving to the Colonial Assembly the disposal of any portion of the lands which might not be appropriated to or be retained by the two Establishments. They differed on the question of sale with the Archbishop.                                           *June 22. [1840].*

## 71: ADD.MS 44819, f. 53

At Sir R. Peel's this day we got through the consideration of five points to be included in a settlement of the Canada Reserves question.

1. That the titles to the existing rectories should be confirmed.
2. That the present actual receipts of the Churches of England and Scotland should be guaranteed to them respectively as a minimum. (Stanley's proposition.)
3. That the monies already received and receivable under the Act of the 7 and 8 George IV, should be divided between the Churches of England and Scotland in the proportion of 2:1.
4. That the residue of the lands should be sold.
5. That the proceeds should be divided as follows:

> To the Churches of England and Scotland⎱
>     by Imperial Act (as 2:1)                    ⎰(left blank)
>
> The remainder not to be appropriated by Imperial Act, but to be surrendered.

(My division under 5 must be with consent of the two Establishments, through their best organs, the best that can be had.)

The points remaining for consideration are

a. To fill up the blank in 5.
b. To determine to what party the surrender should be made.
c. To limit the times and rules of sale, and mode of payment.
d. To consider of future reservations under 31 George I [sic].

*June 24. 1840.*

## 72: ADD.MS 44819, ff. 53–54

Saturday morning [27 June 1840] Peel sent to me for my memorandum[1] and in the afternoon I saw him at the Carlton: where he told me in strict confidence that the Archbishop of Canterbury appeared to have made some strange mistake in proposing to Lord John to acquiesce in the Ministerial project provided the present amount of income were guaranteed to the Church. He said jocularly, 'Gladstone, we must not again trust the Archbishop as our representative on Church questions.' He said he had recommended the Archbishop to go to Lord John and release him from any engagement into which he might have entered with respect to an accommodation, and to explain more fully his views. He said the Archbishop's memory appeared to be failing and that the Archbishop had expressed himself to that effect.

At the previous meeting the Archbishop had spoken of himself as a person noted for and reproached with timidity among the clergy: when Sir R. Peel said no, the reproaches cast upon him were the proof of his wisdom—and he had no doubt that he would be able to support any plan on which the Archbishop might finally resolve.

Today I went to meet Graham and Goulburn at Sir R. Peel's, on the British Guiana Civil List. My own opinion was, that Lord John Russell's tacking the Immigration Ordinance to the new Civil List was a proceeding, on the part of a Government, so enormously unconstitutional and arbitrary, that it demanded and justified parliamentary censure, whatever the conduct of the colonial body with whom he had had to deal. But Peel and Graham both thought that on the whole the case would not afford a good ground for a vote of censure: that the

---

[1] This memorandum has not been found among the Gladstone or Peel Papers at the B.M.

Colonial Combined Court had been refractory—that they had in rejoinder to the Government proposed inadmissible conditions—that Lord Aberdeen had evidently contemplated coercion—that the proceedings in Canada would lead Parliament to interpret favourably any proceedings having for their object the attainment of a Civil List—that though Lord John had proposed too great an amount, and had put himself in a false position by mixing up the two measures instead of allowing each to be judged upon its own merits, yet it was probable that he might now have been led to change his position and to put simply and categorically the demand for a Civil List. Under all the circumstances that it would not be wise to move unless he should come to be more clearly and entirely in the wrong. After explaining my own sentiments as well as I could, I freely deferred to their opinions and abandoned all idea of moving upon this subject for the present: and wrote to Mr. Downie accordingly,[1] with advice to separate the subject of Civil List from that of immigration. *June 30. 1840.*

## 73: ADD.MS 44819, ff. 54-55

In the division on Tuesday night (Church Extension) Stanley said to me as the last man came into the lobby (who when we win usually tells us how many we are) 'No need to give out the numbers tonight!' I said, 'We don't seem to have one of the loose fish while many of our own are away'—'No', he replied, 'such a motion as this is enough to shake the tightest fish—a most unwise move.'

Peel on Tuesday expressed his dissent from my argument respecting Bishops' Council: seeming to think it could not work, while the Bishop and the Chapter may be appointed by very different patrons, and successive Bishops so widely varying. He does not take into his calculation that daily growing knowledge of Church principles which is extending and consolidating the broad common ground of faith and discipline upon which Churchmen can afford to hold in peace their minor differences while even of these they will be in the very best position for getting rid. Last evening at Lambeth Palace I had a good deal of conversation with Colonel Gurwood about the Duke of Wellington and about Canada. The Duke has been very anxious about the question until relieved by his speech last night. He thinks

---

[1] See ADD.MS 44357, ff. 139–140.

he will alter the Bill or else reject it on the third reading. The Duke has been so much engrossed about it, reading through the whole of the parliamentary papers, as to be very irritable when interrupted: Lord Keane went four or five times to see him on his return from India, and failed.

Lord Seaton he says declined the peerage until advised by the Duke to accept it: with full avowal from Lord Melbourne, that he was under no obligation to Government and perfectly independent.

Colonel Gurwood found fault with Sir R. Peel's argument from Lord Seaton's despatch: said it was an assumption and that no statesman should deal in assumptions. I defended it as being this: that if Lord Seaton had been decidedly of opinion that union was bad in principle, and that another clearly preferable measure could be adopted, it was fairly to be expected that he would have made known that sentiment to the Government. And I wondered that he had not taken the opportunity at least of correcting Sir R. Peel in the House of Lords.

He told me however an anecdote of Lord Seaton which throws light upon this peculiar reserve, and shows it to be a modesty of character, combined no doubt with military habits and notions. When Captain Colborne, and senior officer of his rank in the 21st Foot, he was military secretary to General Fox, during the war. A majority in his regiment fell vacant. General Fox desired him to ascertain who was the senior captain on the *command*. 'Captain so and so of the 80th' (I think). 'Write to Colonel Gordon and recommend him to His Royal Highness for the vacant majority.' He did it. The answer came to this effect: 'The recommendation will not be refused, but we are surprised to see it comes in the handwriting of Captain Colborne, the very man who according to the rules of the service ought to have this majority.' General Fox had forgotten it and Captain Colborne had not reminded him! The error was corrected.

He (Gurwood) said he had never known the Duke of Wellington speak on the subject of religion, but once: when he quoted the story of Oliver Cromwell on his deathbed—and said, 'That state of grace in my opinion is a state or habit of doing right, of persevering in duty —and to fall from it is to cease from acting right.' He always attends the service at 8 a.m. in the Chapel Royal—and says it is a duty which ought to be done and the earlier in the day it is discharged the better.

*July 2. 1840.*

## 74: ADD.MS 44819, f. 55

I have seldom heard any thing with greater dismay than last night
when Acland (saying at the same time that he had suggested it to Peel)
asked me whether it might not be advisable that a suggestion should be
made from our side of the House of Commons to increase the grant for
education! This I do not take altogether as a mark of the individual,
but more as a sign of the times: for when he is so forgetful, what must
others be. An objection to the grant which we hardly expected to
arise, namely the difficulty of making an arrangement with the Church
for the distribution of a part of the money, has been removed; the
objections which were most felt and most urged by the whole strength
of our party and by the people out of doors remain: the dangerous
character of the Committee of Privy Council—the power of erecting
normal establishments of general religion, or of none—and the power
of lending the aid of the State to education in every creed alike.

I think Acland only needed to be reminded.            *July 21.* [*1840*].

## 75: ADD.MS 44819, f. 55

Peel said one day of Lord John Russell, during the registration conflicts,
'He does the greater things in the House very well, the smaller ones
very badly.'

Hope tells me that Dr. Hume the Duke of Wellington's physician
told him that the Duke said he would rather have cut off his hand than
passed the Cathedrals' Bill: but his reason for agreeing to it was that
it came to him recommended by the persons of highest station in the
Church.                                          *August 1.* [*1840*].

## 76: ADD.MS 44777, ff. 63–64

Mr. Grenville told us yesterday that he saw Mr. George Spencer (the
Hon. and Rev.) after his return from Rome and learned from him that
he had had an interview with the Pope (Gregory XVI) at the express
desire of the latter immediately before his quitting that city. He made
no secret of stating what passed at the audience. He listened, and the
Pope spoke: and he most urgently and particularly warned him on

having any intercourse with Mr. O'Connell and his compeers, or lending them any countenance.

Mr. Grenville, however, had heard from a third party that G. Spencer, apparently in contravention of this command, had called on O'Connell in London, and after some hesitation and effort asked him whether in his political conduct he acted with integrity? to which O'Connell replied by a solemn assurance in the affirmative. By this we are I suppose to account for Spencer's having since I think symbolised in some way with him politically.

Mr. Grenville went on to say, that Spencer afforded a remarkable example of the perverting power of the Romish religion. He had known him from his cradle: and Lady Spencer said to him when George was very young that he was of such purity and singlemindedness that he seemed the very Apostle of Truth.

When, however, after his coming to England he settled at West Bromwich he came over here to see his sister and Lord Lyttelton. Lord Lyttelton was speedily apprised that all the time which he spent out of their presence was occupied in efforts to turn to Romanism the servants and villagers of Hagley. In consequence when he next came to pay a visit Lord Lyttelton stated to him that however much delighted to see him he had a duty to perform towards these comparatively defenceless parties, and he must require from him an assurance that he would make no such attempts for the future. Upon this George Spencer hesitated considerably which induced Lord Lyttelton to become more pressing: at length he concluded by desiring George Spencer to repeat the words syllable by syllable after him—and then pronounced a sentence to the effect that 'he pledged himself as a man of honour and a gentleman that he would not directly or indirectly use any means which he might possess through his visits to act upon the minds of the people, with a view of turning them to Romanism.' With this Lord Lyttelton was satisfied: and George Spencer repeated his visit. What was Lord Lyttelton's surprise to find, that he had adopted precisely his former conduct after the pledge! He saw him on the subject: put it to him distinctly whether Lord Lyttelton had not spoken the words of the engagement to abstain from all means of proselytism—whether he Spencer had not repeated those words after him—and whether he had not now been acting in direct defiance of that promise. Spencer admitted without qualification that all this was true—and stated that the superior considerations of what was due to religion were his warrant for having set aside the treaty. It had, how-ever, also been set aside without any kind of notice! The consequence was that Spencer's journeys to Hagley have been altogether dis-continued.

This is a most remarkable tale in itself: and it also relates to one who may yet have some part to play in the mixed and shifting drama of the nineteenth century. *August 29. 1840.*

## 77: ADD.MS 44819, f. 56

April 3. 1841.
Two or three nights ago Mrs. Wilbraham[1] told Catherine that Lord Stanley was extremely sorry to find, after his speech on the Tamworth and Rugby Railway Bill, that Peel had been very much annoyed with the expression he had used: 'that his Right Hon. friend had in pleading for the Bill made use of all that art and ingenuity with which he so well knew how to dress up a statement for that House'—and that he showed this annoyance very much by his manner to him (Stanley) afterwards. He upon reflecting that this was the probable cause wrote a note to Peel to set matters to rights, in which he succeeded: but he thought Peel very thinskinned.

William Cowper told me the other day at Milnes's that Lord John Russell is remarkable among his colleagues for his anxiety during the recess for the renewal of the session of Parliament: that he always argues for fixing an early day of meeting, and finds pleas for it, and finds the time hang until he recommences.

## 78: ADD.MS 44777, ff. 65–71

On Saturday [1 May 1841] at 2.30 there met at Sir R. Peel's

| | | |
|---|---|---|
| Lord Stanley | Lord F. Egerton | Sir G. Clerk |
| Sir James Graham | Lord Sandon | Sir H. Hardinge |
| Mr. Goulburn | Sir T. Fremantle | W.E.G. |

to discuss the course to be taken with reference to the discussion of last night.

Lord Stanley inclined to moving a vote condemnatory of the

---

[1] MS: W—m. Wilbraham later written above in pencil by WEG.

financial statement and including a declaration that the House of Commons could not feel any confidence in the present Ministers as persons qualified to meet the emergency. To this Sir James Graham seemed a little to lean.

Peel mentioned also the measure of a general vote of want of confidence: and that of an attack on the proposition with regard to the sugar duties only: saying that *if* there were a good case upon the sugar duties undoubtedly that would be the best point on which to join issue. He thought, however, that it might be better under certain circumstances for the West Indians to relinquish their monopoly: and was averse to introducing any words having reference to the question of slave or free labour. I stated some points with regard to the working of the present proposition. Sandon strongly urged that we should fight this particular question at least in the first instance. There was a strong sense that some measure must be taken: and no one seemed inclined to think that if a single point were selected for our opposition, instead of a general motion, any other than sugar could be chosen.

Today we again met, with Lords G. Somerset and Eliot added to our numbers. Sir R. Peel announced that since seeing us he had held consultations with the Duke of Wellington, Lords Aberdeen, Lyndhurst, Ellenborough, and Ashburton: as well as Stanley, Graham, and Goulburn: and that they had come to an unanimous conclusion—his own views having been modified by the information he had received—in favour of resistance to the proposition respecting the sugar duties. He read to us a statement in detail of three courses, with the reasons for and against them: a motion for a committee on the state of the nation, a vote of want of confidence generally, and a vote of want of confidence on the Budget specifically. For the argument in favour of the course relating to the sugar duties, he read to us a most able letter from Lord Sandon.

He observed that no party could dissolve the Parliament until a Sugar Duties Act had passed—unless it were done immediately, in which case an Act might be got in a new Parliament before the 5th of July on which day these duties expire.

A vote of want of confidence, he remarked, if not successful recoiled on those who made it. It never had been successful in its avowed object of displacing a Ministry, though it had been carried in the House, as by Mr. Fox and Mr. Stuart Wortley.

To lose a motion of this kind under present circumstances would place us in the most disadvantageous position with respect to our resisting the items of the Budget on their own merits. To make it would entail an exposition of policy regarding all questions, and especially the Poor Law. To carry it would leave the Conservative party in the possession of power—with the Queen against them, with a majority in the House of Commons against them, and without the power of resorting to a dissolution in consequence of the state of the sugar duties: while the country would be agitated for a length of time with respect to corn and on that question the Government must stand, not a good one for the purpose. He conceived that their financial course would require time for its thorough consideration and in the mean time that a loan would be required for the services of the year.

Graham said he too had much leaned to the notion of a general condemnatory vote founded on the Budget but that his mind too had been changed and that he entirely concurred that we ought to fight the sugar duties.

Peel expected that we should succeed in this by a considerable majority—that the Government might very probably retire upon it— that even if they did not we should then be in a position of comparative advantage for considering the circumstances and mode of seeking that *decisive* sentence from the House of Commons which in some way or other he thought *must be had*.

The feeling evidently is that although we are strong enough to beat the Government on their proposition relating to corn, they would dissolve upon it and that it would be comparatively a disadvantageous question for us as a party upon which to go to the country.

There seemed to be little or no difference as to the eligibility of the question of sugar: and Lord Sandon as representative of a great commercial community was earnestly requested by Peel with the concurrence of almost every one present to make the motion to which he with modesty and reluctance agreed. Fremantle wished Peel himself to do it—he dissented, because it would divest the movement of its commercial character: besides which he must be held in reserve for any subsequent and general motion which might possibly be found desirable hereafter. So accordingly it was settled: and another meeting arranged for tomorrow to consider the words of the resolution.     *May 3. 1841.*

Opposite [f. 71] will be found a list of what I had myself sketched as a list of possible courses.

I may add this piece of confession. I was anxious, ambitious perhaps, to have had the opportunity of stating the sugar case in the House of Commons: and black malignant jealousy lay at the bottom of my heart when I heard Sir R. Peel pressing it upon Sandon and most persons joining with him. Not but that common understanding tells me it might act ill for the party were the motion to be made by one personally connected with the sugar trade: and that it might be well that Sandon in particular should do it: and even I hope that there was a predominant feeling of acquiescence and satisfaction, and that if I could I would not in my true and ruling will have had it otherwise: yet there was the bad, presumptuous, usurping sentiment of my selfish life, unextinguished even if in a degree suppressed.              *May 3. 1841.*

Perhaps I was partly influenced by recollecting that on Molesworth's motion in 1838, Stanley said to me in the debate that he wished I could have introduced it.                                          *May 4.*

[f. 71]
1. To move a vote of want of confidence.
2. To move a vote of want of confidence, grounded on a condemnation of the Budget.
3. To move a condemnation of the Budget, without any further specification.
4. To move the rejection of the proposition with regard to sugar, in the way of a simple negative.
5. To move such rejection by a resolution glancing at the slave trade.
6. To combine with either of these two last, a (subsequent) motion to refer the timber duties to a select committee, in consideration of the present circumstances of Canada.

## 79: ADD.MS 44819, f. 56

May 4. [1841].
Another meeting at Sir R. Peel's yesterday to consider the terms of Lord Sandon's resolution. Sir Robert Peel was averse on Saturday to introducing any mention of slavery and the slave trade into it: but today he had prepared a draft which laid considerable stress on them and the resolution as finally determined on gives to this topic a prominent place. Much care was bestowed on it in a long conversation: but the opinions of all present appeared to be substantially agreed.              *May 4. 1841.*

## 80: ADD.MS 44819, ff. 57–61

Sunday evening. May 9. 1841.

I sit down for a few minutes of the evening of this peaceful day situated as it is between one stormy past week and another probably yet more stormy to follow it, to place on paper some matters which I may not have another opportunity to state as calmly, and which are not ungenial to the season.

It *may* be that the Melbourne Ministry after the defeat on the sugar (or slave) question which now seems to impend will resign at once, or that they will cling to office and dissolve. What I have to say relates only to the former alternative—and it involves the assumption (for argument's sake) of the further contingency, that Peel should tender me some office. If so I must not accept or reject it according to my liking for the particular post, or the reverse: it must be upon larger grounds.

All my reflections have brought me more and more to the conclusion that if the principle of national religion (a principle, which is my bond to parliamentary life) is to be upheld, or saved from utter overthrow, it must be by the united action of the Conservative party: not necessarily of every member of it, nor only of its members, but yet of the party as a whole and moving under its leaders. The principle of party has long predominated in this country: it now has a sway almost unlimited: and this I think belongs to the nature of a system of what is termed real representation. If Members of Parliament be really *chosen* by the people and if the actual effective power over Government be there, they must be chosen upon grounds few, simple, comprehensive: minutiae and shades of creeds cannot be duly appreciated by constituencies: they cannot make policies the study of their lives individually: they must pin their faith upon some general and leading terms, and by these terms must be defined and determined the great parties which are to contend for mastery in the State.

I differ therefore from those who say, let the holder of Catholic principles stand aloof from the political organisation of the Conservative body, and proclaiming truth in the House of Commons from an independent post, trust to her power to resume in due time her authority. In my opinion those who thus reason seem to forget that the direct mission of Christianity and of pure truth is to the individual heart, not to the mixed bodies by which affairs of vast human combinations are directed.

When truth has gained an ascendancy over those mixed bodies, has been fully acknowledged, has incorporated herself in the entire framework of public institutions, has long had her abode there; and then when her points of juncture with them are at length worn by time, when her theories have been discredited by abuse, when her subjective power over the general mind is waning, there are I think two modes of proceeding: one to work within the cincture of those public institutions, the other to leave it and frankly revert to the original and proper action of the Church, to the work of reconquering the nation by overcoming one heart and another and another.

If the former course [were] to be taken, labour will I apprehend in great measure be lost, unless it be carried on under this limitation: that it must conform to the laws and conditions which those bodies require. In times when individuals are great in proportion to masses, and form and mould them, they give laws and habits to bodies: but now individuals are *small* in proportion to masses—whether in governments or in multitudes—and receive laws from them: we take a wrong measure of the period in which we live, as I think, if we judge otherwise. When a constitution has disqualified itself essentially for abstract truth, it must be cured from without and not from within. When it has lost the virtue of a national religious life with which it had once been impregnated, that virtue can only I apprehend be reinfused by the method which Christ ordained—converting and baptising: not by wholesale proclamations of a gospel of results to men unprepared to receive them, without ordinances, without authority, without principles and motive powers. Were I an American, enamoured of the principle of national religion, I should not seek an entrance into Congress in order to propagate it: for being in Congress, I should not have the requisite *data* from which to argue. Should England nationally repudiate the Catholic Church, it is not I apprehend, by parliamentary evangelisation that she can be recalled to a sense of her duty because what is done in Parliament must be evolution of its own recognised laws and constitutive ideas. On this ground it has been often said of demagogues and with much truth that the way to disarm them is to put them into the House of Commons. How few of them retain any sway there! Their crude and outrageous notions are in no harmony and proximity to those constitutive and governing conceptions under which Parliament, in great measure insensibly to itself, lives and acts. My belief therefore is that Parliament is to be governed, according to its (now) fundamental conditions, by a party: if at all well governed, by the Conservative party: consequently that if the Catholic Church is to be maintained in its position of nationality, it must be by that party: and that the most hopeful way of promoting this design, or of obstructing the counterdesign, is to abide within the organisation of that party. But supposing that party abandon altogether the recognition of the Church, I mean of the Church as *the* Church—which recognition still remains almost unimpaired in Ireland, still more near to absolute entireness in England? Then to act upon the same principle in a diverse application: and still to accept the conditions of the age upon which it has pleased God to cast my lot, to leave a way which is hopelessly barred, and to resume that ancient path which led the Twelve forth from Jerusalem to turn the hearts of all nations to the living God. The meaning then is that leaving out of sight the arrangement of particulars I am of opinion that the time said to be that for resorting to individualised action in Parliament is rather the time for abandoning parliamentary action altogether. If I have differences from my leader, they are as I am convinced not political but religious. I think both his cast of sentiments and of abilities such as to be a great providential gift to this country, wonderfully situated to her need: thus I have ever thought since knowing him. I have the most implicit confidence in his integrity and honour. If I believe in the Catholic Church historical and visible, and consequently in claims generically different from those of sects, and if he does not, this will naturally lead me to aver some things which he must, and on his own principles I think reasonably and consistently, shrink from upholding: but *even if* I be right in my belief as far as it may differ from his, I set down that difference to the periods and circumstances of education. *May 9. 1841.*

## 81: ADD.MS 44819, f. 56

On Friday the 7th I spent some time at Sir R. Peel's in going over the details of the sugar question with him: and thought it worthwhile to observe that he had the tradesmen's books of his household laid on a desk seemingly as if for his inspection. (*May 14.*)

It is told that Lord John Russell who made so able and adroit a speech on Friday the 7th had been refused by one of Lord Minto's daughters on the day preceding. This is not out of keeping with his amazing faculty of self command: still, the harmony may have been the cause of the fabrication of such a story.                               *May 15. [1841]*.


## 82: ADD.MS 44819, f. 61

Graham told me on Tuesday, my speech of Monday had been a perfectly safe one. It is necessary of course to consider in public affairs the conflict and equilibrium of principles and not to give overmuch weight to one so as to derange the rest. It is certainly true that in this debate we are deriving aid from those whose instinct of fear makes them apprehend danger to their interests on corn; and also we have an advantage virtually given to the principle of Protection, by the (probable) defeat of a Government which has moved in a manner on the whole hostile to it: these, however, do not make it the less true, that in the intrinsic merits of the case we have a solid ground of humanity, which is really as it is professed to be the determining element.

Grey's series of misstatements in his speech were the most reckless that I ever heard in Parliament: I am sure he could not have made them in cold blood: yet I confess they were such as to diminish somewhat my respect for the man. God save me from the like and worse.

*May 14. [1841]*.


## 83: ADD.MS 44819, f. 61

It was told me today by Lord Eliot that Ministers had a very stormy Cabinet this morning—they at length determined to abide by Lord Spencer's advice, and *not* to dissolve. He added, that they were to divide on the present motion—then after a short speech from Lord John to divide on his resolution against Lord Sandon's—and herewith to close and to resign. The Archbishop of York reported to me that Lord Grey is loud in condemnation of them—declares the idea of dissolution intolerable—and says they ought to have resigned a year ago.

*May 15. [1841]*.

Baring Wall told Sir A. Grant that the course for Government to take was this—to come down and request that the standing orders might be suspended and a new Sugar Duties Act passed without delay, in order to enable the Government to dissolve without delay and take the sense of the people on the Budget: and contended that Peel as a fair man could make no objection to such a course!! He is supposed to speak the sentiments of Labouchere.                                                                    *May 15.*

## 84: ADD.MS 44777, ff. 74–76

May 18. 1841.
Lyttelton tells me that hearing there was some obstacle to the appointment of William Selwyn as Bishop of New Zealand after he had been recommended by the Archbishop of Canterbury, he went to Lord Melbourne about it, and was referred to Lord John Russell. To him he went and inquired what was the difficulty: I should add that he moved at the request of Mr. Few, the Secretary of the New Zealand Church Society. Lord John Russell said that he had hesitated to appoint him from hearing that he was a 'Tractarian': and that he would on no account appoint a man of such detestable (Lyttelton's word) principles. Lyttelton proposed to bring this matter to issue and said it would hardly do to ask him as he would of course disclaim belonging to any such party—and the point Lord John put was that he must know whether Selwyn did or did not belong to the Oxford party: but Lyttelton proposed, to ask his Bishop (Allen). To this Lord John assented and said he would take his opinion. Accordingly Lyttelton made application to the Bishop who answered that Selwyn could not be said to belong to such a party. This he sent to Lord John: but having heard nothing from him or of the affair after the lapse of several days he was in some apprehension when I saw him which was I think on Friday or Saturday.

Tuesday, May 18.
Eliot's story of Saturday about the decision of the Government not to dissolve is now superseded in common rumour by the idea that they took no final resolution: it is thought they will not in any event go out upon an adverse division, or rather two adverse divisions at the close of the present debate, and that they will present to us a Sugar Duties Bill in order to set their hands free for dissolution, and await the further discussions which may be expected to take place on timber and on corn. I conceive this much more probable than that they should retire at once upon the divisions.

Ashley tells me that he believes Lord Melbourne stands almost alone in energetic opposition to dissolution: and that he is plied mainly with these arguments—

1. that by a resignation he will break up and dissolve the 'Whig' Party—
2. that he will give countenance to the imputation which has been thrown out, viz. that the Administration had brought forward these measures and without any serious intention to make an effort to carry them—

and says that he does not much mind the latter plea, but winces under the former.

Should they remain in office and propose a Sugar Duties Bill on the basis of the present duties, I apprehend that Peel however averse, from temperament and from experience, to votes of want of confidence, will think that at all hazards such a course must be adopted: considering as greater than the evil of so strong a measure, the other alternative, in which the Government would for a length of time fret and inflame the whole country by the promise of cheap bread.

Tuesday, May 18.
O'Connell has been asking his ultramontane witness on the Newfoundland Committee, Captain Geary, whether it be not obligatory upon Roman Catholics to attend Mass upon all Sundays and holidays of obligation, unless in case of some insuperable hindrance: to which Captain Geary replies, that to neglect it is a *mortal sin*: which O'Connell receives with gravity.

I remember, however, that in the year 1834, it happened that O'Connell, George Sinclair, and I, were appointed a sub-committee of the Inns of Court Committee, to go down some fifty miles into Essex, in order to examine a disabled witness named Skingley. The question was what day we should choose to go down—the journey both ways requiring the whole working-day—and I remember that upon some slight question arising as to the engagements of the parties who were intended to go, O'Connell proposed to go on the next *Sunday*, to which I objected and he at once withdrew it and another day was fixed.

## 85: ADD.MS 44819, ff. 61–63

May 22. [1841].

Macaulay made his reply to me on the 11th and after it we went behind the Chair. He had understood that I had accused him in particular of laxity of principle. On the contrary, I told him, that which I intended in employing such a phrase was the gradual descent of a Government professing identity with the principles of Lord Grey, by successive abandonments of its own established and avowed positions, in compliance with the emergencies of their party—a charge which if true could scarcely at all apply to any who like him had come recently into the Cabinet professing the popular opinions which he had avowed in his manifesto. 'With respect to infatuation', I said, 'let me add a few words: I am sensible how strong a case is required to justify me in the use of such terms—you will pardon my repeating them as it is with a view to soothe. What I meant was, that the course Government have taken with regard to these sugar duties appeared to me to be the one which they would have rightly selected if the object had been to damage as much as they possibly could their own professed designs respecting trade.'

On Thursday [20 May] a meeting of twenty was held at Peel's to consider whether any announcement should be made on that day. The almost universal opinion was in favour of silence: 1. because a meeting was to be held in Lincolnshire yesterday which would test the feelings of agricultural Ministerialists with respect to a vote of confidence: 2. in order to be well aware of the scheme of the Government, of which it was then only privately known that they would ask a Sugar Duties Bill: 3. because the general feeling also was that we had better go on to the corn question, unless Government should farther postpone it, without interposing any vote of confidence, on such grounds as these—

a. that we could not with certainty carry it,
b. that if we did it would yield a much smaller majority than the corn,
c. that it would not displease the Government,
d. that the Government would not allow us to finish such a debate on the Thursday and Friday of next week and that consequently we could not after all get the vote probably before the Corn Law division.

In the course of that conversation Lord Darlington intimated his willingness to see a reduction in the present scale of duty. Peel said he was delighted to hear him say so, as in his opinion on the willingness to entertain such a question would depend the practicability of maintaining protection for agriculture. On that day we were summoned again for Monday but yesterday there came a summons for today instead of Monday. The opinion had gained strength that some measure must be taken in the interval; and consequently the meeting was held, of about the same numbers as before, Stanley absent.

It did not seem *certain* that any of the Ministerial men who voted with us on Tuesday would do the same on a vote of confidence: but some would probably stay away: Fremantle reported that it would be an extremely near thing but on the whole we were likely to carry it by a very small majority.

Peel said that if such conduct could be made intelligible to the party and the country, the best course upon its abstract merits would be to wait for the corn debate and enjoy the benefit of the progressive majority—but as such was not the case, he believed it was best under all the circumstances to run the risks, and for him to give notice on Monday that on Thursday he would move a vote of want of confidence in the Administration. He must, however, consult the peers in the interval, and nothing therefore must be either disclosed, or considered as decided. The very general feeling of the party was today strongly in favour of interposing a vote of no confidence: Graham perhaps excepted—while on Thursday it was the other way. Then both Graham and Stanley were against it—while both in the first instance had argued for it as preferable to a motion on the sugar duties, Peel being then inclined to agree with them. In point of fact the crisis is so delicate and so complex, that a very little seems to turn the scale in the most stable minds.

We are agreed in this: that the object is to provide that if there be a dissolution it shall be speedy and shall be followed by an early reassembling of Parliament say in September.

The vote of want of confidence seems to me to have these specific recommendations. A dissolution on confidence is upon the whole more favourable to us and to the peace of the country than a dissolution upon corn: if we carry our vote of no confidence, it will be a new stretch, a new violation of constitutional principle for an Administration sustained by neither House of Parliament to proceed to propose in Parliament a new and great measure of the kind they have announced; and it is not impossible that our vote may thus force them to make their election between resignation and dissolution: 1. at the earliest possible moment, 2. on the better of the two questions.

On the other hand this calculation throws out of view the chance of our being beaten on that vote, which would give them a new lease: it is so very difficult fairly to compare conflicting considerations when they are not *in pari materia.*

On Wednesday when we dined at Peel's he said without naming his informant that at a stormy Cabinet that day it had been decided to ask a Sugar Duties Bill—to take the discussion on corn—and then to dissolve. At the Palace on Monday evening a lady said to Lord Melbourne, 'They say you have given in'—and he replied he had not and would not. It is supposed that he gave in on Tuesday.     *May 22. 1841.*


## 86: ADD.MS 44777, ff. 77–81

June 4. 1841. (Friday).
On Wednesday I had a conversation with Mr. T. Godfrey with regard to treating at Newark—which is noticed in my journal.

Yesterday morning with Rio about O'Connell. I spoke to him to this effect: 'I view with extreme regret that the Roman Catholics of England are allying themselves more and more closely with O'Connell: receiving him at their meetings and making him a prominent figure there. Now the prejudice of this country will be strengthened and inflamed by this course. It may be a necessity of their position—I do not presume to blame it or decide whether it be or be not blameworthy: but it is of most unhappy tendency. We consider that O'Connell, so far as he is to be understood by his habitual conduct, is a man regardless of all laws divine and human: whose career affords the most flagrant instances of abuse employed as an instrument of personal vindictiveness, of falsehood, and of pecuniary corruption. Of course it is not ours to judge him as a moral agent, as a man standing before his God—but such is the aspect his public life presents to us (I do not mean that it presents nothing *else*): we cannot explain it on any supposition which presumes him honest: I assure you that I do not use the language of mere vituperation —that I speak from public occurrences of which I have been cognisant since entering public life though their mass be such that it would be difficult to give any adequate view of them on the instant.' He said, 'I do not think you do O'Connell justice: he is a Christian sincere and earnest in his religion: every Sunday morning he hears two Masses, which is considered a sign of great devotion: and receives the Communion; I see him going into an obscure part to avoid observation.' 'And do you really know', said I, 'that O'Connell receives the Communion every Sunday?' 'He does', said Rio—'he has often said things that have made me bite my lips with pain but consider what he is— consider that in him are represented the wrongs of a people, in him are concentrated the passions to which those wrongs have given birth—I always feel that if I had been an Irishman I should have been shot in 1798—I should have been so wrought up by vindictive recollections that I might have assassinated men: I remember having that desire when I was a boy and when my mother spoke to me of the bones of my grandfather—allow then for O'Connell's intemperance and do not believe him insincere in his religion.' I said, 'The charges against O'Connell are charges which in no degree apply to the rebels of 1798 or to any violence or exasperation connected with the remembrance of wrongs received— all these I set aside: it does not become *us* to make them a matter of reproach: but I do not think if you had lived in 1798 you would have been regardless of truth, or personally vindictive, or stained with corruption, more than you now are. Well, the English people, reading O'Connell's character in that mode and degree in which one is absolutely compelled to form as it were provisional or conditional judgments of one's fellow creatures, consider as infamous whatever voluntarily allies itself with him—the more those of your communion associate with him the more they will embitter our religious prejudices. You know you have not for a long time been in a condition to be fairly judged by us—suspicions of political disaffection have always attached to you in this country and your religion therefore has been viewed under unfavourable predispositions, tending to cause an exaggeration of differences, and exasperation of minds, and a violent revulsion on our part from the Roman Church in the mass—we who desire to cherish every legitimate means of sympathy, and in conformity with both truth and charity to attain to dispassionate views of our relative positions, we are certainly bound to grieve when we see a course taken of which the effect must be to prolong the confusion of our religious questions by the admixture of foreign matter.' 'Yes', he said, 'it is true—our people, however, are fearful of an oppressive reaction under Peel, from the language that has been held with regard to the repeal of the Relief Bill —not that that would be done directly, but they apprehend something of that character might take place: therefore they draw towards the Irish, and unfortunately that almost means drawing towards O'Connell.'

He stated his case with an admirable union of warmth, frankness, and good temper: it is most instructive to hear these things and to learn how far the excuses for even the most flagrant cases may really go. But the great rule of course is to remember that even if we are obliged to form judgments of men to a certain extent, i.e. *quoad* the purposes of action, still we must not suffer our minds to rest on and contemplate them as truths, but refer them to the all merciful Father.

Yesterday evening at the Palace I had some conversation with Molesworth on the Corn Laws and state of parties. He said, 'We who do not really belong to either the Whig or the Tory party in the House of Commons are in a most painful position—for my own part I do not consider that I have given an independent vote since I voted with you in 1839 on the Jamaica Bill.' I said, 'Doubtless compulsion has been put upon you —you have been voting for the Government as the choice of two evils— and whether you have in your own sense been acting rightly or wrongly I do not know and rejoice that it does not belong to me to decide.' He said, 'You will now get a majority, perhaps of fifty, I do not think more: Peel will not have a strong Government, nor do I see how the materials of a strong Government are anywhere to be found: and his Government will break up on these very questions which have now been brought forward in the Budget in a manner that I do not at all like though firmly attached to the principles of free trade. Peel will do something on the Corn Laws—he will be opposed in it by many of his own agricultural supporters and he will alienate them to such a degree that they will withdraw their general aid from his Government and break up his party. The great institutional questions are gone to rest—we have endeavoured to carry them and have failed—the ballot and short Parliaments and extension of the suffrage will not be formidable to him: having failed on those questions we have fallen back on the inquiry, what can be done to improve the material condition of the people—the answer is in the application of the principles of free trade.'

He did not think the Government proposition about corn sufficient really to move the country so as to affect the elections at large.

He allowed there was strength in the argument for maintaining the production of wheat at home on a scale nearly adequate to our consumption, drawn from the dangers and losses to which we should be liable when placed in a state of dependence upon foreign nations: even though we might not depend on one only, and though it be improbable that supposing us dependent upon a number, all of them should combine against us.

## 87: ADD.MS 44819, ff. 63–64

June 7. 1841.

I mentioned to Rio, O'Connell's proposal to me to spend the Sunday, in 1834 in a journey on parliamentary business: he observed that O'Connell probably meant to hear Mass before setting out—and I understood him that in such case the employment would not have constituted a servile work or have violated the obligation of the day—which seems strange.

On Saturday morning [5 June] the division in the House of Commons presented a scene of the most extraordinary excitement. While we were in our lobby we were told that we were 312 and the Government either 311 or 312. It was also known that they had brought down Lord Douglas Hallyburton who was reputed to be in a state of total idiocy. After returning to the House I went to sit near the bar, where the other party were coming in. We had all been counted, 312, and the tellers at the Government end had counted to 308: there remained behind this unfortunate man, reclining in a chair, evidently in total unconsciousness of what was proceeding, his eyes vacant themselves and staring upon vacancy, his mouth also wide open, his arms and feet extended and motionless—loud cries had been raised from our side, when it was seen that he was being brought up, to clear the bar that the whole House might witness the scene and every one stood up in intense curiosity—there were now only this figure, less human even than an automaton, and two persons, R. Stewart and E. Ellice junior pushing the chair in which he lay—a loud cry of Shame! Shame! burst from our side; those opposite were silent, but I imagine in pain and disgust like ourselves—Stanley of the Treasury turned white and seemed to bite his lips, not usual with him—these three were counted without passing the tellers and the moment after we saw that our tellers were on the right in walking to the table, indicating that we had won. Fremantle gave out the numbers, and then the intense excitement raised by the sight we had witnessed found vent in an enthusiastic (quite irregular) hurra with waving of hats.

Stanley was told that Lord D. Hallyburton's vote would be challenged —and he begged that it might not be done, as we had won without resort to this measure: which otherwise would doubtless have been taken: to prevent the sentence of the House of Commons on an Administration from being decided by the vote of an idiot.

Upon looking back I am sorry to think how much I partook in the excitement that prevailed: but how could it be otherwise in so extraordinary a case?

I thought Lord John's a great speech—it was delivered too under the pressure of great indisposition. He has risen with adversity. He seemed rather below par as a leader in 1835 when he had a clear majority and the ball nearly at his foot—in each successive year the strength of his Government has sunk and his own has risen.          *June 7. 1841.*

## 88: ADD.MS 44819, f. 64

On Monday June 7 [1841] a meeting of 25 was held at Peel's to prepare for the decision which Lord John was to announce in the House at 5. All were agreed that the great object would be to *hasten* the dissolution, presuming it inevitable and leaving to the Government the whole responsibility. It was resolved to ask of Lord J. Russell an explicit declaration to the effect that Parliament should be dissolved at once and likewise reassembled on the earliest possible day—in the event of his making it, to assent to the proposition of supplies for six months—which as Peel observed *might* possibly be more convenient—and if not to limit the supplies to three months except in any case when it could be shown that the public service would require more—this was taken as the best means of constraining Government but it seemed to be thought that they might if so inclined elude the necessity of meeting early and that they would have money enough. However, in the House Baring shook his head at the three months when Peel mentioned it and intimated that it really would not do, even supposing Parliament to meet on the earliest possible day. Peel executed his task admirably, ascertaining all that was wished and keeping clear of all approbation of the dissolution. Lord John seemed to feel the irksomeness of his position as holding the Seals, without a foundation for any energetic administration of his department.          *June 10. [1841].*

## 89: ADD.MS 44777, ff. 82–85

Hawarden. July 8, 1841.

This morning I went with Mr. Neville Grenville to see Lord Westminster's tenants again: knowing that a carriage was to come at 8 o'clock to carry them to the poll. They are:

1. Jones, farmer under Lord Westminster but his Flintshire qualification a freehold.
2. P. Mitchell, farmer under Lord Westminster.
3. J. Mitchell ditto.
4. R. Higginson ditto.
5. J. Reynolds ditto.
6. Price, a blacksmith dependent for custom.

All these men are warmly for Glynne. I had already seen all of them except No. 5, him I saw this morning and so can speak of all.

Yesterday I saw all except (4) and (6) and they agreed to meet at Jones's house and to sign a letter to be addressed to Lord Robert Grosvenor stating their wishes for Glynne, and asking on that ground (not an immodest request) to be allowed to be neutral.

But a letter from Mr. Taylor last evening announcing simply that he would 'by the blessing of God' call with a carriage and take them off at 8 this morning had completely daunted them and I found on calling this morning on the Mitchells that nothing had been done.

We found J. Mitchell, Higginson, and Reynolds, and Mr. Neville Grenville said why not at all events write *now* rather than not at all? It was about half past seven. A young man in the cottage sat down and wrote words suggested by Mr. Neville Grenville as follows (exactly):

'We the undersigned should much prefer voting for Sir S. Glynne, and we therefore beg to be allowed not to vote at all if we may not to vote for Stephen Glynne.

J. Reynolds X his mark

J. Mitchell X his mark

Richard Higginson

To
Lord Robert Grosvenor.
Bretton. July 8. 1841.

With this they went (and we to meet them) to H—'s publichouse on the Chester Road where the omnibus was to come. There we found P. Mitchell who was of the same mind but said he dared not sign.

By and bye came up the carriage with Taylor the agent and voters. All went into the publichouse and having travelled four miles they began to drink. By and bye I went in to speak to Mr. Taylor and found him with the letter in his hand. I stated who I was: and he said he had seen Lord R. Grosvenor last night and that 'he seemed very angry to hear that Mr. Gladstone had been *tampering* with Lord Westminster's tenants and had written a letter for them to sign and send to him'.

'Was that the case indeed', said I: 'I think I had better take down those words; pray let me have pen and ink.'

'Well, Sir', said he, 'I will withdraw that word "tampering" if you please: but Lord Robert said he would rather lose an election than canvass one of Sir S. Glynne's tenants.'

About this time Mr. G. N. Grenville came in.

'Well, Mr. Taylor', I said, 'you see that three of Lord Westminster's tenants have signed a letter to Lord R. Grosvenor asking to be allowed not to vote—have you read that letter?'

*Taylor.* 'No Sir I have not.'

*Gladstone.* 'Will you read it?'

*T.* 'No Sir I have nothing to do with that: my orders from Lord Robert are to take every man and poll them for Mostyn.'

*G.* 'Then Sir I will read it to you—but do you have the goodness to look on in order that you may see that I read it correctly.'

I then read the letter under his eye and said, 'Now Sir will you poll these men before you give time to get an answer from Lord Robert Grosvenor?'

*T.* 'Certainly I will Sir.'

*G.* 'Against their own wills which you know to be for Glynne?'

*T.* 'I know they are so inclined, or at least that they were so last time.'

*G.* 'And you will poll them without waiting for an answer?'

*T.* 'Certainly I will Sir.'

*G.* 'Then I will if you please make a note of it': I then made a note of the words as follows:[1] and read it over to him.

By this time he had considered matters coolly (the taking notes of the conversation having this advantage for us both) and he said:

'Well Sir if you will send that letter to Lord R. Grosvenor I will not poll the men until there is time to have his Lordship's answer.'

I said, 'Very good Mr. Taylor that seems as fair an answer as *you* in

---

[1] ADD.MS 44729, f. 109.

your capacity can make me—and we will if you wish it send the letter, but I think it would be more satisfactory to Lord Robert if you would write a line to him at the same time, stating the arrangement you had made that he may know it is not a trick of ours.'

T. 'No Sir I have received my orders from Lord Robert, they are peremptory and I would rather decline writing at all.'

I said, 'You will understand that I have not asked them to vote against their landlord but I thought that if their landlord knew their wishes he would allow them to remain neuter.'

The men were called in and I said in Taylor's presence what they had done with regard to the letter, and what their feelings were. Taylor spoke to Mitchell who said 'I wish to vote for Sir Stephen but I do not wish to offend my landlord.'

Mr. Taylor directed us where to find Lord Robert Grosvenor—agreed finally not to take the men to the poll until ten o'clock tomorrow morning—but said if any one else asked them to vote for Mostyn today and they chose to do it he could not help that. They went with Taylor in the omnibus 'to see the fun', and they stepped into it like sheep—but they declared they would not vote until they heard from Lord Robert.

Mr. Neville Grenville put in a plea to the same effect for Peter Mitchell but Taylor of course refused to allow the compact to extend to him and he was carried off to vote forthwith.

Upon returning to Hawarden I wrote with Mr. G. N. Grenville's aid a letter to Lord Robert of which the copy is annexed[1]—and added the following P.S.:

'P.S. I need hardly add I understood that none of the parties in question had promised their votes.'  *Mold. July 8. 1841.*

## 90: ADD.MS 44358, ff. 56–57

*Gladstone to Lord Robert Grosvenor, 8 July 1841*
*Hawarden.* I trust that you will deem the subject of this note an apology for the great freedom which I use in addressing you.

While canvassing on behalf of Sir S. Glynne I have called on several persons, who are tenants of Lord Westminster or otherwise dependent on him, and I have found them one and all desirous to vote for Glynne,

---

[1] No. 90.

but unwilling to go against their landlord. Upon this I have said to them in substance, 'I will not ask you to go against your landlord but I think if your landlord knew your conscientious inclinations he would not compel you to vote for Mr. Mostyn.' I therefore recommended their plainly stating their own wishes in Lord Westminster's absence to your Lordship as his representative on the spot in these matters. And I confess I thought it but fair on the part of the tenants to their landlord that they should apprise him of their inclinations of which he could not otherwise be supposed to be informed.

Under this advice from Mr. Neville Grenville and myself three of Lord Westminster's tenants have this morning written and signed the accompanying letter[1], and have shown it to Mr. Taylor who called, as he stated by your Lordship's desire, 'to take the men to poll for Mr. Mostyn'. Mr. Taylor seemed quite aware of the favourable inclination to Glynne and anxiety for his success, and after seeing the letter said (at the close of some conversation which I need not here repeat, and after having first expressed a different intention) *he* would not poll the men until time had been given for your Lordship's answer to be received: and he finally stated he would refrain from soliciting them *until ten o'clock tomorrow morning* for that purpose. They are gone with him to Mold.

Mr. Taylor declined however to write to you on the subject and required of Mr. G. N. Grenville and myself that we should convey the letter to you and return the answer: which I only regretted, because I thought it would have been more satisfactory to you to have heard from Mr. Taylor himself of the arrangement that he had made: but he said his instructions from you were peremptory and that he had nothing more to do in the matter.

I am therefore obliged thus to obtrude upon you and I have directed the bearer of this letter to await your Lordship's pleasure: I think however that I have noted with accuracy what passed with Mr. Taylor, and Mr. G. N. Grenville agrees with me in his recollection.

P.S. I need hardly add I understood that none of the parties in question had promised their votes.

---

[1] See no. 89.

## 91: ADD.MS 44819, ff. 65–68

Saturday, August 21. [1841].
At 12 I met at Peel's:

| | | |
|---|---|---|
| Sir R. Peel | Lord Lyndhurst | Lord Ellenborough |
| Sir J. Graham | Lord Stanley | Sir H. Hardinge |
| Lord Granville Somerset | Sir Thomas Fremantle | Mr. Goulburn |

to discuss the general nature of the amendment to the Address.

Peel said, that the motion of last session, moved by him against the Ministers, had laid down a bad precedent: namely a constitutional dogma that to do so and so was 'inconsistent with the spirit of [the] constitution'—that it would be taken advantage of and justly.

The most embarrassing case he observed would be that in which the Queen should recommend generally to our consideration the laws relating to the import of foreign corn: it would be 'difficult to take, dangerous to refuse' in Graham's words. If the Speech should express a preference for a fixed duty, that would be easily met. But the decided inclination was, to decline entertaining any proposals whatever from the Government on the score that it did not possess the confidence of the House of Commons.

I said, 'Do you at all entertain the idea of pronouncing a censure on the dissolution?'

Peel said, 'No: a dissolution is a popular act in its nature and is the only defence of the Crown against a House of Commons: the House of Commons therefore complains of it with an ill grace: and besides, though it may be open to us, we could not well do it after having said to the Government, we insist on your taking one of two courses: either resign or dissolve immediately.'

Lord Lyndhurst said, 'We have other grounds which are better'— Lord Ellenborough, that we had made ourselves parties to the dissolution. I of course did not argue the matter at length: but I much regret the dissolution is overlooked, for such reasons as these—

1. Immediate appeal to the people on a given measure or set of measures is an experiment only requiring frequent repetition to make our Monarchy a mockery.
2. On the question of food, it was sure to produce great excitement and irreconcilable divisions between classes: these evils have been

partially mitigated by the extreme good sense of the English people: quote Lord John in June on the Poor Law.

3. There was no discord of the two Houses or reluctance to legislate which could tend to justify it.

4. If it is possible that there may be circumstances which may warrant the act, this must be when the nation is really with the Minister: not when as now it is against him and he is condemned by the tribunal to which he appealed. In the abstract a dissolution may be fair and popular: but we know that it is attended with expense, trouble, and moral evil almost beyond computation: a Minister has no right to say 'I appealed and I acquiesce' and be *off*: he is bound to know something of his grounds for dissolving and his ignorance or miscalculation even taken alone is a political offence, and an additional proof that he is unworthy of confidence.

However, I think that Peel and others have in retrospect the dissolution of January 1835, and Stanley and Graham that of the spring of 1831: and that they fear that these cases might be so introduced as to break in argument the effect of any direct censure of the dissolution.

*August 23.*

There was another meeting held yesterday—Sunday—at Lord Aberdeen's (Peel being beset with spies) and attended by the same parties as that of Saturday except that the Duke of Wellington and our host were present and Fremantle was not. They sat from a quarter past two to half past three for the purpose of rough-hewing an amendment: it was agreed that we could not properly either promise or refuse to take the Corn Laws into consideration: Lord Ellenborough produced a draft, and Peel several, in which he made revenue and deficiency the central point: and without any difference of opinion it seemed to be thought the discussion of the questions on their merits must be barred by a preliminary declaration of want of confidence. Peel introduced, however, a hope that the case might be met consistently with a due protection to domestic agriculture and with the interests of our colonial possessions. I ventured to observe, that if allusion were made to colonial interests, there should also be a notice of the argument connected with slavery, which formed a main part of our ground last session: that that argument was valid, and told, however scouted by our opponents, and that if we continued to adhere to it we could not well pass it over—that colonial interests alone would not have won our battle, nor would have justified our refusing to go into committee upon the Ministerial proposition.

Lord Aberdeen who came to town last night resumed the point which I hazarded yesterday and seemed to consider that a censure ought to be passed on the dissolution.                                                   *August 23.*

I may as well add a word on my attendance yesterday: it was doing a servile work on the Lord's day, an infringement of the Christian's blessed rest. I did it as a work of necessity, that is of high urgency—so much of human destiny may hang on the deliberations of these days, the occasion is so special and rare—on these grounds I did not think it right, after taking some time to reflect, to absent myself, and trust I was warranted in that sentiment.

Today the same parties met at the same place 3–5.15 p.m. Peel had omitted from the proposed draft of yesterday the allusion to domestic agriculture and colonial interests; as affording a handle for various constructions and not really conveying any thing.

By and bye in came a cover from Lord J. Russell containing the Speech of tomorrow confidentially communicated: Peel read it. It 'more especially' charges on us the subject of finance and on corn says 'it will be for us to determine' whether the present law does not 'aggravate the natural fluctuations of supply, embarrass the operations of trade, derange the currency, and diminish the comforts and increase the privations of the people'—nearly such are the words: a studied invective. Nearly all were surprised. Stanley declared it wicked. He proposed or threw out voting our regret that H.M. had been advised to prejudice the discussion of this great question by describing the law in such a manner as must (here I am not very precise) materially increase the difficulties of the subject: this it was observed by Graham would be taken by the Queen as a personal censure upon herself, and might be made a justification for some violent measure, such as a second dissolution. Peel said, 'How is it possible the Queen can give her confidence to us within a week after delivering such sentiments'—and seemed to apprehend very mischievous results from the promulgation of such opinions in her name. Goulburn apprehended an intrigue and overthrow of the new Administration by it in the interval before February— Lord Aberdeen thought that from *such* a Speech there might be something in the background—Graham that they really intended to prorogue at once, and dissolve us upon the new register. Stanley would not entertain the idea of a dissolution as contemplated by them.

The Duke of Wellington wrote in pencil a few lines proposing to state to the Queen that the present Corn Laws had been enacted with great pains and deliberation under high authority, and that we did not conceive they produced any of the evils ascribed to them in the Speech: he said he thought a plain but civil contradiction might be advisable. Lord Ripon was for mentioning corn specifically in the amendment, or the country would not understand—Lords Aberdeen and Lyndhurst urged that we should set up *confidence* against *corn*, and that we should narrow and lower our ground if we argued the corn case: Graham and I think the general sense was for silence, that is for not going beyond a general allusion to 'trade and revenue and distress'—but Peel could not make up his mind apparently to his own satisfaction and appointed another meeting which it was finally settled should be at half past ten tonight: the Duke to attend after his dinner party. I was surprised to see the idea so much entertained that another dissolution could be contemplated. Peel said, if the present men counselled the answer to the Address it would be that in deference to the wishes of her Parliament she had changed her Ministers: but that her sentiments were such as had been expressed—he was astonished that Lord Melbourne could have concurred in advising such a Speech. Graham thought the Queen's inclination would even be to come down to the House and deliver the Speech herself, and that the Ministers must themselves have stopped her.

In my poor opinion we ought not to mention argumentatively the Corn Law in our Address because:

1. We can safely decline discussing it with the Administration, inasmuch as this was the course taken in the last Parliament when the corn debate was intercepted by the vote of want of confidence: and that it has been approved by the country, as the results of the election sufficiently show.

2. If we argue the measure in answer to the Speech we *pro tanto* recognise the Administration as a Government and depart from our own ground that it is a necessary preliminary to our entering upon these questions that the Administration should have the confidence of Parliament.

3. Our counterargument places us still more palpably at issue with the Queen before the country and pits our sentiments on measures against hers, as well as our simple disapprobation of her Ministers.

4. Such counterargument may easily be construed into censure and if so taken must have a real effect in exasperating against us the mind of the Queen: which we have a right to presume is as yet not the case.
5. It would be in the nature of a disclosure of Peel's case and future intentions: and would enable the Government to worry the question more effectually and prolong the debate in the hope of again exciting the country.

A Conservative party as such is I think apt not to trust to the good sense of the country as much as it ought.                    *August 23.* [*1841*].

## 92: ADD.MS 44819, f. 68

At the evening meeting last night the Duke produced a letter from Lord Melbourne, 'My dear Duke' and 'Yours faithfully', transmitting to him a copy of the Speech: the most familiar, as I understood, he had ever had—Lord Ripon still seemed inclined to put an answer to the corn paragraph into the amendment: but there was no dissentient from Sir Robert Peel's proposal, to mention corn only in the sentence acknowledging the Queen's communication, and to make the rest general— The Duke fell asleep at one time but wakened up again like a young soldier.

Lord Wharncliffe and Fremantle were present with all those of the former meeting.                                        *August 24.* [*1841*].

## 93: ADD.MS 44819, ff. 68-69

Last night I spoke to Goulburn about the notice of China in the Address. It seems to commit us to approbation of the demands made by the plenipotentiary. It may however be said that having no official or precise knowledge what they are, we may equitably presume their justice upon the faith of Her Majesty's declaration.

A more serious question remains. Is the Conservative Administration to adopt as a legacy from its predecessors the demand upon the Chinese Government for compensation in respect of the surrendered opium, and to enforce that demand by war?

If it could be shown that the Chinese Government itself continued to the last such a connivance at the opium trade as to bely their proclamations against it, then the contrabandists might indeed treat them as a mockery and their property might be entitled to the usual protection. But does it not appear that the Chinese Government had waged earnest war against the trade for some time before the seizure? If so *was* the opium entitled to protection? If so can we without sin exact requital for it? There are deep questions of justice and duty here involved, visible to the eye of God. ιεεῖνται νόμοι ὑψίποδες.[1]

There are other matters connected with the war into which I do not enter. Also there are considerations of policy and prudence connected with this matter, that are of themselves most important. But this question of compensation for the opium, to be demanded on its own merits, is a stumbling block at present in my way—if I am right in assuming that it is Sir R. Peel's intention to tender me some situation connected with the Government. May God grant me in this juncture a cool head and earnest, resolute heart that I may neither be bewildered by imagination on one side, nor by interest or vanity or even a *general* desire to serve the country on the other. *August 25. 1841.*

I rejoice exceedingly in having had on Monday night a very good opportunity of naming to Stanley for a West Indian bishopric (as there is likely soon to be one opening or even more) the sons of Mr. Wilberforce—as enabling him to make from among them a most excellent, and also an exceedingly popular appointment. He had before named another person: but he received the suggestion extremely well.

*August 25. 1841.*

## 94: ADD.MS 44819, f. 69

The effect of perusing today some papers and evidence relating to the opium trade in China, is by no means to weaken the impression, that the Imperial Government were manifestly sincere for a considerable time before the seizure—that they were even extraordinarily (according to their measure) energetic and effective for a certain time before it—that they had given signs of their desires and intentions which could not be

---

[1] Apparently a reference to Sophocles, *Oedipus Tyrannus*, 866–7: νόμοι πρόκεινται ὑψίποδες ('there are laws established, sublime and far above us').

mistaken by fair minds—that to none of these signs was any due attention paid by those engaged in the trade—that the siege of the British mercantile community (every house being implicated) was the only measure within their power which was at all likely to be effective—that the confiscation thus produced was in itself just—that if the means were irregular and illegitimate, this does not establish our title to a compensation, which can only be owing to us on the supposition that the act of confiscation itself, and not merely the manner of setting about it, was questionable. In a long conversation with my father, he seemed at first to think that if office be offered me I should remain silent on this question: but afterwards to agree that I ought to make moderate and of course amicable statement of my difficulties: he approved of my plan, to converse with Lord Sandon. *August 26. 1841.*

## 95: ADD.MS 44819, ff. 69–71

August 31. 1841.
In consequence of a note[1] received this morning from Sir Robert Peel I went to him at half past eleven. The following is the substance of a quarter of an hour's conversation. He said, 'In this great struggle in which we have been and are to be engaged, the chief importance will attach to questions of finance. It would not be in my power to undertake the business of Chancellor of the Exchequer in detail: I therefore have asked Goulburn to fill that office and I shall be simply First Lord. I think we shall be very strong in the House of Commons if as a part of this arrangement you will accept the post of Vice-President of the Board of Trade and conduct the business of that great department in the House of Commons, with Lord Ripon as President. I consider it an office of the highest importance and you will have my "unbounded confidence" in it.'

I said, 'Of the importance and responsibility of that office at the present time I am well aware: but it is right that I should say as strongly as I can, that I really am not fit for it. I have no general knowledge of trade whatever: with a few questions I am acquainted, but they are such as have come across me incidentally: and speaking not all in vague professions of incompetency nor as modesty might dictate, but as matter of

---

[1] ADD.MS 44275, f. 51.

fact, it is the case that my mind has not been accustomed or turned to them, they have not been among my pursuits.'

He said, 'The satisfactory conduct of an office of that kind must after all depend more upon the intrinsic qualities of the man, than upon the precise amount of his previous knowledge. I also think you will find Lord Ripon a perfect master of those subjects, and depend upon it with these appointments at the Board of Trade we shall carry the whole commercial interests of the country with us—I hope it will be Lord Ripon—possibly Lord Ashburton. There are two men, either of whom I consider competent to act as Vice-President of the Board of Trade—Sandon would I think fill the office properly, and yourself—of these I should much prefer to have you.'

I here interposed that I thought Sandon eminently and admirably fit for it, and, what I know to be the case, that I am not for a moment to be compared with him.

He resumed, 'If there be any other arrangement that you would prefer, my value and "affectionate regard" for you would make me most desirous to effect it so far as the claims of others would permit. To be perfectly frank and unreserved, I should tell you, that there are many reasons which would have made me wish to send you to Ireland: but upon the whole I think that had better not be done—some considerations "connected with the Presbyterians of Ireland" make me prefer on the whole that we should adopt a different plan. Then, if I had had the Exchequer, I should have asked you to be Financial Secretary of the Treasury: but under the circumstances I have mentioned, that would be an office of secondary importance; and I am sure you will not estimate that I now propose to you by the mere name which it bears'—he also made an allusion to the Admiralty of which I do not retain the exact form (I think to the possibility of Clerk's having gone there. WEG. September 16) but I rather interposed and said, 'My objection on the score of fitness would certainly apply with even increased force to any thing connected with the military and naval services of the country—for of them I know nothing. Nor have I any other object in view—there is no office to which I could designate myself. I think it my duty to act upon your judgment as to my qualifications: if it be your deliberate wish to make me Vice-President of the Board of Trade, I will not decline it: I will endeavour to put myself into harness, and to prepare myself for the place in the best manner I can: but it really is an apprenticeship. With regard, however, to the business of the House of Commons, I have this consideration to take into account, that from the present importance of matters connected with trade, you, and Mr. Goulburn too, must very much concern yourselves in the parliamentary business of the department.' He said, 'I hope you will be content to act upon the sense which others entertain of your suitableness for this office in particular, and I think it will be a good arrangement both with a view to the present conduct of business and to the brilliant destinies which I trust are in store for you.'

I answered, that I was deeply grateful for his many acts of confidence and kindness: and that I would at once assent to the plan he had proposed, only begging him to observe that I had mentioned my unfitness under a strong sense of duty and of the facts, and not by any means as a mere matter of ceremony.

I then added that I thought I should but ill respond to his confidence if I did not mention to him a subject connected with his policy, according to my anticipations of its probable course, which might raise a difficulty in my mind. 'I cannot', I said, 'reconcile it to my sense of right to exact from China, as a term of peace, compensation for the opium surrendered to her—I do not now speak of the national questions of insult or injury, which seem to me to be distinct from the other—I earnestly hope you will never be called to take a decision upon this point, I mean, that Sir H. Pottinger may in some way or other settle it during the present season—still it might possibly arise in the form of a difficulty, and I have thought it best frankly to mention it.'

He agreed that it was best to mention it: observed that in consequence of the shape in which the Chinese affair came into the hands of the new Government they would not be wholly unfettered: seemed to hint that under many other circumstances, the Vice-President of the Board of Trade used not to much mind what was done in other departments, but *remarked* that at present every question of foreign relations and many more would be very apt to mix themselves with the department of trade: he thought I had better leave the question suspended, and said that in the event of my finding the Government policy incompatible with my convictions of duty, my retirement upon such a ground, as being collateral and peculiar, would not be attended with the mischief of a retirement on account of general want of confidence.

I hesitated a moment before coming away and said it was only from my anxiety to review what I had said and to be sure that I had 'made a clean breast' on the subject of my unfitness for the department of trade.

Nothing could be more friendly and warm than his whole language and demeanour.

It has always been my hope, that I might be able to avoid this class of public employments: on this account I have not endeavoured to train myself for them: the place is very distasteful to me, and which is of more importance I fear I may hereafter demonstrate the unfitness I have to-day only stated. However, it comes to me, I think, as a matter of plain duty: it may be all the better for not being according to my own bent and leaning: and I must forthwith go to work, in sum, as a reluctant schoolboy meaning well.

On perusal, I think these notes pretty accurate.

*August 31. 1.30 p.m.*

## 96: ADD.MS 44819, f. 71

On Wednesday [1 September] at Grillion's Stanley expressed a high opinion of Roebuck as an able man and particularly clear speaker likely to make a figure in Opposition. Cobden also was noted as a resolute perspicuous man, familiar with all the turns of his subject.

*September 3. 1841.*

## 97: ADD.MS 44819, f. 72

This day I went to Claremont to be sworn in.

When the Council was constituted, the Duke of Buckingham and Lord Liverpool were first called in to take their oaths and seats: then the remaining four followed, Lincoln, Eliot, Ernest Bruce, and I. The Queen sat at the head of the table, composed but dejected—one could not but feel for her, all through the ceremonial.

We knelt down to take the Oaths of Allegiance and Supremacy and stood up to take (I think) the Councillor's oath—then kissed the Queen's hand, then went round the table shaking hands with each member, beginning from Prince Albert who sat on the Queen's right and ending with Lord Wharncliffe on her left: we then sat at the lower end of the table, excepting Lord Bruce who went to his place behind the Queen as Vice-Chamberlain. Then the Chancellor first and next the Duke of Buckingham were sworn to their respective offices. C. Greville forgot the Duke's Privy Seal and sent him off without it: the Queen corrected him and gave it.

Then were sworn the Secretaries of State and the Chancellor of the Exchequer. Greville again forgot the seals of the Secretaries: Lord Aberdeen kissed hands first, under his orders, and went off before receiving his seals, while Stanley knelt down to kiss hands: but the Queen again interposed with the seals, and gave them in the right order beginning with Graham as Home Secretary and taking Lord Aberdeen next, instead of following the rank of the parties as Greville had erroneously done.

Then were read and approved several Orders in Council: among which was one assigning a district to a church: and another appointing Lord Ripon and me to act in matters of trade. These were read aloud by the Queen in a very clear though subdued voice: and she repeated 'Approved' after each. Upon that relating to Lord Ripon and myself, we were called up and kissed hands again.

Then the Queen rose as did all the members of the Council and retired bowing.

We had luncheon in the same room half an hour after, and went off. The Duke of Wellington went in an open carriage with a pair: all our other grand people with four. Peel looked shy all through.

I visited Claremont once before, 27 years ago I think, to see the place, soon after the Princess Charlotte's death, as a child. It corresponded pretty much with my impressions.

G. Anson authorised me to ascertain whether Lyttelton would be one of the Prince's Lords: and said the Queen would give the most entire confidence (of which I said I did not believe any one doubted in the smallest degree) to her new Government: and that she was an extraordinary person.

I am *lag* of the Council.

Brougham, with his lady, stationed himself on the hill beyond Putney in his britschka to see the people go by to Claremont!

*September 3. 1841.*

## 98: ADD.MS 44819, f. 73

September 16. [1841].
Upon quietly reviewing past times, and the degree of confidence which Sir Robert Peel had for years, habitually I may say, reposed in me, and especially considering its climax, in my being summoned to the meetings immediately preceding the debate on the Address in August, I am

inclined to think, after allowing for the delusions of selflove, that there is not a perfect correspondence between the tenor of the past on the one hand, and my present appointment and the relations in which it places me to the Administration on the other. And that it was not determined in Peel's mind to offer me the situation I now hold, at the time when he summoned me on the 21st of August. He may have made up his mind at those meetings that I was not qualified for the consultations of a Government, nor would there be any thing strange in this, except the supposition that he had not seen it before. Having, however, taken the alarm (so to speak) upon the invitation at that time, and being impressed with the idea that it savoured of Cabinet office, I considered and consulted on the Chinese question which I regarded as a serious impediment to office of that description: and I had provisionally contemplated saying to Peel in case he should offer me Ireland with the Cabinet to reply that I would gladly serve his Government in the secretaryship but that I feared his Chinese measures would hardly admit of my acting in the Cabinet. I am sorry now to think that I may have been guilty of an altogether absurd presumption, in dreaming of the Cabinet. But it was wholly suggested by that invitation. And I still think that there must have been some consultation and decision relating to me in the interval between the meetings and the formation of the new Ministry, which produced some alteration.

Already, however, it is easy to recognise the mercy and wisdom of God in the arrangement as it stands. I am now not a member but a servant of the Government, officially responsible (unless in some strong case) only for my own department—with plenty of homely useful work before me, such as brings with it far less anxiety than the great moral questions of politics—and with a conscience free on this head, in the thought that I am not self-designated to my office, and am not in holding it gratifying any desire or realising any idea of my own.

In confirmation of the notion I have recorded above, I am distinct in the recollection that there was a shyness in Peel's manner and a downward eye, when he opened the conversation and made the offer, not usual with him in speaking to me.

I am glad to find he told Sandon he would have wished much to have had him with him in the Cabinet. *September 16. 1841.*

## 99: ADD.MS 44819, ff. 73–74

I wrote yesterday a letter to Fremantle and a draft proposed letter to [the] editor, *Morning Advertiser*, (see my letters and letterbook[1]) on the subject [of] a recent article, which alleges that I have denounced Peel as 'devoid of all religion' etc.

It would have been a relief to *me* if my referee had allowed me to send this draft—but he consulted Goulburn, Lincoln, and Peel himself by L[incoln]'s sensible advice (which course I purposely left open to him). They were all, with Peel, strongly for my remaining silent and Peel commissioned Fremantle to tell me that he felt perfectly satisfied nothing at all resembling or partaking of the nature of such a sentiment could ever have come from me. They seem to think I did right in making the reference. *October 9. 1841.*

Yesterday I saw Mr. Dodge, an American who has been employed on a commercial mission in Germany. I asked him if much were said of our Chinese war, and begged a candid answer. He said as it was asked he would give it: and stated that the subject was much talked of—that it was considered we ought never to have gone into such a war—that the sympathies of Europe were with China—that it was extremely doubtful how long it would be protracted.

This evening Bunsen showed me a letter from Peel dated October 10th about Germany—in which he hopes that that noble people will always remain united, and devoted to its nationality and will in the centre of Europe maintain its equilibrium and order. He writes with great *verve*, alludes to the song, 'They shall not have the Rhine' and says 'no *they*'—meaning evidently the French—'shall not have the Rhine', if Germans feel so and so.

Bunsen asked if such a letter might be published in Germany. I thought clearly not: but that as it was not marked private it might be shown to his King and that that was probably intended by the writer. *October 14. 1841.*

---

[1] Nos. 100 and 101.

## 100: ADD.MS 44527, f. 37

*Gladstone to Sir Thomas Fremantle, 8 October 1841*
*Carlton House Terrace.* Please to consider the enclosed note, and to give
me a candid opinion upon sending it or not (consulting any one you
please), by which I shall be bound. It relates to a small point, perhaps,
but not one so small as I can either prevail upon myself to overlook or to
decide without aid. The article from which I quote is one of a series, each
consisting I am sorry to say of little else than a tissue of untruths from
beginning to end, all the rest of which I gladly pass over. Silence I know
to be usually and almost always the right *and* the convenient course on
these occasions: three months ago perhaps it would not have occurred
to me to notice this: but placed under Sir R. Peel in the Queen's service,
ought I to allow a slander to go abroad aimed through me (for I am too
small game for the editor of the *Morning Advertiser*) at him?

I have written the note as the most convenient form of explaining to
you the sense in which if at all, I should address myself to this said editor.

## 101: ADD.MS 44358, ff. 145–146

*Gladstone to the editor of the* Morning Advertiser, *[8 October 1841]*
*13 Carlton House Terrace.* My attention has very recently been called to
a leading article in your paper of the 24th September last, in which I
find it alleged of me, that in a work on Church and State I have
'within the last twelve months denounced' Sir Robert Peel as a man
'devoid of all religion' and 'as a person who consequently, though
possessed of "considerable abilities" as a politician, is altogether unfit to be entrusted with the destinies of the State'.

Anonymous statements affecting myself personally in your or any
other publication, I have never thought fit to notice; but having the
honour to serve Her Majesty under Sir Robert Peel, I think decency requires of me that I should not allow such an assertion to pass without
examination.

I therefore request of you to point out where either in the work and
within the time you have named, or at any time, and through any other
channel public or otherwise, I have denounced Sir Robert Peel as a man
'devoid of all religion' and altogether unfit to be entrusted with the

destinies of the State? or used any language, or conveyed any sentiments, with relation to Sir Robert Peel, bearing any degree of resemblance to such as you have been pleased to ascribe to me?

## 102: ADD.MS 44819, ff. 74–76

Some time ago Sir R. Peel gave me a memorandum which he had prepared to be read to the Cabinet on the subject of the Corn Laws: and at
the same time expressed himself favourably as to the detailed paper
which I had lent him.

Yesterday he sent for me and read to me a paper in draft which he had
been preparing for the Cabinet of which the object was to fix with some
precision the two points

1. What may fairly be considered a remunerating price to the British
   grower?
2. What is the price at which a considerable quantity of foreign corn
   can be imported?

On the first question he named 56/-: the point which I also had assumed
as the general result of my inquiries: as to the second when he came to it
he stopped suddenly and desired me to name a sum—I remarked that
every thing depended on what he meant by a considerable quantity—
that considering the diversity and complexity of circumstances any
answer must be conjectural to a certain extent—that also his declaration
must be borne in mind that we are not to judge from exceptional cases
of minute import—that under these cautions I thought it perfectly safe
towards the agriculturist to say

1. That not more than 1,000,000 quarters of wheat could under any
   ordinary circumstances be brought here at 40/-;
2. That not more than 2,000,000 quarters could under any ordinary
   circumstances be brought here at 45/-.

Such appeared to be his general view. After an hour's conversation (in
his dressing room where he had been writing all day) I said it was really
painful to me to profess before him opinions upon the Corn Law: but
that as he wished it I had thought it best to speak with perfect freedom,
and not to trouble him with repetition of apologies, and that I should so
continue to do.

Today I went again with Lord Ripon and Sir James Graham: Peel read the results and part of the details of his paper of yesterday—in the points already stated there was an entire concurrence. (I ought to have mentioned that yesterday Peel said to me he believed in his own mind that 54/- was a remunerating price.)

He then went on to his scale: and they discussed

1. The question of a maximum duty. It was determined that 20/- was sufficient: and would be generally prohibitory below 50/-.
2. The scale upwards which Peel had drawn provisionally—but as in his opinion the best after considering all that he had seen—I think thus as nearly as may be—

| | | | | | |
|---|---|---|---|---|---|
| 50/- .... 20/- | 57/- .... 15/- | 63/- .... 9/- |
| 51 .... 19 | 58 .... 14 | 64 .... 8 |
| 52 .... 18 | 59 .... 13 | 65 .... 7 |
| 53 .... 18 | 60 .... 12 | 66 .... 6⎤ |
| 54 .... 18 | 61 .... 11 | 67 .... 6⎬ |
| 55 .... 17 | 62 .... 10 | 68 .... 6⎦ |
| 56 .... 16 | ———— | 69 .... 5 |
| ———— | | 70 .... 4 |
| | | 71 .... 3 |
| | | 72 .... 2 |
| | | 73 .... 1 |

The leading points in his mind appeared to be those at 56/- and 62/-. My scale was produced and I argued freely in favour of

1. The contraction and acceleration of the slide.
2. The breadth of the level in which it virtually terminates.

I have made this level 10/2 tints (to use Sir J. Graham's expression) *broad*—less might do but I think it the safe side to err on—mine is 20/- to 54/-

Descent by 2/- for 1/- rise in price to 6/- at 61/-

6/- uniform to 71/-

4/- ...... 72/-

2/- ...... 73/- with deductions etc.

Sir R. Peel I think inclined to modify his thus far:

| | | |
|---|---|---|
| 60/- .... | 12/- |
| 61 .... | 10 |
| 62 .... | 8 |
| 63 .... | 6 |

|     |      |     |     |
| --- | ---- | --- | --- |
| 64  | .... | 6   |     |
| 65  | .... | 6   |     |
| 66  | .... | 6   |     |
| 67  | .... | 6   | Here Lord Ripon pleaded for the descent to 1/- to commence but Graham who entered very much into the doctrine of the level urged rather |
| 68/- | .... | 6/- |     |
| 69  | .... | 6   |     |
| 70  | .... | 6   |     |
| 71  | .... | 4   |     |
| 72  | .... | 2   |     |
| 73  | .... | 1   |     |

or some such conclusion.

In one or other of these forms, however, Sir R. Peel's scale is to go, it was understood to the Cabinet. He said it would not do to propose to the agriculturist 6/- at 61/-: and that he thought he might claim 10/- at 62/-. I think in his own mind he would not be averse to abatement—but wishes to feel the pulse of the agricultural folks. For my part I should not be very sorry to see 6/- even at 60/-: and though it might be right to take it I should regard 12/- at that point—especially with altered averages—as a measure of relief considerably short of what the country has a claim to receive.

The present law I am sorry to say appears to me to have been a very stringent and severe one.

Lord Ripon told me on our way back that Lord Ellenborough had confessed to him that in the celebrated amendment of 1827, they, the victors, had the worst of the argument—and that they had done it by way of showing their power.                                    *January 21. 1842.*

## 103: ADD.MS 44819, f. 76

I placed in Sir R. Peel's hands a long paper on the Corn Law in the month of November which on wishing to refer to it he could not find: and he requested me to write out afresh my argument upon the value of a rest or dead level and the part of the scale of price at which it should arrive: which I did.[1]

---

[1] ADD.MS 40469, ff. 134–137.

On Monday I wrote another paper arguing for a rest between 60/- and 70/- or thereabouts: and yesterday a third[1] intended to show that the present law has been in practice *fully* equivalent to a prohibition up to 70/-. Lord Ripon then told me the Cabinet had adopted Peel's scale as it originally stood—and seemed to doubt whether *any* alteration could be made. On his announcing the adoption I said in a marked manner, 'I am very sorry for it'—believing that it would be virtual prohibition up to 65/- or 66/- and often beyond, to the minimum: and not being able, in spite of all the good which the Government is about to do with respect to commerce to make up my mind to support such a protection. Considering the agricultural majority, the importance of a settlement, and the general interests of the party I can just bring myself to support 12/- at 60/- provided it fall to 6/- at 63/-: with this I think importation will generally begin, in quantity, about 62/-. Lord Ripon read my papers and sent them to Peel. I wait the result with some anxiety—what I have written on the last page[2] expresses my present feelings, and it was penned before I knew what Government would do. I see, from conversations with them today, that Lord Ripon, Peel, and Graham are all aware the protection is greater than is necessary.

*February 2. 1842.*

## 104: ADD.MS 44819, ff. 77–79

This day met Sir R. Peel, Lord Ripon, Sir J. Graham, Lord Stanley, Lord G. Somerset, Mr. Goulburn, Sir E. Knatchbull, Sir G. Clerk, and I, on corn—at Sir R. Peel's house. After long conversation on the various provisions relating to averages—which seemed to shrink after all into very narrow dimensions—I asked whether the upper parts of the scale viz. beyond 60/- must be regarded as definitively fixed. There appeared to be a considerable disposition to admit the principle of the

---

[1] Ibid. ff. 142–149 and 150–155.

[2] 'My apprehension and belief is that with a graduated scale of less rapid descent than the present one, the result would still substantially be, that no quantities capable of affecting general prices would be introduced upon a rising market until the duty had arrived at the actual (or *virtual*) termination of its descent, or within one or two shillings of it: and that in order to do justice among all classes this circumstance must be taken for granted and kept steadily in view in adjusting the particulars of any new scale of duties upon foreign grain.'

rest, but it was thought an alteration could not be made after the Duke of Buckingham had retired upon the scale as proposed in the Cabinet— as though it might be considered a breach of the terms offered to the agricultural interest. I put that their part of the scale was that below 60/- and that above it we had only to consider the consumer—but of course it was vain to resist. I therefore asked permission to speak to Sir R. Peel afterwards—and represented to him that I had such serious doubts on the subject of the scale as proposed that I thought it right to mention them— and to him rather than to any other person. I feared it *might* still be found to operate as virtual prohibition up to 70/-—that I should like to think somewhat more upon the point—and I hinted at retirement as being perfectly ready to adopt it if that could be done without perplexing the Government. He said the retirement of the person holding my office on this question immediately before his introducing it would endanger the existence of the Administration—and that he much doubted whether in such a case he could bring it on. I said that in that case I thought my higher duty was to suppress my doubts upon this particular measure, rather than cause embarrassment of such a nature —which I was bound to presume would ensue, if he anticipated it: though I had not done so. He said that he was so entirely taken by surprise that he hardly knew what to say—he was thunderstruck—he considered me to have assented to the scale when he propounded it (January 21) to Sir James Graham, Lord Ripon, and myself. I said in reply that I had then argued for the long rest—that I had also stated what I believed to the effect of continuous or nearly continuous descent in the duty, and had proposed to investigate the point more fully by reference to the entries under the present law—that he had not put a question to *me* upon the general admissibility of the scale—that while Lord Ripon and Sir J. Graham said it would do, I had remained silent, not conceiving myself a party whose consent was to be regarded as of necessity or authority—that likewise further thought and inquiry had made my apprehensions more and more determinate—that I felt it would scarcely be honest to suppress them. He said he quite understood me to argue for a different scheme but had not the remotest idea I hesitated about giving a cordial support to this—that the point on which I stood seemed a small one—that it was impossible for every one to have precisely that which he thought best—that on account of the Duke of Buckingham he had delayed his proposition until the latest moment—that if he had understood me to regard the structure of the upper part of the scale as fundamentally objectionable he would have made a different proposition to the Cabinet. I said I never could have presumed to think any opinion of mine could have affected his proposition to the Cabinet: that Lord Ripon had learned from me immediately on my hearing that the scale had been adopted that I still felt strongly the objections—that I had written a paper to present them[1]—and that Lord Ripon seemed to consider the arrangement above 60/- might still be open to consideration for the benefit of the consumer and as not belonging to the protective part of the scale—repeating too that if I had misled him unintentionally I must abide the consequences. And that the *right* course for me would obviously be to continue to serve the Government as warmly and faithfully as I could. (I meant right, because the interests involved are greater and higher matters than any such difference in the structure of this year's corn-scale—and I may mention, that I do not think I should have been justified, so far as I can yet see, in giving a general opinion on the scale when Sir R. Peel seemed rather to pass me over—very properly as I thought, and conformably to my position as an inferior called in to argue and give information. A day or two after Christopher wrote to me about the scale: and Lord Ripon happened to say to me, 'What business has he to write to you—he has no right to assume that you know anything about what the Cabinet are doing?'—which I thought quite reasonable and it seems to show it was not self-evident that I as Vice-President of the Board of Trade became a sort of concurrent or coordinate authority with the members of the Cabinet.)

I fear Peel was much annoyed and displeased for he would not give me a word of help or of favourable supposition as to my own motives and belief. And indeed I am a poor creature, vain enough I suppose and yet not enabled even by vanity to know what is expected of a person in my office. I wish I could have seen that he was at all soothed: he used nothing like an angry or unkind word, but the negative character of the conversation had a chilling effect on my feeble mind. I came home sick at heart in the evening and told all to Catherine, my lips being to every one else, as I said to Sir R. Peel, absolutely sealed: upon my own *ex parte* statement she thought with me that I had done right in not taking upon myself to give an opinion on the fitness of the scale to be proposed to the Cabinet, without being individually invited: I told her I was

---

[1] ADD.MS 40469, ff. 142–149.

particularly careful not to *look* assent—and I feel that if the question had been put to me about the *necessity* of a long rest, or some equivalent arrangement, I should either have affirmed it, or at least have asked for time to consider it. May my sense of weakness lead me unto Thee O fountain of all strength.                                       *February 5. 1842.*

## 105: ADD.MS 44819, f. 79

I have been much struck throughout the private discussions connected with the new project of a Corn Law by the tenacity with which Sir Robert Peel firstly by adhering in every point to the old arrangements where it seemed at all possible, and since the announcement of the plan to Parliament by steadily resisting changes in any part of the resolutions has narrowed the ground and reduced in number the points of attack and thus made his measure practicable in the face of a popular excitement and a strong Opposition. Until we were actually in the midst of the struggle I did not appreciate the extraordinary sagacity of his parliamentary instinct in this particular.

He said yesterday to Lord Ripon and to me, 'Among ourselves, in this room I have no hesitation in saying, that if I had not had to look to other than abstract considerations I would have proposed a lower protection. But it would have done no good to push the matter so far as to drive Knatchbull out of the Cabinet after the Duke of Buckingham; nor could I hope to pass a measure with greater reductions through the House of Lords.'

He was not well and his doctor called. Sir J. Graham, who had come in, said in his absence, 'The pressure upon him is immense—we never had a Minister who was so truly a First Minister as he is: he makes himself felt in every department and is really cognisant of the affairs of each. Lord Grey could not master such an amount of business. Canning could not do it: he is an actual Minister, and is capax imperii'—to which Lord Ripon assented.                                       *February 26. 1842.*

## 106: ADD.MS 44819, ff. 79–80

Speaking of the probable operation of the new Corn Law today Sir R. Peel said he thought we should get our three or four millions of grain annually—and that at present foreign agriculture was depressed by the present 'horrible law'.

Lately when Hawes (I think) was complimenting him for his liberality at the expense of his colleagues, Lord Stanley said to me, 'It is a little singular to hear this continually when one recollects whence Peel and his colleagues came respectively: especially when I remember to have heard Tierney and his friends habitually complimenting Canning on the very same score, and Peel then held up as the leader of the illiberal party.' I made a remark about Canning to which he said, 'Yes Canning's mind was of the highest Tory character.'     *March 5? [1842]*.

## 107: ADD.MS 44819, ff. 80–81

It may be well to note the propositions which have led the Government to determine not to propose during the present year any change in the sugar duties.

The possible forms of such change were these:

1. To lower the duty on British sugar without touching that on foreign.
2. To lower both largely—say British to 15/-, and foreign to such a duty as would admit considerable quantities to consumption.
3. To lower both partially, say British to 18/- or 20/- and foreign in the same proportion to the existing duty of 63/-+5% = 66/- nearly.

The first was impracticable because of:

1. The parliamentary difficulty of lowering the duty in favour of a monopoly.
2. The uncertainty whether we shall have such a supply as would admit of a large increase of consumption by reduced price.
3. The circumstances that without great increase of supply the sacrifice of the revenue would be made wholly in favour of the planter.

The second was impracticable because:

1. The intimate connection of the sugar duties with questions relating to slavery, as affirmed last year, renders it wholly inadmissible to open the market to foreign sugar without previous arrangements with regard to distinction against slave produce, *or* with regard to the abolition of slavery.

2. Such arrangements are not in a state of progress to warrant any parliamentary measure. *Communications* have however been made to Brazil and therefore the primary steps have been taken. An opening *may* also be made in the direction of Holland before any length of time has elapsed.

3. There is such promise of supply that we need not fear extravagant prices during the year, nor therefore any extraordinary pressure.

The third was impracticable because it opens every topic of objection, and does not ensure *any* of the advantages.

1. Government would be charged with deserting its ground in respect to slavery—and justly.

2. At the same time, with maintaining virtual monopoly, and this at least plausibly.

3. Likewise with making a change of which it would be very doubtful whether it would diminish price sufficiently to effect a material increase of consumption.

I also note the argument I used yesterday for reducing the duties on colonial timber to a nominal rate.

1. In any change to take effect immediately Government must preserve to colonial timber its relative advantage in the British market: or it becomes obnoxious to the charge of breach of faith, and of neglect of the recommendation of the committee of 36, with regard to the wood already out for the season.

2. The relative advantage is somewhere about 32/- per load over all, on timber and deals together.

The nominal duties being

|  | Colonial | Foreign |
|---|---|---|
| Timber | 10 | 55 |
| Deals | various, | ditto, |
|  | average payment | average payment |
|  | 8 | 38 |
| Average payment over all, of each origin | 9/- | 41/- nearly |
| Advantage to colonies | 32/- |  |

3. Such being the case, no real reduction can be effected on Baltic timber, without bringing it down at any rate as low as

Timber 30/-          Deals 35/-

say averaging 33/- since the present average is but 41/-.

4. Comparing these propositions, in order to maintain with precision the relative position of the colonies, only a nominal duty can be taken: i.e.

Timber   1/- against 30/-:   advantage 29/-

Deals     2/-        35/-           33/-

Average advantage as nearly as possible the same as now.

5. But with so large a reduction of actual payment, the amount of relative preference would bear a moderate reduction without injury to the protected timber: say therefore

for Baltic     30/- and 35/- for one year

                25/- and 30/- thereafter

for colonies    1/- and 2/- at once

which would after a twelvemonth reduce the preference to 24/- and 28/-, a change which would not on the whole it is imagined put them to any disadvantage.

Sir J. Graham said to me on Monday, 'This measure (corn) is the euthanasia of the Corn Laws: if we can maintain it ten years I shall be satisfied: and then I trust that our agriculture will not want it.'

March 9. [1842].

## 108: ADD.MS 44819, f. 82

(Motion for introduction of income tax bill)[1]

On Friday night I thought Sir Robert Peel appeared in an attitude of conspicuous intellectual greatness: and on comparing notes the next day with Sir J. Graham at the Palace I found he was similarly impressed. Sheil delivered a very effective rhetorical speech. Lord Stanley had taken a few notes and was to follow him. He was winding up just as the clock touched twelve. Lord Stanley said to Peel, 'It is

---

[1] On the report of the Committee of Ways and Means, Friday, 8 April 1842.

twelve—shall I follow him?—I think not.' Peel said, 'I do not think it will do to let this go unanswered.' (He had been quite without the idea of speaking that night.) Sheil sat down, and peals of cheering followed. Stanley seemed to hesitate a good deal and at last said, as it were to himself, 'No, I won't, it's too late.' In the mean time the adjournment had been moved: but when Peel saw there was no one in the breach, he rose. The cheers were still, a little spitefully, prolonged from the other side—he had an immense subject, a disturbed House, a successful speech, an entire absence of notice, to contend against: but he began with power, gathered power as he went on, handled every point in his usual mode of balanced thought and language and was evidently conscious at the close of what no one could deny, that he had made a deep impression on the House.

(The Monday after) [*11 April 1842*].

## 109: ADD.MS 44819, f. 82

Peel showed me lately in the House a letter from Lord Ellenborough and an address from him in Council to the Commander of the Forces: both very able. In the latter I was pleased to find that the idea of keeping Afghanistan was altogether discarded. In the former I noticed particularly that he complained of *want* of ability and efficiency in the discharge of the public service in India: which I had been accustomed to hear popularly stated the other way. I grieved much to see that he wrote of the China War without the least symptom of an intention to move against the opium trade: referred to the opium revenue as reviving without any apparent dissatisfaction: and proposed for consideration the occupation of trading posts or factories off the coast of China for the purposes of commerce without the least trace of a design to give them aid or redress concerning that noxious and shameful trade.

On Tuesday night [10 May] Peel opened the Tariff anew—and laid down in a manner which drew great cheering from the Opposition the doctrine of purchasing in the cheapest market. Stanley said to me afterwards, 'Peel laid that down a great deal too broadly.'

Last night he (Lord Stanley) sat down angry with himself and turned to me and said, 'It does not signify, I *cannot* speak on these subjects, I quite lost my head.' I merely answered that no one but himself would have discovered it.　　　　　*May 14.* [*1842*].

## 110: ADD.MS 44730, ff. 127-128

Memorandum

Yesterday having read Dr. Wiseman's letter of the 6th to my father[1] I went up to announce to Helen my having done so.

On entering I took her hand, then sat down and asked if she had received a letter from me last week—yes: had she read it? 'I decline to answer'—I repeated the question, she repeated her refusal, apparently with a great effort.

My next purpose I then told her was to notify to her that it *might* be necessary for me to state hereafter the nature of the religious relations between herself and me for many years past as there would not be wanting those who would connect what has happened with my name. I told her she must be aware of this and likewise it might the more be expected since she had referred to Mr. Ramsay and me as having influenced her—she said she had not ascribed any idea or intention of the kind to us—that she regretted having mentioned it, but that it was true. I told her I had no complaint to make of her having said it, did not doubt she believed it, and moreover could not be a judge what *influence* any one might derive in any manner from me or any other— but that the intercourse between us on religious subjects, except what was altogether superficial, had ceased for many years, indeed before the recent controversies and their subjects had been definitely in my mind—that we had never, as I confidently believed, had a conversation upon them, certainly never one which entered into the groundworks of those questions. She said my conversation had afforded her means of judging my sentiments: I replied it was scarcely possible to discourse generally for half an hour with any one without giving indications of that kind: but I did not believe she had even read what I had written upon them. She said she had read parts of the first book when it came out—had read the second book—and had not read the first book in its enlarged form. Anxious that I might not overstate the case (as I told her) I pressed her to tell me as clearly as she could which portions she had read—she said it was rather an extraordinary catechism: she remembered reading with interest a comparison of the position of the two Churches in the *Church Principles* and remembered reading on private judgment and toleration (I naming the subjects) in the first;

---

[1] See no. 111.

but could not say more. She said she had very often gone to church with me in London, since my father came to live here in 1837—I said perhaps six or eight times. She mentioned that on the way back from St. James's I had once spoken of the different feelings with which different parts of the English Communion Service had been written —she thought in 1837 or 1838—I said the very distance showed little could have passed, and also this that at that time I had read nothing to acquaint me with the history of the English Communion Service. She said if I made declarations of this kind respecting her it would be construed into an anxiety to save my wordly position. I replied that was too trifling a matter to be considered in such circumstances. She said she knew some suspected me of being what she was: and intimated that fear of injuring me had been a retarding motive with her. When I said that it would be my duty beyond all things to defend the Catholic principles of the Church of England from being charged with what had occurred by a statement of facts, she replied touchingly, 'You may declare—I shall not contradict you.'

In the course of this part of the conversation I said, 'I am far indeed from denying that a view of these principles which is superficial, which is in the imagination, and is not attended and sobered by the correctives necessary for all such inquiry, may be a means of seduction'—she interrupted me and said, 'Pray do not speak so—it can serve no other purpose but that of giving me pain.'

I then mentioned my having read Dr. Wiseman's letter to my father and put my answer[1] (of the 7th) to it into her hands. She complained that I had not *first* come to her, that she might have made a disclosure to my father. I told her I had not thought that my duty: though indeed the subject of her not having made that disclosure was a very solemn and awful subject.

She stopped in reading my letter and said, 'What does this mean that you apprehend but a small part of the case has yet come under his view?' I answered, that expression is fully explained by my letter of last week to you.

She stopped at the last sentence and said, 'Do you mean that all persons who are to have intercourse together must be in the communion of the Church?' I said, 'No, for then I should not have written any letter to Dr. Wiseman.' 'Do you mean that all must have the same

---

[1] No. 112.

religious opinions?'—'Certainly not', I replied, 'I wrote with no reference to sameness of religious opinions—indeed I wrote without reference to you, but the principle undoubtedly is general—and I meant what I have said, that doubtless it is wise and just that all personal relations should be liable to convulsion, which are not founded in the communion, and I mean the realised communion of the Church.' She said, 'I do not understand it.'

Rising I took her hand and said 'God bless you'. She was entirely passive, and made no reply.

More passed but this is I think the substance. We were together perhaps three quarters of an hour.  *Sunday, June 12. 1842.*

## 111: ADD.MS 44359, ff. 117–120

Dr. Wiseman's letter to WEG's father of 6 June 1842 is not among the Gladstone Papers at the B.M. The following letter from Wiseman to Gladstone was written on the same day.

*St. Mary's College, Birmingham. Private.* If my purpose in writing to you were of a personal nature, I should certainly hesitate before presuming upon the casual, but to me most gratifying, intercourse which I have enjoyed with you. But the object which I have in view concerns your domestic happiness so much more than any interest of mine, that I trust you will bear with me, in all charity and patience, if I enter at some length into it, so as to show the motive of my interposition, and the interest I have acquired in it. You will easily conjecture that this letter has reference to your sister. Some months ago I received a letter from a lady, who concealed her real name, communicating to me her unhappy state of mind with regard to her religious views, and her strong impulse to join the Catholic Church. I replied, and this led to a correspondence, in which however there was nothing controversial. She promised indeed to send me her difficulties at some length, but to this we never came. She described herself as an invalid, unable to leave home or see any priest, or to receive any one at home. I exhorted her to patience, to hope, and principally to prayer, and assured her that God would open a way to her to attain what she so much desired. After some time she offered to reveal her name etc.— but I declined being made acquainted with it, because I felt that I should act far more disinterestedly and without bias from any secondary considerations, if I knew not with whom I was treating, and therefore had no motive save my duty to God and my neighbour. At last she wrote to me that she would be at Tunbridge Wells, where she would enjoy more latitude than in London, and as other business called me to town, I wrote to her that I would try to see her at Tunbridge Wells. As I was entering the carriage to begin my journey, I received a letter from her, which I could only read after starting, and which for the first time made me acquainted with the real name of my correspondent, and her near relationship with you. I learnt that she was leaving the Wells two days before I could be there. I have given this long account, to show that whatever part I have taken in this matter has had no reference to individuals, but has been the result of a feeling of duty. But, having learnt the distress which the event has caused yourself and your worthy father, I have taken the liberty of addressing you, in the hopes that you will be induced to act as mediator between your sister and her grieving parent, towards whom she has always expressed so much affection, and the dread of causing whom pain has been almost the only obstacle which she has felt to doing what she has.

The question now is what is best to be done for securing both her happiness, and the peace and harmony of her family. It is possible that a feeling may exist that it is not yet too late to draw her back from her present position, and make her abandon the faith which she has embraced. If so, I think I can securely say that such hope will prove unfounded. Her conviction is strongly seconded by her natural disposition and her feelings, and will not I am confident be easily shaken. But I feel it right to confide to your prudence and affection for her, what I believe she has not herself made known to her father, but what I have her consent to communicate to you, that she has taken those decisive steps which join her to our communion, so that her being a Catholic is no longer merely possible or prospective, but actual and real. The knowledge of this circumstance will, I fear, cause *you* pain: but I feel that it is better that the whole truth may be known to you so that whatever course you may think of pursuing may not be based upon an erroneous view of the state of things. I am sure that you would not allow yourself to be swayed by considerations of a mere temporal character; but still you will not help feeling how painfully your domestic and individual position may be affected and your happiness more than ever disturbed by any such measures of a harsh character, as will give publicity to what has occurred, and draw the attention of enemies as well as of many others to a matter so domestic and personal, in the heartless way in which such things are usually treated. You might indeed have perhaps thought this worth risking, if all had not been accomplished—but now that this has taken place, nothing but pain and evil *could* be the result. But now under these circumstances looking at your sister's own position, I would put it to your own feelings, if it will not be more conducive to her happiness, as well as to domestic peace, if, now that she cannot be expected to recede, she be allowed quietly and undisturbed to enjoy the consolations which her religion alone can any longer afford her, and which she most earnestly longs for. To deprive her of them can only make her wretched, and prove a source of temptation to her to seek without permission what is denied her. But if, as I trust, you will now interpose to procure for her indulgent treatment, no publicity need be given to what has happened, or it will become so gradually known as to be unattended with any painful notoriety. It is to these considerations that I wished in the first instance to draw your kind attention. Should they be favourably received by you, and should you feel yourself justified in offering your mediation, it will be easy to enter into such arrangements, as will allow your sister the comfort which she so much wants, and secure your family from all public observation.

I assure you that it is painful and humiliating to myself to write thus on such a subject, and to appear to treat as a matter of human expediency what my own feeling would prompt me to write of in very different terms. But this apparent coldness will not I hope be attributed to me, but to the unhappy state of separation, which compels us to treat with one another on the most solemn things with cautious reserve, as though worldly prudence, rather than more sacred motives had principally to influence us.

I beg sincerely to apologise for thus intruding upon you.


## 112: ADD.MS 44359, f. 121

*Gladstone to the Rev. Nicholas Wiseman, 7 June 1842*
*Whitehall. Private.* I hasten to reply to your letter of yesterday: and it may be well that I should in the first instance beg of you to take the trouble to address me at my private residence No. 13 Carlton House

Terrace which will secure your letter from any risk of falling into wrong hands.

My answer to your letter must at least for the present go little beyond the inquiry whether it was intended for communication to my father. It is obviously impossible for me to keep back from him information in which he has so deep and direct a concern as that which you communicate. The best manner of conveying it I conceive would be by submitting the document itself: but I do not wish to do so without having previously stated to you the mode in which I propose to proceed.

Your request has no relation to my own personal course of action with regard to my sister: which is wholly unconnected with any question as to external treatment, and which is definitely and clearly marked out by religious and fraternal obligations. I will only here in passing express my hearty satisfaction that you for the sake of higher considerations have forbore to suppress that of which you well know that the disclosure could not fail to cause pain: I likewise have resolved to adhere to this principle cost what it may: and in the particular instance I fear it will cost much.

With regard to questions of external and temporal relations they are for my father's judgment. I do not feel myself, amidst the daily and hourly pressure of public business at this juncture, mentally qualified to embrace the whole subject: this may surprise you but it is right I should add that but a very small part of it I apprehend has yet come under your view. I shall abstain however for the present from all general professions and simply state that I do not think I can act more justly and equitably in the case than by placing in my father's hands a pleading which proceeds from you.

I might here conclude: but feeling the dreadful nature of the subject which is now opening between us I must indulge myself for a moment in cordially reciprocating the kindly feelings with which you refer to our slight and casual intercourse some years ago. It is I trust allowed to cherish such sentiments: though doubtless it is wise and just that all personal relations should be liable to convulsion which are not founded in religious communion, or which lie between persons who recognising the duty fail notwithstanding of giving it effect.

P.S. I shall trust to hearing from you at your earliest convenience.

## 113: ADD.MS 44819, f. 83

A short time ago, perhaps a fortnight, when I was dining one day at Mr. Grenville's he said: 'If he were called upon to state what was the most remarkable social change which he had witnessed in the course of his long life, he should say without doubt the change in the character of the clergy. In his earlier days, the young clergy were almost as a matter of course gentlemen indeed but unconcerned, in any serious sense, about their parishes or their duties: whereas now the rule was completely reversed and they were as a body zealously and devoutly set upon the work of their office.'

Lord Delamere—only some ten years younger—said that in Cheshire when he was a young man the clergy were the life and soul of all kinds of amusements: the foxhounds were kept by one of the body: and they always mustered in the field stronger than the laity! Whereas now he did not know a clergyman that hunted: and on the other hand he did not know a parish in his neighbourhood that was not looked after as it ought to be by men personally acquainted with their parishioners.

Lord Monteagle some four or five years ago rendered in conversation with me the same testimony as to the Irish clergy and said their only fault now was that they were a little too fond of being persecuted. Baring Wall, before he became a Radical said to me that the fault of our clergy was that they were becoming too active: that they were quite active enough and if they grew more so they would be meddlers. I must say I had great misgivings about him from that sentiment.

Mr. Rogers told me a week ago at Mr. Grenville's that the Duke of Wellington had from the first prophesied evil as the result of the march across the Indus—had said too that we should gain possession of the country well enough, but that we could not keep it. Also that the Duke caused the withdrawal of Sir James Graham's motion, directed against the India war (Easter 1839?)—on the ground that it would dishearten our troops and embarrass the operations without preventing them.

Today at the Foreign Office there were Lord Aberdeen, Sir R. Peel, Lord Ripon, Sir J. Graham, Mr. Goulburn, and I—to discuss the proposal of the Spanish Government for a treaty of commerce in conjunction with a loan, whereof the interest and sinking fund should be payable from the proceeds of the duties chargeable upon our goods sent to Spain, such duties accordingly to be payable in England.

Graham anticipated that upon the conclusion of such a treaty

France would pick a quarrel with Spain and that we should be drawn in. Peel said that the thing was just—that our own manufacturers had a right to expect that we should seek openings for their goods—that France had behaved to us as ill as possible—that Spain must be exhorted rigidly to maintain her independence—that it would be a great stroke in European policy to establish a good understanding with Spain and to support her independence that at the backdoor of France there might be something to keep her in check.

The proposed arrangement does not stipulate for an exclusive advantage to us: and one much resembling it in principle was adopted by Lord Palmerston in 1837. Every one present seemed to think this new and most important project on the whole decidedly desirable.

*November 7. 1842.*

### 114: ADD.MS 44819, f. 84

Lord Aberdeen has differed from the Board of Trade with respect to the Portuguese Treaty: Lord Ripon was half inclined to move towards him: I drew a memorandum[1] and suggested reference to Sir Robert Peel— and I was glad to find that his letter in reply to Lord Ripon adopted the view that our terms were already quite sufficiently liberal. We have not erred there I am sure on the side of too little.

At Lord Aberdeen's on Saturday night Sir R. Peel said he had had a letter from Sir John Tyrrell wishing to be allowed to contradict on his authority a rumour which had gone abroad to the effect that he had given it as his opinion that the existing Corn Law could not be maintained: and that his reply was he had not even heard such a rumour and could give no authority with respect to it, but that as to the fact of his having made such a statement upon the practicability of maintaining the Corn Law, no animal in Essex had been more dumb upon the subject than he had been.

*December 7. 1842.*

### 115: ADD.MS 44819, ff. 84–85

I met Philip Pusey today at the Carlton. Meat according to him had fallen a penny in the pound—and this owing to the tariff: the fear of a

---

[1] ADD.MS 44731, ff. 14–21.

large importation having produced the effects which the large importation itself would have produced. He is disappointed too in the Corn Bill
which he had thought would have kept prices steady at about 56/-—
and says a great deal of land is being taken from its barley turn for
wheat in the rotation, so that the breadth will be great. The farmers are
much alarmed from a notion that Peel is going to make some further
change—from his having spoken of the present measure as an experiment.

I told him I had not heard of any change (not considering the
arrangement with regard to Canada to come within the meaning) and
had no idea whatever that any would be made. But that I was very glad
of the statement Peel had made: laws of this kind were not Magna
Charta, they were in their nature mutable, and particularly in this
country at this time, regard being had to the increasing pressure of the
population upon the production of food. That to speak in entire confidence my own private impressions, of which I was not aware that I had
at any time said so much to any one, I did not see why the law should not
live over some seasons if they were favourable, but I doubted whether it
would stand bad seasons, particularly if it should prove that the new
averages could be *worked* as much as the old ones by the dealers—that I
thought nothing would be so fatal to the law as the prices being driven
up to 73/-, say next spring, if the oncoming harvest should promise to be
late—that the people had been sadly ground down by the high prices of
provisions for the last four years and I was convinced they would not
bear it again. That whenever it should be established as a *rule* that the
growth of the country was less than its consumption, then the graduated
scale, as Lord Ashburton had said to me, meant prohibition up to the
point of the minimum duty: that was not yet established, but it had
seemed to be upon the verge of being established. *When* that was clear, it
would be impossible to maintain the law. I lamented the agricultural
distress, and said [it] seemed to me the fall of prices proceeded mainly
from the poverty of the people, not from the tariff.

He said that the county Members had gone with Sir R. Peel to the
very utmost point they could with respect to corn: and that to speak
plainly, if Sir R. Peel should become convinced that a further change
was requisite, they considered that he ought to leave it to the Whigs to
carry it, and resign accordingly. I said of course he would be governed
by his convictions of what might be requisite for the safety and well being
of the country in judging hereafter of the question whether the law

ought to be maintained or not and so it was clear he ought to be, independently of the further question what course he ought personally to take as to remaining in office. *December 8. 1842.*

## 116: ADD.MS 44819, ff. 85–87

On the 17th [January 1843] I went to Sir R. Peel on Mint matters when he introduced for the first time since I have been in office Church affairs, that is to say the question of the increase of pastoral care, in connection with that of the management of the capitular estates. The gist of his communication was that the value of the estates was very great and that from them efforts ought to be made to relieve spiritual destitution rather than by calling on the State—a call which would be met by pointing to the lavish and wasteful system of management and the resources which might be realised by economy, not by denial in the abstract of the duty of the State. He gave me papers by Sir J. Graham, the Archbishop of Canterbury, Mr. Hobhouse, and Mr. Murray to read —and asked me who I thought in or out of Parliament were the persons most likely to be useful upon such a subject.

In this and subsequent conversations, I ventured to tell him I was convinced that the *whole* question of the episcopal and capitular property would require to be dealt with sooner or later—that if there were no House of Commons in existence still it was desirable for the Church to do her own work from her own means rather than by a public grant—that the system of fines was a secularising and demoralising system—that it was in his power *so* to frame his measures as not merely to render it tolerable but to call forth a great amount of sympathy from the best friends of the Church—that there would be great advantage in somewhat decentralising, in any new plan—that there would be little disposition comparatively to stickle for the proprietary principle, but much for the diocesan—that I thought Hope and Manning the two most valuable persons for aid in such a question.

At one of these conversations I introduced the question of the trade with the American Union: the certainty that the tariff must be modified —the uncertainty as to the degree—the power which this country would have of influencing proceedings with respect to it by intimating a disposition to negotiate—the number of articles on which we might make remissions of duty material to America, without opening the question of wheat—(cotton, (stalk) tobacco, rice, maize, salted provisions, bacon and hams, butter, cheese, etc.) and the advantages there would be in a good system of reciprocity with America, as a means of acting upon the restrictive policy of the continental states. He would not say any thing positive upon the subject but adverted to parliamentary difficulties: and this too only in the form of trusting that he was as little sensitive to them as any man. Still it was for the time an extinguisher.

As to the questions of Church property he said his view was, *fair* consideration for the lessees, and subject to this a management of the property which would realise the full value—local, but subject to central controul—and with this a measure to give effect to the law of church rate.

Today he had a meeting attended by

| | |
|---|---|
| The Archbishop of Canterbury | Sir R. Peel (in mourning, I suppose for Drummond) |
| Lord Stanley | Mr. Hobhouse |
| Sir J. Graham | Mr. Murray |
| Mr. Goulburn | WEG |

The Bishop of London was not well enough to come and the Bishop of Lincoln had had a letter misdirected to him. The conversation lasted from twelve to three. Sir R. Peel said it was desirable to notice the question of increased pastoral care in the Speech: but not to raise any expectations to the fulfilment of which they did not see their way. He alluded to the great excess now anticipated in the value of the estates vested in the Commission, over the former calculation: spoke of public advances on the credit of the future incomes of those estates—repayable with interest, for if interest were not demanded it would be a grant: stated the arguments against a grant: among them the desireableness of preventing the House of Commons from meddling with the administration of Church property, and the democratic tendency which any thing of that kind would have. He thought perhaps that for the sake of this claim those most hostile in Parliament would not be reluctant to vote money.

The Archbishop did not appear to see difficulty in such a plan of advances with repayment after a given term: but Sir R. Peel gradually got on to a broader view of the subject involving the entire question of management of the episcopal and capitular property—the establishment of a provision that the consent of the Commission should be requisite before any incumbent could renew, to the conditions of renewal —and the payment of fixed incomes to the Bishops, instead of requiring fixed payments from them.

The reply of the Archbishop was taken by Sir R. Peel, Stanley, and Graham, to be a refusal—and they said accordingly that they could not recommend the mention of the subject in the Queen's Speech: and appeared to be disappointed.

I did not understand the Archbishop to refuse but to hesitate: to desire to know in the first place the intentions and views of Government —and to consult his brethren the Bishops who he said would be much offended if their advice was not taken—and also that whatever the measure might be, there was sure to be a difference of opinion among them. Peel said that to consult the whole would probably be the way to break up the plan.

The Archbishop told them how he had laboured to quell the opposition to the Chapters Bill—and with what little effect: that though it was *well* received at first, yet before it passed the clergy generally had become very averse to it—that there was a great deal of soreness still remaining on the subject, and that all the old feelings would certainly be revived, but that he was prepared to face unpopularity in the discharge of his duty. He said touchingly when pressed for his opinion that perhaps some would say he was superannuated and that his judgment was less fit for such matters than it had been, and complained of his memory. But that on which he appeared to me to lay stress was that the end in view should be of sufficient magnitude and that they should not interfere with the proprietors in their management for the sake of a small result—such as a sum of 30,000 a year.

Peel spoke strongly of the responsibility lying on the heads of the Church in the present state of things—feared the question would fall into the hands of a hostile and powerful party—insisted that the interests of Ministers should be set aside and those only of the Church and of religion kept in view—considered that the recent Acts (respecting Bishops and Chapters) had produced the favourable change in the position of the Church in popular estimation *now* as compared with what it was some years ago—but felt so strongly the evils which would follow from placing the Government and the body of the clergy in opposition one to another upon a subject of this kind that he would not bring forward any measure, if he had reason to anticipate such an effect.

The Archbishop adverted to the Church Commission and its acts, and said it was very happy that the short Government of Sir R. Peel had enabled him to set it in motion, for he thought the suspicion with which the late Government was viewed was such that it would have been impossible under that Government to make or carry those proposals.

The meeting ended with the whole subject at sea—but nothing is to be said in the Speech. I was a deeply interested listener [the] whole time. Peel, Graham, and Stanley argued with the Archbishop: the last somewhat *keenly*.                                              *January 31. 1843.*

## 117: ADD.MS 44819, f. 87

Sir James Graham showed me on the same day [31 January 1843] memoranda containing his plans: I told him it appeared to me that

1. With respect to proceeds to be obtained from the episcopal estates, there would be the greatest objections and resistance unless the foundation of new bishoprics were contemplated from them.
2. With respect to new funds from capitular estates that it would be most desirable to introduce into the rules for distribution a recognition of the diocesan principle.
3. That the Archbishop of Canterbury would certainly consult the Bishop of Salisbury for one.
4. That there was a difficulty in reasserting and enforcing the law of universal liability to church rate without at the same time doing some thing for the correlative right of universal reception of the inhabitants, by some blow at the pew system.

## 118: ADD.MS 44819, ff. 87–88

In my speech on Lord Howick's motion I was supposed to play with the question and prepare the way for a departure from the Corn Law of last year: and I am sensible that I so far lost my head, as not to put well together the various, and if taken separately, conflicting considerations, which affect the question. Now the Corn Law has more of the slide in it (practically) than I at the time thought necessary: but regarding it as in the nature of a settlement for a period at least I am not prepared to refuse to depart from it. But it so happens that besides this I spoke under the influence of a new and most sincere conviction, having reference to the recent circumstances of commercial legislation abroad—to the effect, that it would not be wise to displace British labour for the sake of cheap corn, without the counteracting and sustaining provisions which beneficial exchange, exchange not distorted by tariffs all but prohibitory, would supply. I do not mean that this conviction is so definite and mature in my mind that it may not in any degree alter its form, or that [it] is ready for decisive action at a moment's notice: but it is one which subject to the conviction of further information I more and more entertain. This it is clear is a slippery position for a man who does not think firmly in the midst of ambiguous and adverse cheering—and I did my work most imperfectly, but I do think honestly. Sir R. Peel's manner, by negative signs, showed that he thought either my ground insecure or my expressions dangerous. He himself most strictly avoided all allusion to legislation abroad as a ground of withholding further commercial change and *vice versa*—and far be it from me to impeach his prudence or defend my own blunders: but at the same time I have so decided a conviction that we could not and ought not to resist a change which would *evidently* increase the demand for labour in the country that I could not avoid giving some expression to this sentiment: as I feel it could hardly fail to influence my future actions. When Graham sat down on the second night Peel highly commended his speech.

Yesterday at Sir R. Peel's it was decided to adhere to our *ultimatum* with Portugal *me valde plaudente*: [1] Lord Aberdeen strongly protested. Peel said, 'These questions of commerce and revenue in the existing circumstances of the country are the really important questions of the day.'

*March 10. [1843]*.

## 119: ADD.MS 44819, ff. 88–89

Monday, March 13. [1843]
Meeting on the subject of Mr. Ward's motion for a committee on agricultural burthens—standing for the next day.

I urged that the friends of the Corn Law had evidently habitually made this one of their points—that it was a subject scarcely capable of being worked out in debate—that we really believed in the existence of these burdens—that any fair committee would probably affirm them or

---

[1] 'Myself applauding heartily'.

indeed could not fail to do so—(in this sense, that the position of land-owners must be viewed with regard to all its circumstances, peculiar burdens on the one hand, protective laws on the other)—that the Government had in its hands the means of securing a fair committee—there might be difficulty and much wrangling, and perhaps no affirmation with respect to the malt tax and the like, but that some at least relative good might accrue from the report, whereas on the other hand the refusal could not stand well in the face of the country. If there were an idea that the inquiry was meant to lead to change in the Corn Law might not that be obviated by declarations from Sir R. Peel giving his own sense to the proposal?

Sir James Graham said there was no good parliamentary ground for refusing the proposal but he thought policy on the whole against it from the tendency to unsettle. Lord Stanley seemed also to think there was weakness in the case—but Fremantle stated strongly the effect which the motion would have on agricultural confidence and Sir R. Peel seemed to think that this defect could not be corrected and advised therefore to reject the motion which was agreed upon. The form of objection (which unless effectually met by declaration is strong) is this—you have legislated—you are not prepared to legislate afresh upon the result of this inquiry—for what purpose then inquire? On the other hand, inquiry was refused last year *because* legislation was pending: if refused now because it is *not* pending, it is to be refused always. And thereby justification of the refusal is the supposition that the inquiry will be indissolubly associated in the public mind with the idea of an intention which does not exist, and therefore by leading to false impressions in the most important matter becomes mischievous.

Graham said, 'The law has not been tried—nor will it be until there is the prospect of a bad harvest—if corn *then* is not to come in until the 1/- duty is reached the law fails: if otherwise it succeeds.' And last night he said to me, 'I keep my mind in suspense as to the effect of the law until that contingency has arrived—that will decide its fate.' I expressed my general concurrence. *March 15. [1843]*

## 120: ADD.MS 44819, f. 89

On Thursday [23 March 1843] Goulburn asked me what I thought of the education clauses. I spoke strongly against *limited* exposition of the

Scriptures: i.e. exposition restrained to what are supposed to be general doctrines. I likewise questioned the wisdom of merely reading the Scriptures to children without exposition. He held a contrary opinion upon the second but agreed with me as to the first.

Graham, however, last night seemed to explain this teaching the Scriptures, or teaching from the Scriptures, as a teaching intended to convey the meaning of the text but without any attempt at proselytism. I do not think such a distinction can be drawn.     *March 25.* [*1843*].

## 121: ADD.MS 44819, f. 90

At a meeting at Sir R. Peel's in Passion Week, he expressed an idea that there might be an union of parties against the Government on the Canadian Corn Bill: and that this was the only question now in view that could produce a Ministerial crisis. But I do not think he regarded the chance as formidable.

Graham represented the difficulties connected with the Irish registration question: that the Irish Government were divided upon it—that Eliot said the matter ought to be settled wholly irrespective of political consequences, while Lord de Grey thought otherwise: and Graham said that any franchise which could be proposed would have very seriously detrimental effects on the representation while as I understood something must be done with the franchise when the question is brought forward.

It was determined to propose to France a separate convention upon cottons and silks: Lord Aberdeen thinking it useless, Peel strongly for it.

At Nuneham the Archbishop of York told me that he saw the King on the day after the dissolution of 1831 and that he apologised to His Majesty for not having been present on the occasion of his going down, and he pleaded that he was not aware any thing of the kind was to take place—to which the King replied that neither was he himself aware of it an hour before hand—evidently intimating according to the Archbishop dissatisfaction at what had occurred. And yet a popular rumour was spread abroad, to the effect that the King had said he would go down in a hackney coach if necessary.     *April 25.* [*1843*].

## 122: ADD.MS 44819, ff. 90–91

On Thursday at Sir R. Peel's the Canadian corn question was discussed. It was determined to exclude all other colonies from the Bill, Canada alone having prayed. I put, however, to Sir R. Peel the probability that other colonies or parties on their behalf will infallibly pray for it—that the same principles will be applicable to them upon their complying with the same conditions—and that the inconvenience of having to introduce new colonial Corn Bills in future sessions for particular colonies would it is likely be greater than that of grappling with the whole question at once and establishing an enactment which would include all cases as they may arise. I do not think he considered this void of weight: but he seemed to view the immediate occasion as that which must on the whole be consulted and decided accordingly.

I learned yesterday that the Archbishop of Canterbury is understood to have refused to allow St. Asaph and Bangor to be saved. If so, I do not see how the Government can go against him, at all events if he should persevere. I, however, must under any circumstances vote for the proposition which is to be made: and looking to the consequences which this may entail I am perplexed by a doubt whether I ought or ought not to take any step for making known my course. I have indeed already, before the session began, communicated my *desire* about the matter to Peel, and to Graham: but whether to say anything further to them or any other, I cannot yet see my way.     *Saturday April 30. [1841].*

## 123: ADD.MS 44819, f. 91

On Friday [5 May 1843] Peel declared that he had a very strong opinion on the subject of the Tract controversy—speaking of it apparently as a whole—and that he had indicated that opinion by his cheers, viz. during Plumptre's speech—but had refrained from any reference to the subject in his own. This plain declaration is a fact of some historic interest. But I am much mistaken if it produce any sensible influence upon the progress of the movement: either upon its progress as a whole —or upon any separation of its spurious and morbid from its legitimate powers and tendencies.

Last night both Peel and Fremantle were pleased with my long dull speech on corn. What I said in February gave much alarm on account of the freedom with which I spoke: a freedom which when there is a general disposition to misconstrue and over construe becomes itself deceptive. Fremantle judges a speech according to its influence on those whom he is to *whip*: Peel in a more complex view made up of the direct influence upon his voting supporters, the good aspect in argument towards the Opposition for debate, and the general relation to public opinion and the character of the Administration out of doors.

*May 10.* [*1843*].

### 124: ADD.MS 44819, ff. 91-94

On Wednesday [10 May 1843], Lord Ellenborough's sister Mrs. Col— [sic] at Sir S. Scott's told me Lord Ellenborough was very much dissatisfied with Sir Robert Peel's speech on the first Somnauth debate —and that he was all but about to resign on it but he thought the second would satisfy him.

At two today I went to Sir R. Peel's on the subject of his letter.[1] I began by thanking him for the indulgent manner in which he had excused my errors and more than appreciated any services I might have rendered, and for the offer he had made and the manner of it. Said that I went to the Board of Trade without knowledge or relish but had been very happy there—found quite enough to occupy my mind, enough responsibility for my own strength, and had no desire to move onwards but should be perfectly satisfied with any arrangement which he might make as to Lord Ripon's successor. He spoke most warmly of service received, said he could not be governed by any personal considerations, and that this which he proposed was obviously the right arrangement. I said that I had thought it my duty when a new sphere of extended obligation was thus opened by his offer, it was my duty to examine my mind and consider whether I had any senti- ments upon points of public policy which I deemed it possible he might think exceptionable. He spoke of the compromises and adjustments of opinion necessary to ensure the cooperation of a Cabinet composed of any fourteen men. I assented, but said of course there were some questions that came closer home than others—as involving matter of principle and of character. I then stated the substance of what I had put in my memorandum,[2] first on the opium question, to which his answer was, that the immediate power and responsibility lay with the

---

[1] No. 125.

[2] No. 126.

East India Company: he did not express agreement with my view of the cultivation of the drug, but said it was a minor subject as compared with other imperial interests constantly brought under discussion: intimated that the Duke of Wellington had surrendered his opinion (I think) upon the boundary question—and added that his own individual sentiments were not favourable to the present Corn Laws.

I then stated the remarks on the education clauses. He said it was somewhat doubtful if they could be carried through, but he thought Graham was disposed to take the sense of the House upon them: this, however, was open for consideration. He inclined to agree in what I said as to the exposition of Scripture but thought this question also to be a minor one in point of difficulty.

I stated my general idea with regard to discipline, observing that after what he had said on the two first I presumed he would consider the remaining two still slighter as obstructing my accession—on discipline he made no remark but when I mentioned what in my simplicity or silliness I thought the least, namely, that of the preservation of the two North Wales bishoprics he said that was a more serious matter as it involved a practical course: and I understood him to add that ten days ago the Cabinet had determined to allow no alteration in the law as it stands: that the movement was calculated to endanger the Ecclesiastical Commission and all its recommendations —that the creation of a Bishop in England not having a seat in Parliament would have a powerful influence in aiding the removal of the present Bishops from their seats—that he had not sufficiently considered the question of additional bishoprics but that he did not think it was closed by the refusal to maintain Bangor and St. Asaph apart, which was mainly on the ground of the assent of Parliament already attained. The Bishop of London thought the time would come when they must found four or five new bishoprics from the Episcopal Fund: and yet I asked would he not save the old one in North Wales? He replied as I understood that the Bishop of London was favourable to its preservation. No one in the Cabinet had objected to the course, except that Lord Wharncliffe said he did not think it material to have a Bishop in Manchester and therefore did not care about destroying one in Wales: but he Sir R. Peel thought the erection of Manchester and Ripon into sees was a great triumph for the Church—although said I two sees were destroyed at the same time in other places? Yes.

I stated that my main anxiety was not on account of the antiquity of the sees, but from the connection of the question with that of the increase of episcopal superintendence in general. That whatever might be thought right as to funds, or as to seats in the House of Lords, it appeared to me most important for the Church of England that the number of her Bishops should be increased. That the efficiency of the system of Church extension depends in great part on the effective combination of the clergy under the Bishop: that at present episcopacy is to England in general something remote and venerable but the Bishop is little seen or felt, and we now find the extraordinary energies of the Bishop of London giving way under the fatigues of his office—that the health of the nation depended in great part on the operation of the Church upon the lower class and thus the question became in my mind one of very great magnitude.

Much was said on this topic.

But at last I observed that as this was a question which I had understood was to be mooted in the House of Commons very speedily—as therefore whether in or out of the Cabinet it would have the same effect upon me—and as he had stated his view of the question of general increase of bishoprics apart from this—I would beg to have the time until Monday to consider the question which he readily gave and renewing my thanks I withdrew. But he seemed to me very tenacious upon the point of adhesion to the law as it stands and gave me the idea that the feeling is very much his own personally. From Lord Stanley I understood that there had not been a Cabinet upon the subject but probably the meaning was the papers had been circulated.

I wished to consult Hope—but he is out of town: then Manning but he too is gone. I have to consider with God's help by Monday whether to enter the Cabinet, or to retire altogether: at least such is probably the second alternative. The question as to this bishopric would have been straightforward, if the enactment had been pending. The question has many elements: may God in His mercy enable me to adjust them.

*May 13. 1843.*

## 125: ADD.MS 44275, ff. 140–141

*Sir Robert Peel to Gladstone, 13 May 1843*
*Whitehall.* I have proposed to the Queen that Lord Ripon should succeed my lamented friend and colleague Lord FitzGerald as President of the Board of Controul.

I at the same time requested Her Majesty's permission (and it was most readily conceded) to propose to you the office of the President of the Board of Trade, with a seat in the Cabinet.

If it were not for the occasion of the vacancy I should have had unmixed satisfaction in thus availing myself of the earliest opportunity that has occurred since the formation of the Government, of giving a wider scope to your ability to render public service, and of strengthening the Government by inviting your aid as a Minister of the Crown.

For myself personally, and I can answer also for every other member of the Government, the prospect of your accession to the Cabinet is very gratifying to our feelings.

## 126: ADD.MS 44732, ff. 141–142[1]

Memorandum

1. With regard to the opium trade, I have great doubts respecting the monopoly. But I am fixed in the conviction, that whether it be legalised in China or not, the British Government ought to act in the same sense as that in which it acts at home with respect to spirits, that is I apprehend in the sense of limiting, so far as may be practicable, the production and consumption; and of aiming, not simply at a maximum of revenue, but at a maximum of revenue from a minimum of quantity.

2. With regard to the education clauses of the Factory Bill, admiring both the intention and the general construction of the plan, I am under these impressions:

First that the compulsory principle, with efficient executory provisions (now for the first time proposed), although I do not say unwarrantable presuming a general concurrence of sentiment, is nevertheless formidable in its possible consequences.

Secondly that a measure of this kind however reasonable ought not to pass if opposed by any large portion of the community.

Thirdly that if it is not to be carried through, then, as it is necessarily rather in the nature of a compromise than of the assertion of a great permanent principle, the House of Commons had better remain unpledged to it.

---

[1] *Docketed:* 'Memorandum and draft made for interview with Sir Robert Peel on Saturday, May 13. 1843'. The draft is ff. 139–140.

Fourthly that the terms in which the intended mode of exposition of Scripture has been described (I hope I may say this without any disparagement to the respect and warm esteem I feel for Sir James Graham) are not capable of being strictly reduced to practice, and would if taken as authoritative and permanent lead to much future heartburning and to charges of bad faith.

3. With regard to the Ecclesiastical Courts Bill, I am strongly of opinion, that the Church of England will never regain her hold over the populous masses of this country without some revival, in a purely spiritual form, of religious discipline. But I feel the great inherent difficulties of this question and I fully admit it to be one requiring in a peculiar degree the exercise of circumspection.

4. I cannot conscientiously do otherwise than vote for the maintenance of both the bishoprics of North Wales.                    *May 13. 1843.*


## 127: ADD.MS 44819, ff. 94–97

On Sunday [14 May 1843], I came to the judgement expressed in my draft letter of that date.[1] But on Monday morning both Hope and Manning came here and upon a discussion urged that considering the question relates to the disturbance of an existing law, and that law one to which the Bishops in general were consenting parties I ought not to join issue with the Government on a point which is narrow when separated as by Peel's declaration of Saturday from the general question of increase of bishoprics.

Finally with their approbation I decided to state to Sir Robert Peel —and I did go and in half an hour afterwards state—

That my private opinion is for maintaining the two sees.

That I do not believe this plan would in any way endanger the general recommendations of the Commission.

That I would easily surrender my opinion as to the see to the sense of the Bishops—as to the funds or the peerage to him.

That I should find myself in a painful situation if the Bishops should vote for the revival in the House of Lords, and I should have to give an opposite vote in the Commons.

That, however, I was prepared to do so considering

---

[1] No. 128.

1. That this is part of an extensive legal settlement;
2. That the Episcopal Bench generally assented;
3. That Sir R. Peel declared the general question of increase of Bishops to be separate and open.

That but for these circumstances I should have entertained an insuperable objection of conscience to concur in any proceeding opposed to the general sense of the Bishops.

That in the same way with respect to ecclesiastical policy in general I could not be a party to measures of Church legislation opposed to the general feeling of the Church.

That I recurred with great satisfaction to a declaration which I had heard him spontaneously and emphatically make at the commencement of the year with respect to the measure for increase of clergy that he was so sensible of the evil which would arise from public opposition between the Church and the Government that he thought it would far outweigh the good of the particular plan and he would at once abandon it. I entirely agreed with this sentiment at the time, I could not at once assume perhaps that it applied on his part to all Church measures, but for me it would be a canon. That accordingly having made this exposition from the belief that it was right to err on the side of too much rather than too little in such a matter, I had no difficulty remaining.

Sir Robert Peel observed that it might likewise be some satisfaction to me to remember that the decision on these bishoprics was taken before my accession—that he thought the local wants of parishes ought to be supplied before the revenues were taken to found the see of Manchester: and seemed to admit that this ought to have been considered in the Act of 1836.

He spoke again of the satisfaction of his colleagues and even said he did not recollect former instances of a single vacancy in a Cabinet, on which there was an entire concurrence. I repeated what I had said of his and their most indulgent judgment and took occasion distinctly to apologise for my blunder, and the consequent embarrassment which I caused to him in February 1842 on the corn scale.

In the course of the conversation I also ventured to assure him that there was a feeling in the Church respecting the suppression of a bishopric, or consolidation, whichever it might be called, very different from and much exceeding any which had reference to the retrenchment of capitular offices, or the transfer of revenues.

After we had finished this subject, he referred to the Canada Corn Bill—said he had the strongest impressions, confirmed by the experience of last year, against yielding to the demand of a party in a case where the decision had been long ago announced and having the features of this case—clearly meaning he would carry it or go. He anticipated my concurrence in these sentiments: which I expressed in the strongest terms.

I should have added that when speaking of the evil of hostility between the Government and the Church I told him in evidence of the strength of my feeling upon that subject, that I had in my own mind contemplated the resignation of my seat as well as my office, in case the misfortune should happen to me of separating from him on a question of that sort: from what I had seen in Parliament of the tendency which exists after a separation made originally in a friendly spirit, towards estrangement and hostility.

What I found upon this is: it has always been my impression that if the present Administration come to a breach with the Church, the battle is hardly to be fought against them in Parliament. Her warfare must be withdrawn, it seems to me, from the places of this world, to more appropriate scenes where the Heavenly Dove can never cease to overhang her banners and where her victory is assured.        *May 16.*

Sir Robert Peel also added that while knowing my opinions he wondered that the particular subject of the North Wales bishopric should have presented a difficulty to my mind under the circumstances in which it stands—and with reference to my general observations said he felt assured that in practice no obstacle or uneasiness would arise.                                              *May 16. [1843]*.


## 128: ADD.MS 44275, ff. 142–143

*Gladstone to Sir Robert Peel, 14 May 1843*[1]
*Carlton House Terrace.* Having made use of the leisure which you so kindly allowed me, I proceed to state what I think both my convictions and my character require of me.

I am deeply persuaded of the expediency of an early increase of

---

[1] *Docketed:* 'Draft to Sir R. Peel. May 14. 1843. Cancelled.'

episcopal superintendence for the efficiency of the Church of England and for the welfare of the community. The question about to be raised respecting the bishoprics of North Wales is I admit by no means the same, but it seems to me substantially connected with it.

My opinion is strongly in favour of the legal reestablishment of the two sees. But this subject, being separate from that of the peerage, and from that of the funds, is one upon which the sense of the bishops in general would carry with me the greatest weight. If that sense be in favour of the continuance of the present enactment, I shall cheerfully surrender my own judgment: but if they consider that the enactment should be repealed, I cannot refuse them my support.

Allow me to say that while I profess these sentiments it is with the sincere intention of respecting the general legislation which has been adopted on the recommendation of the Church Commission. I must add of my own knowledge that there is a very different feeling upon the subject of suppressing a see, from that which applies to the retrenchment of cathedral institutions or the transference of revenues. I doubt whether those who composed the Commission in 1836, would renew this particular recommendation in 1843. The argument from want of funds has received a double solution: first that they exceed what was assumed, secondly that less is now thought of the income of a bishop and more of his spiritual functions: the exigencies of the Church are differently measured both on the bench and elsewhere, not merely as I believe in the minds of any section or school, but by a general progression, of which almost every one consciously or otherwise has undergone the influence.

I have no means of estimating what the intentions of the bishops actually are: nor what the probabilities that after the discussion in the House of Lords a vote will be taken in the House of Commons: for I have avoided as far as possible mixing in the subject, conceiving it my first duty to communicate with you and to ascertain the views of the Administration.

Subject to the obligation I have above described, I am only desirous to take the course you may judge most convenient, or least likely to be attended with inconvenience. Upon this point I felt that I could explain myself with less indelicacy to some other Minister, than to the head and organ of the Cabinet: and having been led by an accident to explain my position to Lord Stanley on Saturday, I [*unfinished*]

## 129: ADD.MS 44819, f. 97

May 15. [1843].
My first Cabinet. On Repeal meetings. No fear of breach of the peace grounded on reasons. Therefore no case for interference. (The Duke however was for issuing a proclamation (May 27).)    *May 20. [1843].*

May 20/20. [1843].[1]
Second. Repeal. Constabulary tainted: cease to give accounts of what is said in the chapels. Deemed advisable to dismiss some against whom this may be proved: and to resume recruiting, which will keep the army at 2,500 more than intended.

Scotch secession. Not deemed advisable to call another Assembly in August.

North Wales bishoprics. In reference to former decision, Duke of Wellington and Lord Ripon requested to uphold the existing law in the House of Lords *as existing*. Archbishop of Canterbury, London, and Lincoln expected reluctantly to support—rest to oppose, the maintenance of it.

Peel dwelt strongly upon an important political argument, not heretofore considered by me: viz. that the party of the late Government at present stand pledged to the recommendations of the Commission and the existing legal arrangement of revenues: but that if the law were altered as to the North Wales bishoprics, this might lead to their breaking loose upon other and vital parts of these Acts in a sense hostile to the Church.

## 130: ADD.MS 44819, ff. 97–98

May 27/27. [1843].
Cabinet: chiefly on Indian matters. General misgiving as to the sufficiency of cause for making the Ameers submit to a new treaty: positive disapproval of the deposition of Meer Roostum and substitution of Ali Nurad—the greatest disinclination to annex Scinde to the

---

[1] This is a method of dating frequently used by WEG. The first figure is the date of the event or conversation recorded; the second is the date on which WEG wrote his account.

British territories—expectation that Lord Ellenborough will return home. The Duke advised to write simply that we did not fully understand the cause of his acts and waited more: Peel said I think most truly that it was impossible at this distance to give peremptory instructions, but we must keep close to the spirit of former dispatches, and must express an opinion as far as there were grounds laid before us— must say that former doubts were not removed—and that we were not prepared to sanction the annexation of Scinde. At the end of a very long conversation he broke out and said, 'After perusing these papers —sent from the Government of India—and without going further, I must say that it is a very bad case from beginning to end, and cannot be defended.'

Lord Ripon I thought showed weak. He had prepared a minute approving, under the circumstances, of the proceedings—up to the point of the annexation, and on that he said he was not prepared to offer an opinion: thought, however, it would be a perpetual burden. The truth is his post *at this moment* requires one of the firmest minds. Further this letter which he had prepared he said he did not propose— but it was only a mode in which approval might be expressed, *if* decided on.

The Secret Committee had written to him expressing strong disapprobation on the grounds both of expediency and of justice.

In Ireland matters grow darker. The Duke has made his military preparations with considerable precision as if thinking speedy outbreaks possible.

## 131: ADD.MS 44819, ff. 98-99

June 3/3. [1843].
Cabinets yesterday and today on Indian affairs—great perplexity. Lord Ellenborough, going out with the error of Afghanistan (not to say the crime) full in his face, has repeated it in substance by his proceedings about Scinde. Peel again declared today the proceedings to be unjust and indefensible. He said there were two definitive courses: one to approve—which he thought would cover the Government with disgrace: the other to recall Lord Ellenborough, and send out a successor—but he did not know whom to send (I think it not impossible that Graham may go before the year is out)—and he felt that they

were all willing to spare if possible a former colleague: that there was a third course, to await the more precise accounts of the engagement subsequent to that of Meeanee—this was a makeshift and the difficulty would recur in the course of ten days—it might enable Lord Ellenborough to complain of the Government for indecision: he had a strong impression that recall would be right but he would not urge it at the moment. On this intermediate basis he framed the sketch of a dispatch.

Lord Ripon again showed weak. He had drawn a draft stating the suspension of the judgment of the Cabinet on the ground of policy, independently of considerations connected with the previous transactions—and the Chancellor prompted him to introduce the mention of justice.

The Duke said it was impossible to judge of the policy of retaining Scinde at this distance, presuming it just: and desired to write in such terms as to gain time—and enable Lord Ellenborough to remain and act if perchance he might be so disposed upon altered views. Three hours sped rapidly away on these topics.

## 132: ADD.MS 44819, ff. 99–100

June 5/10. [1843].
I missed the Cabinet on Monday not knowing it. The dispatch for India was finally considered, as Goulburn told me, according to the substance before agreed upon.

June 8/10.
A Cabinet, on Irish affairs chiefly—question whether to legislate or not. Graham said if no legislation that probably the anti-repealers would meet on the accustomed days in July—and collision would ensue: when considering the state of the country it would become impossible to maintain the peace.

The Duke has written in a note to Stanley circulated on Thursday, 'We shall probably have war in Ireland: perhaps in Canada'. He came late to the Cabinet and on being called upon to give his opinion spoke to this effect—'We are a Government and we must act as a Government, we must endeavour to maintain the dominion of the Crown in that country. We must act by Parliament if Parliament will enable us, and if not we must act by such powers as the Crown possesses. I am for putting down the evil which presses: that is, the evil of these mob meetings: the organisation we cannot get at, the other we can: and they will put the State down unless the State puts them down.'

Peel pointed out, as elements in the case, the evil of placing the parliamentary [sic] in apparent and qualified alliance with the repealers, by any proposal of legislation which they should resist: the certainty that the plan of moving adjournments would be resorted to, and the great excitement that would be raised in the country, where there are parties ready to take advantage of the Irish movement. The difficulty of legislating against the meetings only would be, that it would leave untouched the root of them, which is the organisation of the Roman Catholic priests: but on the whole he seemed to lean to this kind of legislation if any, as strictly bounded by the necessity of the case.

Lord Lyndhurst said a Bill against the meetings would be reasonable, so would one against the organisation of tribute and associations, but he must leave it to the Commons to judge of the expediency of proposing it. The other alternative was a strong military force. It was clear that nothing could be effectually done with Irish juries under the present law.

I sat by Sir H. Hardinge and observed to him that I did not see that the foundation of the case was sufficiently laid, namely *such* apprehension and of *such* breach of the peace as to warrant an application for altering the constitution—that when any Bill was taken it ought to be strong and sufficient—that there was immense danger and evil in demanding one—that it seemed better to wait, employ all the existing executive means, and urge the nobility and gentry to exert themselves to keep the anti-repealers from all collision with the repeal party. This was his feeling—and perhaps Lord Stanley's. Nothing was decided except that the law officers should prepare drafts of Bills in both forms as quickly as possible.

## 133: ADD.MS 44819, ff. 100–102

June 11/17. [1843].

On Sunday Cabinet met at Lord Aberdeen's to consider whether the state of Ireland was such as to require legislation. The nature of the emergency seemed to me entirely to justify the interruption of the Christian rest.

There was a turn in the current of feeling. The Law Officers had prepared the two Bills, one against meetings, the other against the discussion of repeal. The latter was too *choquant* and Peel read a most able letter from the Irish Attorney General showing the inefficacy of the former. Graham had now I think come to the view that legislation was unwise. There was much discourse: the peers for the most part —including the Duke of Wellington—leant to legislation. Peel against it, at the same time thinking it would probably be required before the session is over, and viewing strongly the evils of such a parliamentary opposition as would be encountered, its effect in the country, and the evils which might arise from the combination of Leaguers and Chartists with the Repealers. It was at length determined not to legislate without some further advance of circumstances (*me valde plaudente*).

## June 15/17.

From two to five a most interesting discussion on proceeding with the educational clauses. The individual opinions of each member were asked and they were as follows—

| For proceeding | Against proceeding |
|---|---|
| Lord Stanley (who led the argument on that side) | Graham (who stated the case) |
| | Peel |
| Duke of Wellington | Lord Ripon |
| Duke of Buccleuch | Lord Wharncliffe |
| Chancellor | Hardinge |
| Lord Haddington | Knatchbull |
| Lord Aberdeen | W.E.G. |

Goulburn told me today that if there he would have been with the Noes. Peel was called on: opinions being so divided, to decide, which he did for relinquishment. The arguments for proceeding were:

1. That the Church had conceded much and we were bound to stand by her and not let her opponents triumph over her.
2. That if this scheme failed there could be no education of the people directly by the State—and either they must remain in the miserable condition described as the ground of the present measure, or
3. Government would be urged to plans of separate and indiscriminate endowment of schools of different sects.
4. Premium on future agitation.

To which Peel added:

5. Evil effect on the character of Government from reunion in such a case.

It was held on the other hand:

1. That the Church acquiesced rather than supported: and would not fear any momentary triumph of Dissenters.
2. That the opposition would be such that even obtaining the Bill this year would be doubtful.
3. That it might connect itself with the other existing and predisposing causes of disturbance.
4. That supposing the Bill got it would become a cause of perpetual dissension instead of a measure of concord.
5. That without concord a plan of that nature could not be worked at all: the 'teaching' of Scripture would be a subject of incessant contest among parties seeking occasion of difference, and such contest as no legal definition could settle.
6. That much might be done (Lord Wharncliffe) in the event of the withdrawal of the bill by the extension of the present grant.
7. That the Bill might be expected to cause resistance to the payment of rates.

I think the consideration that concord was an essential condition of working the measure in such a way as to make it a benefit and save it from being a new evil weighed most in bringing the Government to its decision.

June 17/17.
Further discussions on education. Whether to proceed with the factory clauses—whether to keep the clause giving power of inspection and of withholding certificate—what answer to the questions (a) if the grant should be extended—(b) if Wesleyans and (c) if other sects should participate.

The two first questions were affirmed.

Lord Wharncliffe on the other said the present Minutes enabled the committee to make grants to Wesleyans, to Roman Catholics, and to all Dissenters: and that some grants had been made by the present Government to Wesleyans, but none since the committee was formed to Roman Catholics.

Lord Stanley did not know any grant had been made to Wesleyans: nor did any one else seem to know it.

Peel said and I think it was felt generally no specific exception could be made in favour of that class. The understanding was that the grant was now given to National and to British and Foreign schools. He thought Government should declare that it had no intention of departing from that practice. Did not see why the Wesleyans should not unite themselves with the British and Foreign School Society and thereby obtain a share. Thought the delicate part of the case was that of the Roman Catholics: and that it was not advisable to draw that into discussion.

Lord Wharncliffe said the opposition of the Wesleyans to the present plan was owing to the Oxford doctrines alone. Goulburn however on my asking replied that they all opposed Brougham's Bill 25 or 30 years ago when that controversy did not rage.

Goulburn thought the Wesleyans had no good reason for not going to Church schools.

It was determined to answer in the sense described by Peel: and that there was no new plan in view to bring forward, at the same time the mind of the Government would of course be directed to the subject: no intention to propose a further grant but if it should appear that there was not enough to meet the voluntary efforts, in that case such a proposal might be made before the close of the session.

I obtained leave, with some dunning, to bring in a Bill to remove the remaining restrictions on the exportation of machinery.

## 134: ADD.MS 44819, ff. 102–103

20/24 June. [1843].
Cabinet on the Irish spirit duties. It was resolved to abandon the addition not from conclusive proof of the failure of the financial measure, but on account of its moral effects.

24/24 June.
Cabinet on Indian affairs. The Duke has sent round a memorandum recommending the sanction of the annexation, but with restoration of Meer Roostum to his possessions and compensation to other Ameers. He holds the command of the Indus to be essential to the defence of our Indian Empire in its vulnerable point, the north-west frontier.

Lord Ellenborough's despatch vindicating to the Government his Somnauth proclamation, declaring that our dominion rests only on force, is hostile to the people, hated by them, and to be maintained by the sword has excited the strongest disapprobation even of the Duke of Wellington. The Duke says those assertions are untrue—and he said of the letter that Lord Ellenborough '*ought to have his nose rubbed in it*'.

But the Duke's memorandum has told on the Cabinet. The tone in general was, at all events to keep Lord Ellenborough in his office—not as a good, but as the least evil. Lord Ripon had prepared a despatch, sanctioning the annexation and strongly recommending the restoration of the possessions of Meer Roostum and perhaps others. Stanley and Goulburn with some others suggested that it would be well at least to name to Lord Ellenborough for his consideration the restoration of the Ameers to a qualified sovereignty. A paper of Major Outram's was read declaring that we could not govern the country except by their means. The Duke I think did not like making this into a positive recommendation. It was, however, quasi-agreed that it should be done: but I fear Lord Ripon in embodying it will reduce its force. I was somewhat disappointed but I felt my ignorance of Indian matters disqualified me for pronouncing strongly the opinions to which my feelings and instincts would lead, the sum of which is that it is not mercy but justice which we are called upon to do largely to the Ameers. At the same time I admit our obligations to the peace of India in general.

## 135: ADD.MS 44819, ff. 103–104

June 27/8. [1843].

I came in late—it was decided that a vote of thanks should be given to the army for the operations in Scinde. Sir H. Hardinge brought me back from Sion and we discussed Indian matters. I said that the Scinde transactions would in my opinion damage the Government much if the Opposition should take them up with energy and make the most of them: nor can I see how the restitutions which are absolutely required by justice can be made in India without great embarrassment. He observed upon Peel's manner of handling questions in the Cabinet viz. that he feels towards the Duke of Wellington as his old master, and to Stanley as originally not of his party and as to both hesitates to take any strong line which might seem dictatorial and with the peers in general as in the case of Ireland feels his way and draws them towards his point before finally declaring. He considers that Peel has been very much influenced in this affair of Scinde by the strong opinions of the Duke as to the necessity of retaining the controul of the Indus.

Peel said on Saturday of the protracted discussions on the Arms Bill that they were formidable on account of their possible reaction on Ireland. He has also stated strongly his sense of the damage to the character of Government from the withdrawal of measures—e.g. the factory education clauses and the spirit duty. A great political truth.

## 136: ADD.MS 44819, ff. 104–105

July 1/1. [1843].
Cabinet on (1) Canada.
(a) Capital—to be fixed at Montreal. More defensible than Kingston, because, says the Duke, we cannot expect to hold a permanent superiority on the lake.
(b) Civil List. Peel dissuades us from breaking with the colonial legislature upon the question now mooted, viz. whether if they are willing to vote a Civil List we shall repeal that part of the Union Act which gives one by the authority of Parliament. Nor having conceded this principle will he break them upon any minor detail—but if the £60,000 which they offer be on the whole enough or thereabouts will take it—deeply regretting that the question should have been raised—and thinking that under the circumstances Sir C. Metcalfe is the best judge of the means of carrying on the Government and must be trusted very largely.
(c) Amnesty. The Chancellor said, 'This is a much easier question—what harm can it do?' But Graham said, 'It is easy as a colonial question: yet the precedent and inference for England and Ireland is most formidable.' Many forms of proceeding were discussed—but here too it was felt that the Government must be trusted to make the *whole* concession if absolutely necessary: and without difference of opinion, though with great reluctance.

Peel said, 'Let us not conceal from ourselves that we are by each of these steps losing ground, weakening the authority of the Crown: and it is especially unfortunate at this time. We may be quite right—we must keep the colony in peace, until we part from it—but the fact is that it is rapidly becoming ungovernable—and we are fast drifting down to the final issue of separation. Who can manage it if this Governor cannot? He has boldness and honesty though the turn of his mind is to concession —he has the confidence of the Government and Parliament and the *prestige* of past success. If he dare not venture on breaking up his Government and a dissolution, we have no choice. An unsuccessful appeal would dreadfully weaken the Crown. But at the same time, although in losing Canada we must lose all British North America, including the naval station of Halifax, yet if demand after demand is to be made upon us, each weakening the authority of the mother country, we must soon consider seriously of the propriety of acquainting the Premier that we can no longer undertake to provide for its defence.' Stanley said, 'I have told them that already.'

On the Civil List, Stanley was for maintaining the office of a permanent Civil Secretary to which the Assembly object. But Peel said that ground will not do for a constitutional battle. And he disapproved a good deal of the system of permanent under-Secretaries in this country.

(2) India.
Today to my great joy Major Outram's views for the government of Scinde through the Ameers came into the ascendant—in consequence I imagine of a letter from the Chairs, which emphatically urges that course. Lord Ripon's draft despatch was therefore thrown over. It was, however, thought impossible absolutely to overrule Lord Ellenborough's discretion—but Peel said, write to him that we think the restoration of the Ameers to qualified sovereignty and our superintendence the most desirable course, while we trust it to his discretion to pursue the best line he can. And this to be written secretly: though it would entail a difficulty upon the production of the other papers in Parliament.

## 137: ADD.MS 44819, ff. 105-106

July 4/6. [1843].
Cabinet on India. Since Saturday week, the inclination of the Cabinet has turned more towards restoration of the Ameers—and I think this would have been ordered but for the distance, the difficulties it places in

the way of positive directions, and the dangers to the peace of India at large from the repudiation of the Governor General's policy and his personal recall. The letter to be sent however is in the sense of the most earnest recommendation—the Duke rather hanging fire and desiring, apparently, that nothing should go beyond mere suggestion. Although support here is promised if Lord Ellenborough decide on perseverance in his course, I think it will be difficult for him to do so in the face of the letter of this mail. The discretion entrusted to a Governor General, as exemplified in his practice, is enormous—far beyond that of *any* subject I think, in point of independent individual action.

Lord Ripon seemed not indisposed to go a step further and to desire him either to *restore* or to *report* his reasons for not doing so.

Major Outram's representations to members of the Government have I think had considerable influence in causing the recommendation now made.

## 138: ADD.MS 44777, ff. 91–94

Saturday, July 8. [1843].

It was first discussed whether in producing the Scinde papers to insert Major Outram's notes of his conferences with the Ameers. On the one hand, they came through the Governor of Bombay to whom they were not sent officially—and we do not know that Lord Ellenborough has seen them. On the other hand without these notes, the case of the Ameers is in no manner shown—and the pledge of giving a fair view of the case is not fulfilled. Lord Ripon to make more inquiry into the circumstances under which the notes were forwarded.

Lord Aberdeen proposed to accede to Brougham's amendment in his Scottish Kirk Bill—by which the power of the Church to judge of objections is not declared but enacted.

The reasons for are:

1. That the Law Lords *una voce* including the Chancellor give their opinion that in its present form it declares the law in opposition to the judgment of the highest tribunal, contrary to all principle.
2. That it is doubtful whether the peers will vote for it in the face of such declarations.
3. That the Scotch judges have swerved in some instances from their first opinions, on which the provision as it stands was founded.

4. That the Kirk of Scotland will attach the same or nearly the same value to the boon.

5. That by using the term enact, you do not determine that the Bill is not declaratory, nor consequently do you pronounce upon the present state of the law: whereas by using the term declare you do so pronounce, and against the House of Lords.

Sir Robert Peel seemed very averse to this course—thinking

1. That the amendment would render the Bill difficult to carry in the House of Commons.

2. That on account of Lord Aberdeen's recent declarations, as well as on account of the withdrawals which have lately been taking place, it would much weaken and disparage the Government.

3. That it would render the Bill unpalatable in Scotland, and make it impossible to maintain the Kirk as [the] national establishment.

4. That the Advocate and Solicitor-General adhere to the opinion that the declaration is *true*—i.e. rightly states the law.

Reference to be made to Lord Aberdeen's speech.

Determined to grant inquiry into the condition of the framework knitters. *July 14.*

Monday, July 8/14.[1]
Found Cabinet in discussion on Lord Brougham's amendment. Sir R. Peel very reluctant—Lord Aberdeen and the Chancellor see no choice. Duke of Wellington willing to take any course which might be thought best by the Government generally. Stanley in the choice of difficulties for the amendment. Graham regarded the change as a very serious evil in Scotland, and as affecting the character of the Government—but under its present general difficulties he would with great reluctance assent rather than break up the Administration. I left the room before all had spoken, only telling Lord Aberdeen I concurred in thinking the change would make little difference in Scotland. The decision, however, was for the amendment.

July 14/14.
Cabinet on (first) Irish debate in House of Lords. Determined not to take up any affirmative position, which would lead to counter motions, but to give a simple negative to Lord Clanricarde's motion.

---

[1] This seems to be a mistake for Monday, July 10.

(2) State of business in the House of Commons. Peel said, 'Within this room I must tell you, I have and always have had my opinion on the Bill—that is not now the question. The character of the Government will not allow it to be given up—on the other hand, *you will not carry it*— the Bill is very ill drawn, no one seems much to understand it, and we are quite disappointed in our Attorney-General for Ireland. Lord John Russell in the first place has lost all power over his party as a whole, they act in bands: besides, he is in connivance with them—had an understanding I believe even with O'Connell (Sir J. Graham through Edward Ellice)—and the great object of this agitation in Ireland is to displace the Government.'

Morning sittings were named—sitting till October—Lord Wharncliffe proposed a declaration of determination to carry the Bill, which Peel declared would produce a counter one and lead to defeat—Lord Lyndhurst modification of the rule of adjournment—Sir R. Peel observed there was no case.

Some discussion but no decision on the Presbyterian marriages— Unitarian Chapels' Bill—and Slave Trade Suppression Bill.


## 139: ADD.MS 44777, f. 86

July 21/24. [1843].
Cabinet on Presbyterian marriages—and on the plan for quieting the Unitarian title to endowed chapels upon proof of an usage of thirty years in those doctrines. As respects the first subject, it was stated that the Presbyterians of Ireland vehemently protest against any scheme which should have the effect of placing them on the footing of the Dissenters under the English Marriage Act of 1836—while the Church and perhaps the Roman Catholics would object to any special recognition of their orders. As to the latter the Unitarians urge it and the Lord Chancellor appeared to have encouraged it.


## 140: ADD.MS 44777, ff. 86–90

[July] 22/27. [1843].
Sir J. Graham announced that the Irish Presbyterians and English Dissenters were likely to oppose vehemently the projected measure for

quieting Unitarian titles. Mr. Goulburn thought the Church would also oppose—it seemed to me there would be little interference from that quarter.

Some alarm excited by a letter stating a case in which a Presbyterian Minister receiving the *Regium Donum* actively supports and collects for Repeal.

Peel announced that the Queen and Prince were anxious to visit King Leopold at his home near Ostend—and a question arose whether Lords Justices must in such a case be appointed and with what powers. It was hoped they would desist from the plan—and Peel said, 'They will be as reasonable as possible—but it does not do to thwart them—I know how to manage them—the way is to receive the proposal without objection and show a willingness to meet their desire—then as difficulties appear they will grow cool.'

[July] 24/27.
Ellice joined me on my way home to dinner and said how desirable it was in the uneasy state of the country to get rid of the session. Ireland, Wales, the iron trade, and now the weather (for the harvest) and the action on the prices of corn formed a threatening combination. What a mistake it was to bring in such an Arms Bill instead of a more continuing Bill. He thought Peel had never pledged himself on any ground of religion to maintain the Irish Church property, and said that in that his position differed from Stanley's and from Graham's—who left Lord Grey's Government in 1834 on the religious ground—though he said I must speak to *you* with some caution on such a point—at that time he said he told them, 'The day will come when I shall be fighting under Peel's banners and you two will lead the Tories.' I replied that I thought if a state of circumstances arose in which Peel thought the settlement of Church property in Ireland could not be maintained that he would leave to others the alteration of it but would refuse to be a party himself. He did not seem to dissent from this but it was quite contrary to what he had himself said. He deprecated the discussion standing for next week as detrimental to the cause.

[July] 25/27.
Meeting at Sir R. Peel's on education. Lord Wharncliffe, Sir R. Peel, Sir J. Graham, Lord Stanley, Mr. Goulburn, and W.E.G.

[July] 25/August 3.

The question was, what answer should be made to Hume's motion, with Colquhoun's and Lord John Russell's suggestions tonight.

In a conversation of two hours, the general views expressed were these. Goulburn said but little.

Graham thought we must adhere to the present ground—that of a distribution to the National and the British and Foreign Societies only. Thought my argument in 1839 unanswered and irrefragable, that indiscriminate endowment of schools would break down the establishment principle by entailing a similar course with respect to churches.

Peel said it would not do to argue that what we did for schools we must necessarily and exactly do for churches—because at present we virtually aid Dissenting schools through the British and Foreign Society —and it appeared that the Committee of Council—or rather Lord Wharncliffe *for no one else knew the fact* had aided one Wesleyan school. He thought it would not do to stand absolutely on the exclusive distribution to the two societies. We had not the advantage possessed in the case of the Church—for as to education we had already abandoned the principle of the Church by admitting the British and Foreign.

Stanley answered that he thought a tenable and intelligible ground still remained under the present practice because according to the constitution of the British and Foreign it taught in its schools nothing peculiar, therefore nothing contrary to the peculiar doctrines of the Church of England, but only certain truths supposed to be common to the Church with many classes of Dissenters. So that there was a principle in the present system—and at the Cabinet on the factory clauses he had stated strongly his opinion that the Government ought not to depart from it.

Lord Wharncliffe evidently leaning to further relaxation said Shuttleworth had told him, that he (Shuttleworth) had learned from Sinclair that the Church would not object to grants to Roman schools, provided no Protestant children went to them. What rumours men will rely upon *with* their wishes! Goulburn differed from this and Stanley emphatically.

I should say the prevalent *tone* of the meeting was a desire if possible to include the Wesleyans, and not to include the Roman Catholics— the latter more decidedly than the former.

I stated that the one thing of which I felt convinced was, the utter impossibility of taking any distinction permanently or on principle between different sects so soon as the rule of two societies was *confessedly* abandoned—either as in favour of Wesleyans and against Roman Catholics, or as in favour of both these and against Socinians: or perhaps even Jews. It was observed that Socinians were not Christians—I replied that we endow them in Ireland.

Peel said he thought he must point out particular modes in which the application of public money might be extended i.e. as to schoolmasters' houses etc.: express generally adherence to the orders and minutes already in existence.

(I hoped that would not necessarily include the adoption of the expressions of the minute of December 1840—which are evidently framed to admit of a very great latitude.)

And if pressed as to Wesleyans or Roman Catholics with any particular instance, to decline any hypothetical reply but say special cases would be dealt with as they should arise.

The absurdity of Colquhoun's proposition was universally recognised.

On the whole we have reason to be thankful that the debate was cut short by counting out.

It was stated that the Dissenters would probably oppose the grant next year unless the range of distribution be enlarged.

## 141: ADD.MS 44777, ff. 95–96

August 3/3. [1843].
At Cabinet today Lord Ripon read a letter from the Chairs stating that a secret Court of Directors were unanimously of opinion that the proceedings towards the Ameers could not be justified and wishing for authority to apprise the (Secret) Court that Government had disapproved of them and was anxious as far as possible to repair the injustice.

Peel expressed his apprehension that the body were about to move decisively against the Governor General and exercise their power.

He sketched a reply stating that on account of the state of Scinde, and of the fact that no imperative categorical instructions had been sent out but a recommendation (I think) to deal as favourably as might be with the Ameers, the Government deemed it premature at this time to disclose the nature of the instructions to the Court. For this a draft of Lord Ripon's was set aside.

It occurs to me here to mention circumstances showing I think that Peel must hold personally what would be called very Low views of the Church. In a debate on the education clauses he said he had a very strong opinion on the Oxford controversy. On another occasion he said it was impossible to read the last charge of the Bishop of Chester without the greatest admiration for that prelate—in which I doubt not he pointed either jointly or mainly at the doctrinal portion of the charge. And at the last Cabinet but one it was observed how desirable it was that some Whigs should subscribe to the National Society's Fund—we mentioned some who had done so—Peel said he wished very much that *Sir George Grey* would subscribe. I said he was an excellent man, but an extremely Low Churchman, rather preferring I believed the Presbyterian system—and others said the same. Peel replied, 'Would not he agree with the *Bishop of Chester*?', seeming to take him as a type and very loth to believe that Grey would not be in unison with him.

After this Government came into office Grey wrote a welltempered article in the *Edinburgh Review* in which he treated my not having been included in the Education Committee of the Privy Council as a favourable indication of the views of the Administration with respect to the education of the people.

## 142: ADD.MS 44819, ff. 106–107

August 8/11. [1843].
I came late to the Cabinet which had sat for Irish affairs, and I brought on the subject of Lord Brougham's Bill for the suppression of the slave trade, and explained as well as I could the anomalous and irregular shape of the measure as it stands, and the delicacy and great importance of the principles which when reduced to order it would involve.

Upon referring to a former discussion in the Lords, it appeared that the Duke, the Chancellor, and several other Ministers there had invited Brougham to frame a Bill and had promised the support of the Government—apparently without any qualification. The Bill had then been allowed to pass through the Lords without any opposition or even I believe observation from the Government—and Brougham was naturally incensed at my remarks on its reaching the Commons.

Upon considering however the state of the measure and the prayer for time and inquiry which I understood was about to be made by petition, the opinion seemed to be that there must be an interposition by the Government. And Sir R. Peel said to the Lord Chancellor and the rest (the Duke had gone), 'You have got us into the scrape, pray do what you can to get us out.' They were to endeavour to prevail on Brougham to assent to the postponement of the Bill until next session.

At a late meeting Sir R. Peel stated that Prince Albert had asked him whether anything could be done for the discountenance and suppression of duelling. He answered that the matter would require great consideration. He spoke in a very good tone about it in the Cabinet and said that he thought society would support any man of known courage who in Colonel Fawcett's position had stated that considering his connection with Lieutenant Monro he would not fight him and should feel himself prevented from doing so by his duty to God. He seemed much inclined to think some step might be taken with reference to the present practices in the Army and Navy—and I ventured to speak for the removal of the *positive sanction* which is actually given by the existing rules.

If we could but estimate our brotherhood in the Redeemer, how would the horror which people feel at the combat between Colonel Fawcett and Lieutenant Monro teach them the most conclusive lesson against duelling altogether.

## 143: ADD.MS 44819, ff. 107–108

August 16/16. [1843].

Lord Aberdeen and I went to Sir R. Peel's this morning by appointment: he observed first that the feeling of the House of Commons as indicated last night was very strong against Russia: was friendly to interposition by remonstrance even in cases where you have no title to go to war: thought Mr. Canning did right[1] to remonstrate with France in 1823. Lord Aberdeen thought otherwise of the policy of 1823, and generally that [we] were placed in an humiliating position by remonstrating without being prepared to back the representation by substantive measures.

2. I got this appointment made yesterday to consider the Stade question, feeling that it would not be creditable to the Government that

---

[1] MS: write.

it should continue longer unsettled. Sir R. Peel said the conduct of Hanover in levying the dues was flagrant: that we should give notice we could not submit to paying them: should throw it on her to show how much over and above the $\frac{1}{16}$ it might be right for us to pay not on account of her title but simply from our own acquiescence: should express a readiness to consider that question: and as to the amount to be given he was not willing to give more than £8,000 a year, the present payment being £16,000 and the $\frac{1}{16}$ about £4,000. Lord Aberdeen thought we must not go very much below what Hanover would have had under the treaty of last year. It was agreed that Lord Aberdeen should send notification to Hanover that we cannot submit to the existing toll.

3. As to Portugal—Lord Aberdeen said he did not believe Palmella was come prepared to grant all that we ask. Palmella had conversed largely on the subject with the Prince who has written a very good letter to Peel on the subject[1] showing I think a tact and capacity for business as well as a considerable command of English. In this the Board of Trade is stated to have been called by Palmella '*un peu doctrinaire*' and he imagined that we require the duties to be *ad valorem*.

Peel said that in his opinion it was very desirable to avoid reopening the negotiations, in which I concurred. He had already written to the Prince a letter in which he intimated that there was much difficulty.

*1843*[2]

## 144: ADD.MS 44777, ff. 97–100

On Thursday, August 17 [1843] I had an interview with Sir R. Peel and others at his house at which he spoke out very freely about commercial matters.

(1) Trade etc. That if he were not hampered by party considerations he should wish to propose a Corn Law with a duty of 10/- from 50/- to 60/-, to cease altogether at 65/- and with a maximum of 14/- uniting the fixed with the sliding principle.

That the revenue of the country showed so little elasticity, that unless there should be improvement during the coming autumn, some further great operation would be necessary next session.

---

[1] ADD.MS 40437, ff. 145–147.
[2] In pencil.

That the income tax must be extended to five years instead of three—according to what he had already intimated in the session of 1842—and he hinted that it would be a very great good if they would raise it to 5 per cent.

That the cotton, wool, and sugar duties must at all events be dealt with next year—and also silk.

And that some further effort to relieve trade might be necessary: that if an increase in the income tax were found requisite it must be combined with relief to the consumer.

(2) Stade duties. He thought the conduct of Hanover all but piratical—praised Ward's memorandum. Considered one half the present payment the outside of what Hanover ought to receive: it was determined that Lord Aberdeen should intimate that we could not acquiesce in the continuance of the present tax. (N.B. Lord Aberdeen came to me afterwards and said he felt a difficulty in receding from the arrangement which was all but signed last year: in which we *intended* to give $\frac{3}{4}$—and in fact gave something more.

I observed to Lord Aberdeen that Hanover seemed purposely to have kept us in the dark at that time as to the facts: that we had now better knowledge: but more particularly it was avowed throughout those negotiations that we were as it were paying a price to keep Hanover out of the Zollverein—whereas now the two questions would be avowedly and wholly dissociated—and this might justify material departure from the terms of last year.)

(3) Portugal. Lord Aberdeen said he thought we were bound to adhere to our offers if Palmella should declare himself ready to accept them. I demurred to the doctrine: and thought that unless bound, which I could not conceive, it was any thing but desirable to renew the negotiations. Sir R. Peel agreed.

(4) America—determined to have a Cabinet.

Saturday, [August] 19.
Cabinet. American overture talked over. The question was whether we might give an assurance that if she should make material reductions on our goods we would reduce upon particular articles, and whether we should name them. Cotton and rice were the two obvious ones: should maize also be included? I said the agricultural interest had been worried twice this year with matters of comparatively small account in themselves—namely the Canada Corn Bill and the Ashburton Treaty clause

—do not again fret them for a small object—either let it be something great and adequate, or nothing at all—they do not argue whether the risk to them be great or small—they complain of the reopening of the question at all.

Sir R. Peel would not quite give up the idea of altering the duty upon maize: and at the same time said that the affirmative could not now be safely promised—therefore the resolution was, not to name specific articles at all—but to reply according to my memorandum[1] of the same date—embodying (as I believe) Sir R. Peel's language.

Graham, Lord Wharncliffe, and Knatchbull dissuaded making any change with respect to maize. They agreed that it might have been done in the Corn Bill of 1842. I remember then urging upon Lord Ripon and Sir R. Peel that it should be done: but Sir R. Peel was unwilling to increase the number of alterations in the Act.

He I think was the father of the sliding scale for colonial corn, an useless change, tending I think rather to make the scale ridiculous, but *quandoque dormitat*, the soundest judgment when required as his is to traverse an immense multitude of details will wink upon some of them.

Sir R. Peel said the main question for the Prorogation Speech was whether the Queen should be advised to make a strong declaration against Repeal. He did not appear at all confident of her willingness to do it and said he had better see her before anything was considered in Cabinet.

I missed the next Cabinet being out of town. I see, however, that the declaration appears in the Speech.                    *Fasque. August 29. 1843.*

## 145: ADD.MS 44777, ff. 101–102

In the account of the conversation on August 17 about Portuguese negotiations,[2] I forgot to state that Sir R. Peel had received a letter from Prince Albert upon the subject which he sent to me for perusal.

This letter showed, as I thought, that the Prince had paid great attention to Palmella's communication, and that he had an evident capacity for business.

Palmella had, it seems to me irregularly and improperly, opened the

---

[1] ADD.MS 40470, f. 51.
[2] No. 144.

subject in a conversation with the Prince and stated his anxiety to renew the negotiations: that he would accept what we offered (i.e. we presumed in the way of reductions in *our* duties), and hoped we would accept what he offered—that the chief obstacle lay with the Board of Trade which was *un peu doctrinaire* and required that the duties should be levied *ad valorem*—this was quite a mistake.

The Prince stated in this letter that the Queen and he felt a sincere interest in the subject and hoped it would be practicable to conclude an arrangement.

In this subject throughout, Lord Aberdeen has been decidedly for closing, and 'protested' against the contrary course in the spring: Goulburn has taken but little part, that little leaning to disfavour: Lord Ripon was somewhat indecisive: Peel hostile, I strenuous the same way even before he had declared.                  *Fasque. September 13. 1843.*

I should further have stated that at the same conversation it was observed by Graham that if in the event of a bad harvest foreign corn should not be entered until the duty got down to the shilling, it would be all over with the Corn Law and *vice versa* that it would survive if corn came in at all equably at higher rates.

Peel I think assented. I have long thought so.

*Fasque. September 16. 1843.*

## 146: ADD.MS 44777, ff. 103–106

November 15. [1843].
Cabinet dinner. Sir R. Peel described Sir C. Napier as in military matters clearly a first rate man. He and others thought Outram sadly damaged by Napier's replies and his own previous letters. It was held that opium could not be excluded from Hong Kong—that the Chinese wish simply to hear nothing about it from us, and that we shall not bring it to their ports. It has been represented that Macao is a formidable competitor to Hong Kong.

November 16.
Cabinet on the measures of the next session.

Factory Bill to be reintroduced without any education clauses. Law requiring certificates to remain as it is; the more so as the great subscription which has been raised makes it more likely to work—the 6½ hour clause to be by all means retained.

Irish Registration and Poor Law England Bills—to be brought in early.

Ecclesiastical courts. Sir J. Graham said he was obliged at length to give up Doctors' Commons. Peel that he could not stand the argument of the necessity of a profession of civilians to be maintained by testamentary business during peace in order that there might be adequate learning for the decision of Admiralty questions during war. The Chancellor said they might be got up *pro re nata*. It was observed that the great will case of Wood was ultimately argued not by civilians but by Pollock, Follett, Wilde etc. Peel did not understand why the Bill of last session had been altered. All seemed to agree that in the altered form it had no chance: and that the monopoly of Doctors' Commons must be surrendered. Goulburn, however, appeared reluctant.

The Attorney General had hinted a committee. Peel said this would have a palpably hostile aspect—the leaning appeared to be towards a commission of inquiry into the constitution of Doctors' Commons—and the notion that the result would open it: and would lead to the establishment of a good system for diocesan courts.

Friday, November 17.
Cabinet—on Ireland, the affair of the demurrer and the plea in abatement on which it was founded. Pollock says the judgment against the Attorney General allowing time was wrong.

Peel went off to Windsor—when I had just opened the question of the Brazilian project of treaty. The discussion became vague after he had gone—not by any declaration but insensibly—a high compliment. We only got to the point that to decide now on the Brazilian project is to decide on our course with respect to the sugar duties for twelve months more from next July.

Monday, November 20
Cabinet.
1. Brazil—decided to reject the proferred convention which takes away not only all the positive advantages secured to us by the present treaty, but likewise all the substantial provisions relating to reciprocity which give value to such an instrument.

2. Portugal. Duke of Palmella's memorandum to Lord Aberdeen of today read. It appears that in reality nothing is there offered except the faculty of resuming the negotiations at the point at which they were

dropped in April—and fighting for one concession after another in infinite detail until their tables should come somewhat nearer to our terms.

Lord Aberdeen fought hard for Portugal: and Peel agreed that Palmella might be told the terms offered by us in April were still open to him. This in my view is much. I fear he will give a paltering answer and that the matter is not yet at an end. Peel has thus far bent, partly to keep up to the terms of special friendship which have prevailed between this country and Portugal, and in part perhaps through deference to Lord Aberdeen.

3. Ireland. Lord de Grey in a letter to Graham laments the Attorney General's temper and manner: and the Attorney General in one of his own is evidently beset by apprehensions, annoyances, and cares relating to his reputation and the attacks made upon him, which must take both from his usefulness and his happiness.

The main question pending for the Government is whether to have a special or a common jury—in Ireland they lean to the latter, but Graham read an admirable letter of his own to the Lord Lieutenant dated October 16 and a subsequent one proving that the former is that to which the Government should look.

I am to prepare a note on the Brazilian question.[1]

*November 20. 1843.*

## 147: ADD.MS 44777, ff. 107–108

November 21. 1843.
Cabinet. Determined to issue a commission to examine into the constitution of Doctors' Commons—the terms of it to be fixed by Sir James Graham with the Chancellor.

State of Ireland discussed: the bonfires, the Waller outrage, which Peel declared to be the worst he had ever known. The Duke of Wellington suggested a local force—Peel feared that persons would enlist in it to train against the Government.

Our demurrer expected to be allowed.

November 22.
Colonel Outram has applied to Lord Ripon for a recommendation to Sir Hugh Gough expressing his wish to go to India immediately—and

---

[1] ADD.MS 44733, ff. 49–95 (draft), ff. 99–109 (copy).

his intention to leave on record at the India House his opinions with respect to the Scinde policy.

It was arranged that the Duke (who expressed a bad opinion of him) should receive the application from Lord Ripon and should as Commander in Chief recommend him as an active and competent soldier for Indian service.

Determined to acquaint Lord Ellenborough of the regret of the Government that he had disjoined the management of Cutch from Bombay and attached it to Scinde without reference home in the first instance.

Determined to acquiesce in the annexation of Scinde not as (Peel said) satisfactory but as having no other alternative. Lord Ripon had a despatch which did not content Peel. He pointed to the polemical and popular character of those of Lord Ellenborough and said the reply must be carefully framed—and on account of him and of the East India Company as well as of Parliament and the public so put as to show both that Government was justified in its doubts and suggestions in July, and in its final decision now. Graham observed that the doubts were so far removed, as not to warrant the disturbance of what has been done. Peel intimated that he was not satisfied as to the treatment of Meer Roostum. The intrigue of the succession seems to me to remain much as it was.

Both the Duke and Lord Ripon expressed a great anxiety that Outram should leave the country as soon as possible.     *November* 22.

December 20.
On Friday Sir R. Peel expressed *obiter* a strong opinion that the next change in the Corn Laws would be to total repeal.

## 148: ADD.MS 44777, ff. 109–110

Cabinet. January 11. 1844. On Irish registration.
Three hours discussion on the question whether an excess of (say) £5 rating over rent, or the declaration of the £10 solvent tenant test should be substituted for the present practice. The Duke leant to the latter: Peel and Graham to the former. Nothing was decided.

January 12.
Peel, Lord Aberdeen, Lord Ripon, and I, met and discussed the Stade duty from 1.00 to 3.30 without much progress.

A new point was started whether the Elbe bordering states would not exceed their powers under the 16th annex of the Treaty of Vienna by establishing a tariff which should raise any of the duties. Lord Aberdeen thought no, the rest of us yes.

Lord Aberdeen, however, pointed out that we did not know what we wanted or were ready to accept. This is true. Peel shows the greatest reluctance to look definitively at this part of the question. I have never seen him more pressed and worried with any subject. Its scale is small, but it might involve an European war by a not impossible progression of cause and effect: and though this would probably be intercepted by the common sense of mankind still to go near it is awful. Still I am not for receding from what we are clearly convinced is right because Germany has shifted and shows a disposition to support Hanover.

Cabinet same day. Found it had been decided to take the solvent tenant test instead of the excess of rating above rent—which I incline to regret, though I am very inadequately informed. _January 12. 1844._

## 149: ADD.MS 44777, ff. 111–114

Saturday, January 13. 1844.
Meeting at Sir R. Peel's on the Bank question with the Governor and Deputy Governor. Sir Robert Peel is very great on this question of the currency and Bank charter. He inclines to an approximation by gentle and voluntary means to a final system of one bank of issue.

Foreign Office at 3.00 on Stade. Sir Robert Peel was prepared to accept under the circumstances a clear deduction of 25% with the power of free distribution on our part. But as an alternative to protest against any decision of the Elbe states which by exceeding the duties levied in 1815 should exceed their powers under the Treaty—and announcing that unless a settlement were made we could not continue to pay either permanently or for any indefinite time while waiting for a sentence.

Lord Aberdeen considered that the Elbe powers have a competency under the Treaty to increase the duties: and that in any event we must continue to pay the duty pending a final award—thus differing from Sir Robert Peel with whom I altogether felt. And he seemed determined to adhere to his opinion.

It was, however, determined that Lord Aberdeen and I should see Kielmansegge on Monday to ascertain further the precise nature of his proposition which Lord Aberdeen thought he was inclined in some degree to modify in our favour. And that we should also see the Law Officers on the subject of the construction of the 16th annex of the Treaty of Vienna. We have done both accordingly—and find Kielmansegge's proposition remains as it was. But strangely enough he contended that the tariff of 1821 was the same except as to any abuses that might have crept in, and modes of collection and such like, the same with the tariff of 1692. I said then why not go back to the tariff of 1692 and so settle the question? He said they were pledged to the tariff produced in 1821. I replied, not to that tariff but simply not to increase it.

Within the present month Milnes has sent an intimation to Sir Robert Peel that he means to propose in Parliament an alimentary provision for the Irish Roman Catholic priesthood. And Eliot has addressed a long letter to Sir James Graham in support of the same measure and of an increase of the grant to Maynooth—the amount of the stipend being I think only £100 or £150 as contemplated by him—although with respect to the former of these he expresses his conviction that all the Scotch, all the Dissenters, many of the Church and of the Conservative party would oppose it, and that it would very probably destroy the Government. The proposition is modestly expressed, and it is evidently founded on conscientious belief that it would tend powerfully to the peace of Ireland.

Sir R. Peel today returned from Windsor, reports that the Queen and Prince Albert express no sort of dissatisfaction with the Irish proceedings but a fear that on account of the magnitude of the risks involved they may lead to some embarrassment—and a desire that it may not be so.

The Queen desires the institution of a new order of merit below the Garter and the Bath for the reward of personal service to the Crown. Peel and Stanley both desire something of the kind for *colonial* persons in particular—but after a long conversation nothing is decided.

*January 20.*

## 150: ADD.MS 44777, ff. 115–118

At Lord Stanley's Cabinet dinner, Wednesday the 24th [January 1844] Sir James Graham read letters from Ireland announcing the progress of

Repeal in the 16th Regiment—it is said by one Barry, a leader, in a letter of his that sixty odd have joined the movement.

The Duke of Wellington told a characteristic anecdote. Lord Stanley said to him speaking of the Spanish soldiery, 'I suppose you would not like to have such fellows as those, Duke, officered by Spanish officers for the foundation of your army.' The Duke said, 'No, no, no. When I commanded the army in France, I have put ten thousand of them under arms, as a punishment, for plundering. I said to them, "If you cannot behave like soldiers of yourselves, I must make you." They talked about the *pun d'onor*—and I told them, "The true *pun d'onor* is, not to do the thing, and then not to object to the punishment."'      *January 29.*

January 29. Cabinet today on the Queen's Speech.
The question was raised whether the mention of the Landlord and Tenant Commission, and of the registration, was to be interpreted as excluding other measures. It was agreed that it could not be interpreted as closing the door against them. Graham mentioned two—the mortmain law, and extension of the grant to Maynooth. He thought it was a great question, but was not prepared to say it might not be well to appoint a committee on Maynooth. Peel said he thought Maynooth was on a bad footing, and that if you had such an establishment it might be asked why not put it on the best basis. Graham also hinted at an increase of the grant upon conditions. Lord Wharncliffe who raised the question evidently assented. No one else said anything.

It was also asked whether corn should be mentioned in the Speech? Agreed we can not—but Lord Wharncliffe said we must speak stout. Peel said it was impossible on that, or on other questions, for the Government to bind itself irrespective of circumstances: but the law had fulfilled our expectations and there was no intention of changing it. The question lay between this law and repeal—at least there was no other step for *us* to take. Lord Wharncliffe said the great matter was to express the opinion of the continued necessity for Protection. Peel rather avoided any answer.      *January 29.*

January 29. 1844.
In Cabinet on Tuesday Sir R. Peel opened the Bank question. Then Lord Haddington again produced his demands to the naval service. Last time he proposed to reduce 39,000, the vote of 1843, to 38,000: today he had got it down to 37,000: and he only got 36,000. He

proposed nine sail of the line at home: this was cut down. Then Sir James Graham reintroduced the question of the ecclesiastical courts. The Law Officers came in and declared their approbation of Nicholl's proposal to have a bill abolishing peculiars, and referring the modes of proceeding in the diocesan courts. Also taking away the jurisdiction over tithes. This to supersede the proposed commission. The plan appeared to be generally accepted. Graham remarked it was giving a new title to the ecclesiastical jurisdiction over testamentary matters. He had previously dwelt much upon the evil of division and opposition from within the Conservative party which the measure of last year produced.

*January 29.*

In Thursday's Cabinet the Bank question was discussed as to its general principles.

*January 29.*

## 151: ADD.MS 44777, ff. 119–126

Increase of Maynooth grant.

1. It will be a great shock to the religious feeling of the country, and will weaken confidence.

2. It will not be possible to establish any efficacious controul over the college.

3. It is doubtful whether the increase of allowances for maintenance will alter the class from which pupils will be drawn.

4. Unless the number of students to be provided for be something like doubled, the college will not be able to supply the demand for parochial priests: and the complaint of an incomplete and niggardly provision will still remain.

5. If the standard of maintenance be thus raised, and the scale of the establishment thus enlarged, the increase in the grant will be such as to attract considerable animadversion on that ground alone.

6. The assistance at present afforded to each pupil must be much above what is given by the bursaries in Scotland, and equal to what is supplied by most exhibitions and many scholarships in England.

7. The enlargement of the vote will raise anew and in full the question of the principle and the policy of the original establishment of the

college: for the present vote has been commonly and perhaps justly represented as a legacy from the separate Parliament of Ireland.

8. It must therefore be considered whether it was wise, and whether it is now wise, to do so much, being prepared to do no more?

9. It is not to be supposed that this concession would have a material effect in disarming opposition, unless in so far as it might be interpreted as an indication of an intention to go farther—unless it were taken as a promise to pay, and that at no very distant date.

10. If there be no intention to gratify the expectations which would thus be raised, it is to be considered whether the present advantage would not be outweighed by the evils of the prospective disappointment: whether by what you now give you do not greatly increase the means in the opponent's hand of extorting what you would then refuse.

11. By reaffirming the principle of a State education for the Roman Catholic priesthood, you bring into more powerful relief the anomaly of the absence of a State provision for them and you tend to precipitate some measure of that kind.

12. But what is it to be? Will Parliament or the country agree to the support of two State Churches throughout Ireland upon the scale of the present Established and Roman Churches? Will not the impetus communicated to the question discharge itself upon the existing Church of Ireland, and if the desire for an endowment of the Roman Catholic priesthood is to be satisfied will it not be satisfied by the abstraction of her revenues?

13. Does not every new act, or rather does not the first direct, unequivocal, spontaneous act of the Imperial Parliament in the nature of endowment to the Roman Catholic Church in Ireland, very greatly weaken both logically and morally the argument for maintaining the Church of Ireland?

14. If I am wellfounded in thinking that under the circumstances of the present day there will *either* be no parochial provision for the Roman Catholic priesthood, or it will be one supplied from the revenues of the Church of Ireland—if it be admitted that the latter alternative is by all means to be averted, and if it be also true that the call for such a provision will grow more imperative in consequence of any extension of the grant to Maynooth—is not such an extension upon this ground highly dangerous?

15. If it be thought that such a provision is practicable in some other way, let the obstacles be considered,

(1) In the feelings of all Scotland—
   of English Churchmen generally—
   of English Dissenters generally—
   of Irish Protestants—
   of the Irish Roman Catholic clergy—
   on the ground of religion.
(2) In the power of the voluntary principle.
(3) In the reluctance to a new and heavy public charge.
(4) In the difficulty of adjusting the stipends so as to make the priest what is termed independent without raising him to a preference above the Presbyterian minister.
(5) In the evident fact that the stipend will not give the State any controul.
(6) In the extreme unlikelihood that the Roman Catholic priesthood will be contented to remain a salaried but inferior body—by the side of a hostile National Church.           *February 11. 1844.*

These my reflections of Sunday night were nearly all brought out yesterday in the Cabinet. I began by observing that perhaps I was scarcely a fair judge of the particular arguments of policy respecting an increase of the grant because I had to a great extent pledged myself in the face of the public (meaning, by my book) against any such increase: that if my views of it were changed, of course it would be my duty to avow the change: but that such was not the fact—and then came out piecemeal the objections noted down above.

Mr. Goulburn alone spoke in the same sense. When Sir R. Peel said, 'Look ahead, in the government of Ireland', he replied, 'Look ahead on both sides and consider the feeling of this country.' When Lord Stanley (I think) said we were committed to the principle as much by the annual vote as by an increase of it, he referred to our annual vote for Protestant Dissenting Ministers in Ireland and asked if we were therefore prepared on principle to entertain a general provision of that kind?

The argument was on the other side that the college as now constituted was admitted to do mischief—that therefore it was a fit subject for inquiry whether its working might not be improved—that literary instruction and thereby refinement might be added—a higher class of teachers secured, the feelings of the priesthood mitigated. I held that no improvement except in secondary respects could be introduced, that the real *gravamen* of the charges against Maynooth after all was this, that the pupils partook of the feelings of their countrymen, and that they were educated according to the discipline of their Church—that inquiry was all very well for those who believed that improvement might result from it but I was not one of them.

When I spoke of the effect this measure would have in precipitating the demand for the payment of the Roman Catholic clergy, Lord Aberdeen said it would certainly be a step to it (which Lord Wharncliffe had negatived) and Sir R. Peel agreed in the opinion that we had passed the day for making such a payment out of the public funds and that if ever made it would be out of the revenues of the Church of Ireland.

The Duke said—'We cannot withdraw it, that is impossible: and I think we must try to amend it—the mode of doing so is difficult to determine.'

Sir Robert Peel and Lord Wharncliffe observed that it was not necessary to make a declaration upon the subject in the approaching debate —but Lord Stanley and Sir James Graham pointed out I thought with truth and force that *now*, with the triumphant verdict in the hands of Government, was the time to explain as fully as possible the policy to be pursued.

I have named the part taken by some. The Duke of Buccleuch was absent. Hardinge and Knatchbull took no part in the conversation— Lord Aberdeen made only the observation I have reported—the rest went with the proposition, on which I fear that Peel's mind is set.

They deluded themselves I thought with visionary hopes of improvement, of controul, of conciliation, all of which by the means proposed are entirely beyond reasonable expectation. This is purchasing peace by the hour. There may be times when that is imperative: but it never can be imperative upon those persons who believe that it involves a sacrifice of the future to the present and barters gold for brass, even though that gold be tarnished.

The decision was postponed to the morrow. A discussion followed on the far easier question of removing the restraints upon private endowment. A memorandum stating the two subjects by Sir James Graham, went round in the evening—in which the Maynooth question was thus stated, whether an inquiry by committees or commission might be promised into Maynooth, with a view of improving the education given and the condition of the inmates, and of rendering the establishment, or the provision, more adequate to the needs of the Roman Catholic population of Ireland.                    *February 13. 1844.*

13 February. 1844.

Today after going over the other points expected to be raised in the Irish debate, the Cabinet returned to that of Maynooth: an inquiry to be conceived and described in the manner to which I have adverted.

The first point raised was whether the inquiry should be by committees of Parliament or by Royal Commission. Every one seemed to prefer the latter: in which I concurred: at the same time Sir R. Peel observed, 'The principle of the measure, to which Goulburn and Gladstone objected, remained the same.'

Then finding that no one spoke—I said I agreed in the opinion that a commission was preferable to committees—that I further felt the force of the arguments used by Sir James Graham and Lord Stanley in favour of an immediate declaration of the policy to be pursued in all its material particulars—that I had, however, stated my difficulties yesterday as to concurrence in such a measure and that they were insuperable.

Sir James Graham then said that such being the case he would at once advise that entire silence should be observed as to any idea of change in the Maynooth grant during this debate. Lord Wharncliffe joined him and Sir Robert Peel said that nothing could be so fatal as any division in the Government at the present juncture.

I said it grieved me beyond any thing to place any thing relating to myself personally in the way of the measures of the Government: that, however, no men would more readily own, none had more emphatically taught both by their words and their actions that considerations of character were not on any account to be set aside—that only a great and decisive change of sentiments could justify my participating in such an act, and that no such change had taken place.

There was at this time a break up: and I expressed to Graham, who stood by himself, a doubt whether their decision was the best: I said that their silence would be noticed—and would be ascribed to a division of opinion—that being once perceived, the Government would be pressed upon it and the disclosure of it would by force be hurried on—while they would lose the advantage attaching to a spontaneous declaration. He said no, he felt the loss, but was confident the decision was wise.

*February 13. 1844. 4 p.m.*

## 152: ADD.MS 44777, ff. 127–128

On Sunday, February 18 [1844] Sir R. Peel sent round a memorandum relating to the debate in progress concerning Ireland and proposed for consideration but as he said for consideration only the following points:

1. The possibility of abolishing ministers' money.
2. Of extending Trinity College Dublin for the Roman Catholics.
3. Of establishing provincial academies for the Roman Catholics.
4. Of reducing capitular establishments in Ireland on the principles of the late reduction in England.
5. Of enlarging the municipal franchise.

On Monday, February 19, a Cabinet was held to consider these matters.

On (1) Lord Ripon proposed that it should be done and that a number of the episcopal advowsons should be sold and the money applied to form a fund to supply the place of ministers' money and for other Church purposes.

But it was observed that the surrender of the ministers' money would involve the principle of the abandonment of Church property—and it would also be open to the objection that it was a waste of a public fund which on the principles of those opposite ought to be carefully reserved for application to public purposes. Sir R. Peel on these grounds abandoned the idea though very anxious to get rid of the conflict into which the Church is brought with occupiers in towns by this fund.

The second was rather lightly passed over as likely to be opposed by the Church and university authorities. It appeared to me possible that under this head something might have been done.

The fourth was likewise passed over as likely to open insurmountable difficulties in carrying new Irish Church legislation through Parliament.

On the third Sir R. Peel chiefly dwelt—he read a letter from Lord Stanley advising that the Government should endeavour to meet the Roman Catholics on the ground of education by making a provision for training their youth both those intended for orders and others in their religion. The terms of Sir R. Peel's memorandum had not gone quite so far—and bearing them in mind I said, is it meant that some system analogous to the system of national education in Ireland should be applied to higher classes and to pupils of more advanced age? Sir J. Graham replied that the proposal meant more than that—it meant a

Roman Catholic education both for the intending priests and others—
and that the question now to be decided was whether in principle there
was any objection on the part of the Cabinet to such a scheme? Sir R.
Peel suggested that he might in debate state to the House 'that there
was no disposition to exclude the consideration of any scheme for extending the means of education in Ireland upon such principles as to
make it accessible to Roman Catholics without any violation of their
principles'. I assented to this—but declared myself not prepared to
assent to Sir James Graham's exposition of the proposal and expressed a
hope that that question need not *now* be decided. (And I must say that
Sir R. Peel in his speech kept *within* the terms he had indicated.) The
burden of obstruction seemed to lie on me alone: which cannot long
endure. Sir R. Peel in leaving the room said, 'Depend upon it, the attack upon the Church of Ireland *can only be staved off by liberal concession*'.

February 27. 1844.

## 153: ADD.MS 44777, ff. 129–130

Last night I read another memorandum of Sir R. Peel's now in circulation, representing the necessity of an immediate consideration of the
measures to be adopted for Ireland, as to the franchise, parliamentary
and municipal, as to facilitating voluntary endowments, and as to
education: in which last in point of fact lies the soul of the whole proposal.

He advises that a commission should be appointed in a spirit friendly
not to Maynooth but to carrying out the principle recognised by the
original establishment of Maynooth—which is to consider what means
of academical education it may be practicable to afford to the Irish
Roman Catholics, and whether to pupils intended for orders in conjunction with other classes of pupils or not: and other kindred matters.

After what passed in the last Cabinets, I regard this memorandum as
a conclusive proof of Sir Robert Peel's conviction that he must make,
and must now make the attempt at furnishing upon a liberal scale from
the funds of the State for the Roman Catholics of Ireland, clerical and
lay, the means of education in the principles of their religion and I have
to consider as God shall enable me the very serious question not whether
I shall assume or avoid responsibility but whether I shall choose on the
one hand the responsibility of participating in that endeavour, or on the
other hand by retiring of giving a signal for disunion, suspicion, and

even conflict in that political party by which alone as I firmly believe the religious institutions and laws of the country are under God maintained.

But I see in this endeavour:

1. No rational hope of conciliating the Roman Catholic body in Ireland.
2. Nor of altering the character of the Irish Roman Catholic priesthood for the better.
3. A further declension in the religious character of the State of these realms, and a great stride in advance as respects the recognition of separatism.
4. An acknowledgment of the Roman Catholic priesthood as the instructors of the Irish people, which will certainly strengthen, and probably accelerate the demand for making over to them the funds destined for that instruction, namely the Church property of that country: and will morally weaken in a very great degree the position which it is a principal object of the Government to defend.

After what I have written and published on these subjects, I incline to think, that even if I wavered in my judgment, nay even if I inclined to the contrary side, it might be no more than a just tribute to public character and consistency that I should retire and leave the opportunity to others less committed, or even give them an independent support—but without relying absolutely and solely on any abstract principle, I must say that my mind is not changed, and unless the time yet remaining before decision shall change it, the path of duty, at least as to one first and material step, for me is clear.     *February 29. 1844.*

## 154: ADD.MS 44777, ff. 165–166

Seeing Sir R. Peel go homewards this evening I plucked up courage and asked to walk with him. Presuming that in tomorrow's Cabinet he would discuss the subject of education for the Roman Catholic clergy and laity of Ireland I represented to him whether it might not be wise before issuing a commission on the subject to make some private inquiry e.g. into the rules of discipline with respect to the separate education of candidates for the priesthood—into the disposition of the Roman Catholic bishops to make terms or admit controul—to consider how far Dr. Murray could speak for the rest—or how far the relations of the rest to the Pope with whom we have no relations might preclude them from entering into an unconditional engagement: which their canonical obedience might override, while the Pope has no relations with us and can give us no guarantee by which he could be held. Also into the French quarrel about education. I said perhaps I was led to this suggestion by a personal interest, but still it occurred to me that before taking so great a step such a preliminary might be requisite, particularly as he proposed to modify and soften the tone of the priesthood by his measure—of which I certainly despaired.

He replied, what are we to say to Mr. Wyse's motion on Thursday week? That we had not now time—that we could not remain as we were—that it might be sufficient to announce that the Government were inquiring into these matters specifically, but that would raise perhaps greater expectations than a commission. *March 1. 1844.*

## 155: ADD.MS 44777, ff. 131–136

This afternoon I went to Sir R. Peel before Cabinet and stated to him verbally, after having looked at the terms of Mr. Wyse's motion, such an answer as it had appeared to me might be given to it.

I likewise stated that I felt it was one question whether I should vote for or against a plan of Roman Catholic education in Ireland—that I felt there were difficulties attending it which I had not been able to surmount, but that it would be my duty to take advantage of all the time that might elapse before the actual proposal of such a plan in order to form and mature my judgment upon it—that I felt, however, adverting to my previous pledges upon the subject, it to be a plan which I could not support as a person holding office.

He said once, what are the words you have used which you consider to pledge you? no one would remember them—but I must in justice add I think this fell from him through inadvertence—it was not the staple of his argument and indeed he never recurred to it. He spoke of the anomaly of the Church—of its revenues nearer £700,000 than £500,000—of their unequal distribution—of the impossibility of governing Ireland without breaking up the Roman Catholic combination for Repeal, of maintaining the law, of looking foreign powers in the face—of the effect that a secession from the Government on religious grounds would produce in raising a clamour, depriving the Government of the support of the Protestants in Ireland, and leaving it open to the attacks of its opponents whom it could not offer enough to conciliate—of the heavy sacrifice entailed by office, of his own fixed intention on his resignation, come when it might, to retire from public life, of his belief that the breaking up of the Government would be followed by the accession of a very democratic Ministry—but that nevertheless it would be a question for consideration whether in the event of a secession from it on this question such a dissolution ought not to take place. He also argued, but indecisively, that others might like me consider themselves committed, e.g. Lord Stanley against the reconsideration of the parliamentary franchise.

He requested me to put down on paper words expressing the extent to which I was prepared to go in meeting Wyse's motion—agreeing that it would on many accounts be advisable to proceed by the ordinary official means in any necessary inquiries, rather than by a commission.

Accordingly I wrote hurriedly the memorandum of this day marked Secret.[1]

He received and treated me with the utmost frankness and kindness.

At 3.30 I went to Cabinet where Sir R. Peel stated his view and mentioned that I saw great difficulties in a pledge on the part of the Government to take up the question of education in the Roman Catholic religion in Ireland.

Different members of the Cabinet entered into conversation upon the questions whether the education should be jointly lay and clerical or separate, and the like.

At length I said it was incumbent upon me to state that I had obstacles in my way anterior to any such inquiry as to the mode of working out the plan. I stated in some detail—encouraged to do so by them—my leading objections—for instance, that they would not break up the Roman Catholic combination nor sensibly diminish its force, though they might soften an individual here and there.

That the concession would not be regarded as one of grace and favour longer than while the arrangements were in course of being made—any plan to claim that character must I thought be much more extensive.

That the Government would fail in obtaining an effectual controul over the Roman Catholic priesthood and in mitigating its character.

That these measures would destroy much of the argument, both in reason and in feeling, that still remained for maintaining the Church of

---

[1] No. 156.

Ireland, and that although they would obtain a temporary relief yet at the end of a short term they would find themselves in a far weaker position than at present.

That they would greatly damage the general principle on which the Church is maintained in England, though their effects here might not be powerfully felt at once.

That they would give a great shock to the feeling of the country and to its confidence.

That feeling what difficulty and what responsibility lay on every side I had suggested previous inquiries, without any preliminary public pledge to take up the Roman Catholic education afresh, which I admitted would as an expedient only gain time but which I contended was the best mode of proceeding with reference to the end in view. That if they meant to have any arrangements on which they could depend they must begin by treating with the Pope, from whom, without having some relations with him, they could have no guarantees: and of course no subordinate persons could afford them on his part. Lord Aberdeen strongly concurred: and Sir R. Peel and Sir J. Graham much inclined to the view that this as an argument was sound.

That I was aware the most insignificant name might in critical times acquire an importance by allying itself with a public or party feeling— but that I believed there were reasons which would prevent this evil from accruing in my case, at least in the usual degree.

That if I retired from the Government on the announcement which was then proposed that it should be declared they were engaged in inquiry with a view to improvement and extension of Roman Catholic (specific) education in Ireland, it would not be as pledging myself to oppose such a plan but it would be with the intimation that considering the pledges I had given to the public, even without reference to the objections which still appeared to me to apply, it was my duty to reserve to myself a free and unfettered judgment, as an independent Member of Parliament upon any such proposal.

The Chancellor said that the effect would be to create an extreme party, and to leave the Government without friends in Ireland. Lord Wharncliffe said that an extreme High Church Protestant party would be organised. Graham that the result of a popular clamour and of a combination must follow whatever my intentions might be. Peel referred to his wish in 1829 to quit office and to support the Duke in carrying emancipation as an independent Member of Parliament: I said I was not so blind as to believe that the two positions were at all similar. The Duke of Buccleuch said he had very strong Protestant feelings but that after careful attention he had no scruple in adopting Sir Robert Peel's proposal.

But I must say no attempt was made in any manner to deceive me. Peel said he would be satisfied with the declaration of my memorandum —but that immediately after making it the Government would be pressed and forced to say whether they did or did not adopt the principle of taking up afresh (i.e. as contradistinguished from the bare continuance of the Maynooth grant) the education of Roman Catholics in the doctrines of their own religion. I suggested that it was hardly fair to exact such a declaration of principle in the abstract before the circumstances had been investigated on which the possibility of its application would depend.

Sir J. Graham and Lord Stanley observed that it was above all things essential that the Cabinet should be agreed upon the meaning of the terms which might be used and should not hold out any expectations except such as they were prepared to realise. To this all emphatically assented. And when I intimated that I was ready to acquiesce in any declaration which would not pledge me in honour as a member of the Government to adopt what I plainly saw would be the certain result of the inquiry, namely a fresh adoption and extension of the system of education in the Roman Catholic religion—no one in the faintest manner intimated that any such declaration as they contemplated would leave me free thereafter to recede.

The pressure was heavy upon me but I was not afflicted with the temptation which arises when the forms of right and wrong are studiously veiled—and the conviction still remained clear before me, that according to such light as I now have, the proposed measure is either too little or too much, and that if it be done it should be done by those who have long approved and advised it: that I ought to make no premature decision upon it, but to place myself in a position where my judgment would be free and where my pledges might be either maintained or retracted with honour, and for this purpose not to be a party to the introduction of the measure.

I left the Cabinet at half past five thinking they would like to talk the matter over in my absence: and they all remained apparently with the purpose of doing so.                                        *March 2. 1844.*
*Deus adjuvet.*

241

## 156: ADD.MS 44777, ff. 161–162

Secret[1].

That the motion of Mr. Wyse as it stands in the Order Book, would without inquiry pledge the House and the Crown at once to provide for the Roman Catholics (and by implication for the Roman Catholics only) of Ireland an university education, in such a manner as to involve either fundamental alterations in the constitution of the University of Dublin, or else the foundation of a new university, equal not only in honour and privilege, but in endowments: for although it speaks of 'other means' as an alternative, it is hardly to be conceived that any means less extensive or materially different would correspond with the spirit of the Address.

That without raising any argument as to the principles implied in it, and even in the view of those most favourable to them, the House is manifestly not at the present moment in a condition to entertain such a proposition.

That Sir Robert Peel has already declared, in his speech on the 23rd ult., that he should be sorry 'to exclude the consideration of the means of providing some system of academical education for a higher class than those educated in the National Schools, but for the present', as he added, 'the Government intended to give an increased vote, to a considerable extent, for the purpose of national education', and he also made a favourable intimation with regard to instruction in agriculture.

That it may be again announced, that the Government is directing its attention to the important inquiry how, and to what extent, public aid may advisedly be given to education in Ireland, so as to meet the wants of persons of higher classes and likewise of more advanced ages, than those for whom the National Schools provide, and so as to be accessible to Roman Catholics without infringement of their principles.

And that with respect to the provision for the purposes of instruction during the time that the Government is thus maturing its views, it has been already declared that the vote for National Education will be increased: and it is not intended to propose any other alteration.

*March 2. 1844.*

---

[1] I have a few matters to look to in my office, but I hope to follow in a quarter of an hour. WEG. [Pencil note at the head of the document].

## 157: ADD.MS 44777, ff. 137-138

I reviewed the memorandum of Saturday[1] (March 2?) this morning and interpolated a little—although much more took place I think it presents a fair view.

I may add—at my interview Sir R. Peel spoke of the readiness of opponents to accept conciliatory measures and of the opportunity now offered of breaking up the Repeal forces and the combination against the Church: also of the sentiment of the Conservative party that a new course should be taken with respect to Ireland.

I said it had not appeared to me that such was the attitude of either party. That I could conceive possible means of acting upon the Repeal combination but not compatibly with the maintenance of the Church.

Lord Stanley in Cabinet said he in his colonial business found by experience that there was a great need of an arrangement with the Papal see.

Some one asked how I could vote for the National Schools grant. I replied that without inquiring whether it were good in itself, it was clearly something wholly different in principle from the adoption of the Roman Catholic religion as the matter of education—because the profession of its conductors had been throughout that it was to be a joint education in common truths—and that points of difference were to be left to be dealt with apart. Lord Ripon noticed that he believed many of the schools were virtually Roman Catholic schools, and that many of the Protestants of Ireland had petitioned to have separate grants for specific teaching by each communion, instead of the present system. I said true—and that was one of my reasons for believing that there would not be so great a shock as some appeared to think: at the same time I believed that confidence would be shaken in this country, secession or no secession.

In the evening I wrote to Lord Stanley asking for a conversation in the hope of showing him by a more free personal exposition than I could decently give in Cabinet that my retirement would not entail such consequences as had seemed to be anticipated, and meaning to test that opinion by shaping out the probable course of circumstances.

*March 4. 1844.*

---

[1] No. 155.

## 158: ADD.MS 44777, ff. 139–148

On Monday evening [4 March 1844] Lord Stanley gave me two hours' conversation in Sir W. Gosset's room at the House of Commons on the subject of our difficulty in the Cabinet. It was at my request, but he took the offensive, and began by representing to me the extreme seriousness of the occasion: that Ireland could not be governed without concessions to the Roman Catholic religion, nor England by any other government than the present one—if the former fact stood alone the Ministry might change and then all would be straightforward—but taking the two together he could see nothing ahead if there were a break up on this question but a civil war. He stated to me that in his opinion my position in the House and the party and in the Cabinet would render his remark applicable with force to my secession, but that any secession under such circumstances from the Cabinet would go far to produce the consequences he apprehended. For his own part he vehemently disliked office, public business, and the House, to which his whole time and powers were dedicated and personally therefore such results would be a relief to him but in a public view he could not exaggerate the danger.

I said I was in the hope of being able to show that although the measures proposed would in any event have a formidable effect upon public feeling in England yet my retirement need not make any considerable addition to that effect. That a very feeble name joined to a cause in which strong feelings were enlisted might indeed as we saw by common experience in Parliament cause a formidable excitement—but that in the first place if I were to retire I should found the act mainly on the pledges I had given to the public and on their rendering it my imperative duty, not indeed at once to resolve on opposing the measure, but to refrain from supporting it as an official person and to reserve to myself the power of exercising an impartial judgment upon it. That in retiring it would be my study to avoid simply giving any factitious importance to the occasion nor should I be at all averse, if I found objections did not exist in other quarters, to say things for the precise purpose of disqualifying myself from becoming an instrument for facilitating a combination to oppose the Government, for example I should have no scruple in urging them to take measures forthwith for the reestablishment of relations with the Pope: firstly because that measure is demanded by the present circumstances irrespective of the new scheme—by his temporal sovereignty—by the number of our Roman Catholic fellow subjects—by the more direct relations subsisting in almost all the colonies—by the qualified relations subsisting in Ireland: but that especially it is essential in order to render the measures contemplated in Ireland so much as rational, and to give them a *hope* of success—for if arrangements are to be made you must know with whom they are to be made, and must go not to sergeants and corporals but to the colonel in order to deal effectually with the regiment.

He seemed to agree in the reasonableness of this measure and to be gratified when I told him that I should not object to being a party to it, not viewing it as introductory to the intended scheme but on the ground of its necessity with reference to our actual position and allowing the other subject to stand over: while further it was my opinion that *if* they contemplated such a plan this was a proper and indispensable preliminary.

I assured him that I was not riding the hobby of any abstract principle—that if I could believe the scheme afforded a better hope of maintaining the Church of Ireland I admitted the argument would bear difficulty—that as to the abstract principle of a religious character in the State I viewed and always had viewed it as an ingredient of great value in its composition, to which it was desirable to adhere as long as possible, but by no means as one for which the existence of a State ought to be perilled, because the lower ends of a State ought to be fulfilled even when its higher ones should have become impracticable: although again a question might arise as to the *persons* by whom the abandonment ought to be made.

I besought him to imagine the Government in the predicament of being solicited to surrender some portion of the property of the Irish Church, and to that end plied with all the arguments now used against it, and with the plea that it would conciliate the Roman body and place them in a condition of greater comfort and respectability—I know that in such a position they would resolutely say 'No—if this be necessary we will retire—and let others do it—whatever be the risks and threatenings of the times we will not dishonour ourselves by the act—and we think that the surrender of a small part instead of securing the rest would infallibly accelerate its destruction.' Such as the position of the Government would be in that predicament, such was very much my own with reference to the present scheme—the leaning of my mind was to perceive in it an almost entire surrender of the means both in point of argument and of feeling by which the Irish Church is maintained. I

245

asked myself again and again *how* after these measures were completely launched and the Church battle was again to be fought, it could possibly be undertaken by the Government? Nothing but reference to their own sheer *will*, to the promises of the opponents and to Acts of Parliament would remain—they would have emphatically recognised the Roman Catholic priesthood as the instructors of the mass of the people and would have taken into their own hands the provision of means for their training upon that very ground, and how then would it be possible in argument to resist the question if they be by the confession of your own acts the instructors of the people why they are not in possession of the national property by which that purpose of instruction was intended to be fulfilled? I must say I do not think he was without a misgiving upon this important head.

He said, do you think it possible looking to the state of the House of Commons, of Ireland, and of the Church of Ireland to say we will take our stand upon civil equality and we will do nothing, absolutely nothing, for the Roman Catholic religion professed by the mass of the people, and yet to hope to maintain the Irish Church and the Union?

I said, I am very doubtful about that—but my feeling is that upon any other footing there is no doubt at all about the matter and that the Irish Church certainly cannot be maintained—that if it is to be upheld as is intended by the Government it must be by men refusing to endow the Roman Catholic religion though giving a full and liberal interpretation in every respect to the doctrine of civil equality—that I *could* conceive the scheme of surrendering the Church—of saying we recognise the principle of the popular will—we allow the property to be made over for the support of the religion of the great majority—we place the Roman Catholic priesthood in the situation of our national clergy for Ireland—there would still remain tremendous, perhaps insuperable difficulties even within Ireland itself in the existence of a Protestant proprietary aristocracy— but still if the experiment really were to be tried of placing that great *actual* power which wields the popular forces in Ireland on the side of the Government and of the Union, this it seemed to me was the form in which to do it full justice it must be tried: and such a trial I trusted never would be made through the agency of the present Ministers but by those who could do it with the claim of sincerity and the grace of consistency.

At one time he mooted the question whether under certain circumstances he himself might not as a choice of evils consent to be an agent in stripping the Church of Ireland—if he said it were in his conscience clear that such a measure was indispensable for higher (he evidently meant more *necessary* though lower) ends—he would not say—he might not be able to look the question in the face—but he expressed a sort of half hope that under such extremity, for the purpose of saving worse alternatives, he might so act.

I replied to him, even if it be so yet how different is your position from mine—you have made proof of your fidelity—and have already arrested by a decisive and welltimed act the course of spoliation—you are like an old general that can in the view of the world well afford to refuse to fight a duel: I am one whose courage never has been tried—I have no position, no rank or stake of property in the country—the public may very fairly regard me as a mere adventurer, if I should part company with character—and I have never had the opportunity of demonstrating that: I came into Parliament while my party was in opposition, came with it into place, and have quietly remained there with it—it is not therefore that I should be suspected, but I should be fairly and reasonably suspected—the solemnly recorded, systematically explained pledges I have given would cover me with disgrace—nay my disgrace would even impart itself to the Government of which I acted as a member and instead of strengthening I should weaken it.

*Thursday, March 7.* [*1844*].

In that same conversation near the commencement I apprised Lord Stanley that if I were obliged at the moment to make up my mind absolutely on the contemplated measures, it would be to the judgment that they were calculated to destroy not to assist in preserving the Church of Ireland—that, however, it was my duty not to precipitate that judgment—that one so circumstanced was not in a condition to join in the proposal—but that in any event, whatever my own final view might be I should regard the organisation of any opposition to the Government on such a ground as one of the greatest public misfortunes —that it would be my absolute duty to avoid participating in it and to do whatever might lie in my power to prevent it, the general character and spirit of the Government remaining the same. Consequently that I should be most anxious to avoid, if it could be done without dishonour, taking a part individually in Parliament against: and that unless I found it would have the character of a cowardly and unworthy act my desire would be to retire from Parliament in order to obviate any risk

247

which there might otherwise be that my separation might act like the spark falling upon combustible materials.

Lord Stanley seemed to be inclined to argue that I could not possibly retire and yet continue to have confidence in the Government and likewise deprecate resistance to the measure which I should by the supposition have chosen to retire rather than support—but I put it to him whether it *was* really a duty in every case *either* to remain and support or to retire and oppose—and whether there might not be circumstances in which it would be right to resign rather than support, and yet having resigned not to resist. And I think he admitted that there might be such cases.

With regard to my pledges I explained to him that I had in my book first in 1838 and then again rewritten in 1841 not three years ago argued for the maintenance of the Irish Church on the religious ground and on the ground that if maintained at all it should be exclusively maintained, and if not exclusively maintained not maintained at all—that I had dealt with the case of Maynooth as one of *quasi* compact and that I did not admit the argument from the practice in the colonies to the case of the mother country. That in my cool and deliberate opinion the sentiments were such and so stated that if I now were to be a party as a member of the Government to proposing a project for taking up afresh and reconstructing by the hands and means of the State the education of the Roman Catholic priesthood, or of the laity in the Roman Catholic religion I should give the world a *right* to point to me and to say 'that man is not to be trusted—after his having written *thus*, and now acting *thus*, no words will bind him'. This I think Lord Stanley was much inclined to allow. He said, 'No doubt you are in a position of great difficulty—you will require to have great moral courage in your decision, whichever way you may decide—and I have no doubt you will pursue a very honourable and highminded course.'

He said, 'At the commencement speaking quite unreservedly I may state that we got Peel to make a very strong declaration about the Church in Ireland—a stronger one I think than he would otherwise have made'—unless, as I understood, it had been concerted among them that a plan of Roman Catholic education should be proposed.

Much more was said but I have given the essence. Next day I had a short conversation of the same kind with Mr. Goulburn: and dwelt strongly on the reestablishment of relations with Rome as in any case the right mode of proceeding: in which he seemed to be disposed to agree.

I must, however, add one more point: I acquainted Lord Stanley that in my view my own position was quite different from that of every other member of the Government—that none of them so far as I knew had given pledges like mine—that with respect to himself and Sir J. Graham for example I did not think any one could even be justly surprised at such a measure's proceeding from them—and that I knew nothing of any other member of the Government which as it seemed to me would render it dishonourable to participate in such a proposition.

I also begged him to believe that in what I said generally but especially with regard to future opposition to the Government I did not speak hastily but most deliberately and should not be sorry if every word I had spoken were taken down.

I also expressed the opinion that although their *act* would shake and weaken confidence there was no one in the House of Commons who could organise a party within the Conservative party against them on the ground of it but I allowed that if there were any person able and disposed to do so it would in itself be practicable as there would be sufficient materials. *March 12. 1844.*

## 159: ADD.MS 44777, ff. 149–150

In the conversation on Monday week (4th March) with Lord Stanley of which I have already made a memorandum, the following observations were also made and I now record them.

1. In speaking of the reestablishment of relations with Rome, I stated that it was right I should freely avow that without entertaining any sanguine or visionary views of reunion I did think the effect in a religious view of making England and the Church of England better known in Italy would be good as it would tend to the mitigation of hostile feeling and of exaggerated opinion.

2. I stated that I had not a thought to reserve and wished to make known the whole subject as it stood in my own mind.

3. Also that I was not afraid of any clamour affecting reputation except such as I felt to be founded in justice.

Cabinet. March 16. [1844].

Discussion whether thanks should be voted to Sir Hugh Gough. The Duke stated he had looked into the particulars of the action of Maharajpoor and that it appeared to him there was no ground for impeaching the conduct of the General. Notice had been given by Sir J. Hobhouse to Baring that the motion would be opposed. Sir R. Peel who had seemed on other grounds indisposed observed that such an intimation ought not to affect the decision of the Government. On the Duke's authority it was decided that unless new information unfavourable to Sir Hugh should arrive thanks should be proposed.

The probable defeat of Government on the Factory Bill was also discussed: and whether if the ten hours were carried Government should adopt that provision or drop the Bill. The alternative of Government's resigning was mentioned but not entertained: so also of Sir James Graham's resigning. He stated that *he* could not adopt the ten hours if it should be affirmed by a majority. Lord Wharncliffe, Lord Aberdeen, and Goulburn appeared to lean the other way. Peel was decided against adopting it—I think rightly. But he does not in this, nor in the Corn Law endeavour 'to stave off by liberal concession' the extreme alternative as in the case of the Irish Church. On the contrary he altogether repudiated the idea of adopting the eleven hours plan as a mere 'confession of weakness'. This is remarkable and worthy of reflection.

There was much interesting conversation on the very powerful bearing which the adoption of the ten hours would have upon the Corn Law: Graham said he did not think the latter would survive it twelve months. Also on the progress of the anti-Corn Law feeling in the House of Commons: the cowed and timid temper of the majority, as shown by the backwardness of the country gentlemen in debate, and by the altered and declining tone of anti-Corn Law speeches, Peel observing that there was no sign so sure of the progress of a cause as when the speech made against it two or three years ago could not be made and was not made now—and that he wished a deputation of Lords could always be present during the debates in the Commons for he believed it impossible for that House in any other way to know the movement of public opinion.

*March 16 and 19. 1844.*

## 160: ADD.MS 44777, ff. 151-154

March 23. 1844.
Memoranda on the position of the Government after the divisions on
the Factory Bill.

1. Are the speeches of Milnes and John Manners, or even of Inglis, fair
indications of the spirit of the party at large in Parliament?
2. If it be said, the party did not disown them—is it not to be recollected,
that the party is a silent party—what reproaches for instance do the
county Members bear weekly from the League, affecting themselves,
without attempting defence?
3. Upon the whole, during the last two sessions, have they not borne
much with and for the Government?
4. Is not the unreasonable and highly inconvenient licence of private
judgment among them a necessary consequence of the fact that each one
of them stands in something of the same relation to his own constituents as that in which the Government stand to him? Is it separable
from our parliamentary constitution taken with the present tone of
thought and feeling in the country?
5. Postponing any question as to the honour of the Government—is it
at this moment the best thing upon the whole for the country

   (a) that an effort should be made to replace the twelve hours—twice
       very solemnly negatived;
   (b) that the bill should be dropped, subject to the chances of future
       agitation, or to being taken up by Ashley;
   (c) that the Government should resign, or
   (d) that the eleven hours should be accepted?

6. Especially or, at all events, if it be the sense of many of the leading
Members among the Conservative party who have voted against the
Government that eleven hours should be accepted as a permanent settlement—and if they declare their intention to take and treat and uphold
it as such, and not as an instalment?
7. Is not Ward's vote an indication, taken together with Sandon's, of a
sentiment, whether just or not, yet probably entertained by many on
both sides, that the Government can no longer resist and ought not
longer to resist some concession to the evident disposition of the House
of Commons?

8. Is the question upon which the Government are fighting a question of principle, or is it a question of degree and of general expediency?

9. Would the acceptance of the eleven hours be an impeachment of the character of the Government or of any member of it?

We have had two conversations today, one early and one before dinner 5.00—7.15—and have postponed until Monday the final decision. Peel was with the Queen in the interval and reported that she was thoroughly frank and kind—evidently contemplating the possible displacement of the Government with alarm—begging him to consider her position—and praising the conduct of Baring and Labouchere without expressly blaming Lord John Russell—also indignant at the late article in the *Times*.

At the Cabinet Peel, Graham, and Stanley were as in the morning strongly opposed to the acceptance of the eleven hours—all felt and spoke bitterly of the treatment of the Government by the party, Graham in particular who said there were matters of feeling in which feeling led us right without reference to reasoning and this he thought was one of them. He also spoke of the coming difficulties of the Government on Irish questions—'even on those respecting which the Cabinet was agreed'.

On being urged with the nature of our parliamentary constitution as the real cause of these difficulties he admitted that the question of the Duke of Wellington recurred with the utmost force—'How is the Queen's Government to be carried on?'

I argued in the sense of the queries which I have written out above. Lord Wharncliffe and Lord Aberdeen were of the same mind. The Chancellor and Goulburn I think doubtful. The Duke of Buccleuch seemed to lean to eleven hours. The rest took little part.

The Chancellor thought the Bill could not be dropped and the Government remain in office. So Lord Wharncliffe and so Graham but he was for abandoning both.

My seeing him so rigid upon this question of material interests is a lesson to me to be firm and cautious in an objection which I have taken and which has relation to principles of unchangeable truth.

Stanley and Goulburn thought the ground too narrow a one for resignation.

Graham read a letter from Mr. Horner reporting from all *his* sub-inspectors: the effect was that both masters and men generally would acquiesce with gladness in eleven hours.

I expressed my readiness cheerfully to acquiesce in what the Government might decide. But I confess that which appears to some to be firmness, to me and with my views of the temper and meaning of the party, seems obstinacy: and this ground on which they deem it a matter of honour not to yield an inch I think the fittest for compromise.

Mahon, Lord F. Egerton, Beckett, Sandon (by note) and others have stated to me last night and today their wish for eleven hours.

*March 23. 1844.*

## 161: ADD.MS 44777, ff. 155-158

This day the Cabinet met at eleven—all present but Knatchbull who was also absent on Saturday: it seems odd to go out of town for 48 hours when those 48 hours include a decision which may involve the fate of the Government.

Peel began by stating his strong opinion against compromise—it would weaken the authority of Government—would lead to further concessions—would purchase no more than momentary peace, and would diminish our strength for resistance.

After some loose discussion Lord Stanley spoke in the same sense. A pause: and then I said that while perfectly prepared to acquiesce with cheerfulness in their decision I was myself strongly in favour of the compromise: upon the combined grounds of:

1. The very extended disposition of the millowners to seek or at least to concur in and accept it—which Lord Stanley while denying its existence had stated to be a capital element in the question.

2. The opinions of the inspectors and their subordinate officers—appointed under auspices not too favourable to the philanthropic view of the question.

3. The votes of the House of Commons—a concession to which must be distinguished from a concession to the mere views of a section or party arranged out of doors.

4. The belief that a large proportion of our own friends would accept the eleven hours as a settlement—and would do all in their power to make it a settlement *bona fide*, so far as the subject matter allows the term to be applied—that I regarded this as essential, and fully admitted that for the Government to propose a mere instalment would be out of the question. Allowing also that if it were felt that honour

was pledged against the compromise that was conclusive: and observing that a great part of the commercial risk and detriment of the eleven hours plan might be obviated by the immediate repeal of the duties on the raw materials of cotton and wool, which must at all events be surrendered as soon as the state of the revenue would admit.

Lord Wharncliffe was the only person who spoke in the same sense. Duke of Buccleuch thought eleven hours might better be proposed some time hence than at this juncture. Goulburn saw difficulties both ways: (in the eleven hours that it might not prove a settlement) and gave no decisive judgment. Peel said he went much farther than the mass of the Cabinet seemed to do for he thought the interference wrong in itself and was not willing to add one tittle to what was already contained in the Bill. Lord Ripon and Lord Haddington expressed their assent to the refusal of the concession: and the rest were silent. It was agreed on all hands that the *mode* of proceeding would be to drop the present Bill and to propose to bring in another which should simply amend the existing law, without repealing and re-enacting which the present Bill does.

Going with Graham from the Drawing Room I asked him what he thought of the likelihood that our friends might feel themselves bound in honour to persevere—and that our adversaries would see before them such an opportunity as they could never have hoped for to take the Government and carry a short time Bill which should in itself supply them with a new and resistless argument against the Corn Laws. He thought this probable enough but seemed easy in mind.

His speech, however, in announcing the intentions of the Government was really the speech of an ultradoctrinarian, and when he had sat down I thought it right to go and say to him that it sounded to me fearfully strong—and nearly or quite as fatal to his own Bill as to the ten or eleven hours plan.                                    *March 25. 1844.*

What occurs to me in these discussions is that the Ministers are not in fact men of mere expediency as they are sometimes thought and called —that they act upon a strong, rigid, and jealous sense of honour, and they are perpetually dwelling on principle as apart from expediency: but my mind is differently turned as to the regions which I consider to belong to these words respectively. I find a fit subject matter for concession where they consider the question to be one of right and wrong: and vice versa—and I am bound to add I feel myself more lax as to the concession in Parliament of what I think principles, than they are of what they consider to be such.                                    *March 25.*

## 162: ADD.MS 44777, ff. 159–160

Another driblet from my conversation with Lord Stanley. In speaking of the necessity of maintaining regard to character, and that so as to be intelligible to the public, I put it strongly that what we have to rely on under God for the maintenance of the institutions of the country is the good sense and firmness of the English people—but that in order to enable them to carry us through, it is absolutely necessary for them to know what they are dealing with and what they may depend on in the characters and professions of public men, as they must otherwise be utterly at fault.

Sir James Graham on this day week in a conversation on the Factory Bill early in the day expressed his extreme soreness at the proceedings and speeches on that subject: held strongly that there were indignities which could not be borne and seemed to intimate that they had been offered to him—and declared that he did not know for what purpose men continued in office if it were not in order to give effect to their own honest convictions regarding the interests of the country.

Alas, thought I, with what immense qualifications alone is that sentiment tenable in reference to present circumstances! and if so high a doctrine is to be maintained with respect to matters of trade and labour, what can be high enough for cases of spiritual concern and of eternal truth?

Not that it is desirable that there should be no qualifications: far from it: but they have now almost eaten out the whole heart and life of the principle which after all Sir James Graham meant to express, namely the principle of an individual conscience in governors, which is to actuate them in the work of governing.            *March 30. 1844.*

## 163: ADD.MS 44777, ff. 168–171

April 2/2. 1844.
Cabinet this day in consequence of an announcement from the Court of Directors, that it is their intention to exercise their power of recalling

Lord Ellenborough—although Lord Ripon had endeavoured to dissuade them from coming to such a resolution.

Lord Ellenborough made a wholesale dismissal of the public officers of Sangor and in communicating it to the Court stated that he was governed in part by reasons which he could not communicate. They prepared a dispatch of sharp reprimand in return, of which Lord Ripon refused to sanction the severest part. What remained, however, still declared that they could not sanction proceedings a part of the reasons for which was to be withheld from them. To this Lord Ellenborough made an angry and offensive reply declaring that he would act upon his own conviction at all times, irrespective of their censure.

A memorandum of the Duke's was read which Peel called I thought justly a most wise and admirable paper, pointing out that Lord Ellenborough had been very wrong but that the Directors also would be very wrong to recall him: and that their proper mode of proceeding would be by procuring the administration of an adequate rebuke: if he should resent it and resign, the responsibility would lie with him.

Lord Ripon read an extract from a private letter of his to Lord Ellenborough, on the subject of the dispatch from the Court which he had castigated. In this he represented that he had expunged much, and had pushed them as far as he could, but that they would not withdraw from what remained.

I observed that this letter went to separate him and the Government in Lord Ellenborough's view from the Court, and to give it to be understood that he did not approve of what the Court had said.

He replied that he considered himself fully responsible for what remained and the more so because he had refused assent to other matter.

But Sir R. Peel asked whether Lord Ellenborough had received this private letter at the time when he answered the dispatch and on learning that he *had*, he observed that Lord Ellenborough must have been greatly encouraged by it in writing his insubordinate reply.

Sir R. Peel, however, very decidedly advised that the Government should deprecate the exercise of power indicated by the communication from the Court—should point out the great evils attending such a step—should refer to the present state of the army and of India compared with that in which Lord Ellenborough found them—and should entirely decline any participation in the responsibility of the measure even such as would by implication accrue if the offer of the Court to enter into preliminary communications upon the choice of a successor should be accepted. He expressed a very strong opinion that if this course were taken the Court of Directors would recede from the resolution which they had expressed.

Considering that it is announced as a formed resolution, often contemplated and only waived for very strong reasons, and at length adopted after full deliberation and experience, I can hardly think that the Directors will be so pliable, at least unless some unusual mode of conveying to them the views of the Government (as for instance by stating the Duke of Wellington's personal impressions) should be adopted.

Lord Ripon thinks the Directors will persevere.

Sir R. Peel advised him in writing to Lord Ellenborough to hold a firm tone and not to humour him, and said Lord Ellenborough's head was turned (as to all matters relating to his personal position, he appears to mean).

Gwalior treaties discussed and draft of dispatch approved.

## 164: ADD.MS 44777, ff. 172–175

On Monday [22 April 1844], Sir Robert Peel said to me,'I am much obliged by your memorandum[1]—I have perused it once and will read and consider it further.'

This leads me to think he 'sees daylight' in it— for he is so strict in the use of words that I do not think he ever would profess obligation for a paper in terms if it caused him dissatisfaction.

On Wednesday at the Duke of Wellington's it was declared that the Court of Directors had recalled Lord Ellenborough—and that unanimously. Peel spoke of the crisis as most serious; and asked how we could hope to find a fit man to go out as Governor-General if he was to receive his instructions from the Queen's Ministers and to have the apprehension of being dismissed for obeying them? He observed it would be the right course to solve the difficulty by applying to Parliament to abrogate the power of the Court to recall the Governor-General, if it were possible: but he did not think it would be possible to carry Lord Ellenborough through the House of Commons—and that the next best was steadily to maintain the tone which had been assumed, and to require to know whether the Court approved of the directions intended to be given to the successor, before concurring in the choice of one.

---

[1] ADD.MS 40470, ff. 201–211.

Today in Cabinet Lord Ripon had prepared a paper to be addressed by him to the Chairs but Peel had also prepared one being dissatisfied with Lord Ripon's as an argument upon the case which went to lower the Crown. His which was adopted with universal preference merely declared intentions and slapped the Court rather smartly.

The Duke was much excited and said in all his recollection of public life he never knew a transaction so outrageous, to pass between one set of gentlemen engaged in the service of the State, and another. He added that on Lord Ellenborough's withdrawal there would be insurrections all over India.

Nor was this from blind partisanship: for last summer when Lord Ellenborough sent home a most mischievous dispatch, the publication of which would have been enough to revolutionise India, the Duke was most indignant and said, 'He ought to have his nose rubbed in it'—and recently when Lord Ellenborough in a private letter contemptuously observed that the Court of Directors could not get rid of the parliamentary fiction of their authority over him, the Duke said with a vigorous gesture, 'That which he calls a parliamentary fiction, is *the law.*'

Peel observed that Lord Ellenborough with extraordinary powers had not the faculty of managing men and that　　　　　　(*Friday, April 26*) the great art of Government was to work by such instruments as the world supplies, controuling and overruling their humours: that it would be recorded as the great glory of the Duke of Marlborough and the Duke of Wellington that in the midst of such disadvantages, thwarted or ineffectively supported by others, they had achieved their victories.

A note of the Queen's was sent in circulation in which she expressed a strong sense of the ingratitude of the proceeding considering the change in the circumstances of India during Lord Ellenborough's government: and stated she should not be sorry if 'those gentlemen' (the Court of Directors) knew her mind.

Yesterday Sir R. Peel sent in a box to a part of the Cabinet a paper forming part of a confidential report from an agent of a great European Court respecting the position of the British Government with regard to Ireland. It was somewhat like the production of an English partisan; it spoke of intimate relations with 'the Catholic Bishop of London'. The representation was, that the Roman Catholic religion was making immense progress—Protestantism crumbling—the Government pledged to an extreme hostility to the wishes of the Irish people—and now incapable of recovering their confidence—Ireland certain of her triumph whether O'Connell be sentenced or not—Lord John Russell and the Whigs awaiting an early return to office—their return could not well be delayed beyond the commencement of the next session—but from the maladroit proceedings of the present Government it might be accelerated—a *ministère de fusion* impossible as Sir R. Peel was the only practical statesman of the present Government and there could be no place for him in the new one—the Irish Roman Catholic priesthood would have lost their power, unless they had placed themselves at the head of the Repeal movement—the tranquillity of the country would have been compromised—it was now secure even in the event of O'Connell's imprisonment—and the Roman Catholic priesthood were not (as he learned from Dr. Griffiths) hostile to the Crown—which, however, would be damaged by the failure of the Administration.

Sir R. Peel in a memorandum observed that this paper would at least serve to show what inferences must be expected to be drawn if Government should avow the intention of communicating on matters of religion with Rome.

But would not the same inference be drawn and yet more formidably in case of new Roman Catholic endowments *without* the reestablishment of intercourse with Rome? *April 29. [1844].*

## 165: ADD.MS 44777, ff. 184–185

On Tuesday [30 April 1844] in the week before last at the Cabinet Sir R. Peel said, 'Before six weeks are over the Crown and the Court of Directors will be committed before the country in a desperate struggle concerning the abrogation of the power of recall.' But on the Friday [3 May] of that week a perfectly amicable arrangement was made by Hardinge's appointment. In that choice Sir R. Peel showed his usual tact and sagacity: but I never was so much struck with exaggeration in him, as when he used the expression I have just cited and some foregoing ones with relation to the affair of Lord Ellenborough.

Today he announced in the Cabinet that he had offered the vacant seat to Lord Granville Somerset—to be held either with his present office or with the Secretaryship at War: and stated that Lord Granville Somerset had been very anxious to be in the Cabinet on the formation of the Government. He had preferred retaining his present office to taking Hardinge's—no wonder. Sir R. Peel went on to state that he had then offered Eliot Hardinge's office with a seat in the Cabinet—if he preferred that to remaining as he is. Eliot preferred the latter—stating that he thought he could be of more use in Ireland, and that he had great satisfaction in his relations with Peel and with Graham. Lastly he thought Fremantle was decidedly the person who had the best claims on the Government from service performed for the Secretaryship at War: and accordingly at a great personal sacrifice he had determined to offer it him: and Fremantle had accepted, behaving very well and declaring himself ready to continue where he was if it were thought better for the Government.

Lord G. Somerset affords I think a remarkable instance of a very good tempered and goodhumoured man with unconciliatory modes of proceeding in business: and I confess also that he seems to me scarcely a statesman, but that he has abundant talents for administration, and a mind quick in finding objections and consequently of great use in the department of intercepting what is crude and rash.

*May 16. Ascension Day.* [*1844*].

## 166: ADD.MS 44777, ff. 186–187

On Monday week [20 May 1844] I fell into conversation with Lord Stanley upon the dearth of young men of decided political promise on our side of the House, and on the other: always excepting Cardwell: and I said I thought there were others with capacity enough but the habits of business and the present mode of composing committees were not such as to afford them easy means of acquiring the necessary habits. He said to me, 'You are as certain to be Prime Minister as any man can be, if you live—the way is clear before you'—I said in reply that I could not dare to speculate on the future. I think too he can hardly have recollected our former conversation.

He spoke of the insubordination of the young men and said he did not think enough personal attention was paid them. I asked how it was possible for Sir R. Peel to do more than he now does—and said that he did the work of three or four already: Lord Stanley replied that he spent a great deal of time in waiting on the Queen and that he thought some might be saved with advantage for the purpose of paying such attentions: adding that he was speaking very confidentially.

On Thursday at Mahon's Lockhart told me, that he considered Newman to be the finest writer of the day. *Saturday, June 1. 1844.*

## 167: ADD.MS 44777, ff. 188–193

A Cabinet was held on Saturday [15 June 1844]. Sir Robert Peel stated the composition of the majority which had defeated us on Friday night —the character of the meeting at his house on Thursday, 'the most unsatisfactory meeting he had ever known'—adverted to the tone taken by the speakers in the debate—the resignation of Lord Melbourne in 1839 on a colonial question with a majority of five—the terms of the vote moved by him in 1841 which declared that the Government ought to withdraw from office in consequence of inability to carry their measures —the doctrine then held, that they ought to have retired on the sugar duties—the substantial resemblance of our position on that question— the impossibility of carrying on the public business in the House of Commons with any certainty or dispatch. He considered that it was too dangerous to try to obtain a reversal of the vote of Friday: and likewise that even if we succeeded the wound inflicted on the character of the House of Commons, after what had taken place respecting the Factory Bill, would be too severe: that we could not adopt the motion of Mr. Miles: and that we could not propose the renewal of the old sugar duties, the very course taken by Mr. Baring in 1841—he saw no other mode of proceeding open and on the whole thought there was nothing for it but resignation.

Stanley and Graham, who had been with him since the debate, concurred.

The Duke of Wellington said, 'G—, I am against quitting: I have seen the consequences of quitting before, and I say continue if you can.'

Lord Aberdeen wished that the defeat had been on the distinction between free and slave sugar which would have made the case a clear one—and said this seemed more like a question of detail—begged that at all events nothing should be done *ab irato*[1] but that we should sleep upon it.

Goulburn saw great disadvantage in resigning upon a question that would not and could not be understood by the country as a matter of principle.

I said that without endeavouring to draw off from the conclusion to which Sir Robert Peel appeared to point I wished to observe that our position with regard to this question was not that of the Whig Government in 1841—they were defeated on the principle of their measure:

---

[1] 'In hot blood'.

the principle of our measure had been affirmed by a large majority in the vote against Lord John Russell's motion, and the amount of differential duty, the second leading feature, had been generally accepted by the House and acknowledged in the main by the West Indians. If we chose now to take the old duties for nine months, our substantial objects would have been attained in the main if not so completely as by our own plan: the distinction of free and slave sugar would stand affirmed—the prices pretty effectually checked—notice given to all parties and the outline of the terms on which they were to compete in the British market.

We also discussed other modes of proceeding mentioned in my notes of Saturday.[1] I argued that two courses ought clearly to be rejected, viz. either to give up the distinction of free and slave sugar or to adopt Miles's motion.

We met again Sunday at two, at Lord Aberdeen's house. Peel said he felt two courses to be incompatible with his personal honour: one, to adopt Miles's motion—the other, to propose the renewal of the old sugar duties whether for twelve months or nine. Much was said by him and Graham of the incapacity of disgraced men to serve their party or their country: and Peel said in reference to the expression of confidence expected from the party before Monday's House, that the way for them to show confidence would be by voting for the plan of the Government.

I said that after Sir R. Peel's declaration I had no more to urge upon the subject of the renewal of the old duties for nine months, although it appeared to me that there were no insuperable or very formidable objections to that plan on its own merits: but that if it was thought fit to combat Mr. Miles's plan in detail so as to bring it back to the plan of the Government we should have a good case for debate in the first question that would arise, which would be to negative the prospective reduction to 20/- in November next.

Lord Granville Somerset asked if there were no means by which a plank might be provided for those who having voted in the majority were anxious to escape but could not absolutely reverse the vote they had given. For instance to take our own plan but only for nine months.

Peel said Lord John would then make and ought to carry the motion to postpone the whole subject until next year.

Some of us, however, differed, I among them, and thought it im-

---

[1] ADD.MS 44734, f. 130.

possible for Lord John to propose with decency or with hope the maintenance for another year of the prohibitory system.

Sir R. Peel had been to the Queen after the Cabinet on Saturday who
was very cordial—said the Opposition seemed to her to have behaved
alike ill with the recusant Conservatives—observed that she hoped no
resignation would be necessary—and laughingly that she could not send
for Mr. Miles.

Graham spoke strongly and in a dark sense of the spirit of the party
which he conceived to be hostile as well as unruly. From this we generally
dissented.

But it is evident that Peel's mind and the others leaning the same way
have been influenced not principally by the difficulties of this individual
question, but by disgust with the immense, uncheered, unrelieved labour
of their position and with the fact that their party never seems to show
energy except when it differs from the leaders.

I confess I think that in choosing to attempt the reestablishment of
our own plan we are too hard upon them and that we ought to have
made some small and secondary concession—but I feel that Peel's final
inclination must and ought to guide the Government.

Mahon came to see me this morning and stated what he has collected
regarding the state of the party—some few, mere units, were discon-
tented and hostile—the great mass firm and cordial—most desirous to
avert resignation—but yet feeling it essential to save the honour of the
House of Commons—and not inclined virtually to reverse the vote of
Friday night by the adoption of the measure of the Government.

I told him with thanks for his communication that I thought we were
all the unconscious instruments of working out at this time great constitutional problems, which are to be solved by the general result of a
series of apparently isolated transactions—that the powers of government are now ultimately in the hands of the Conservative majority but
subject to certain conditions as to their exercise, which I fear we do not
yet properly understand—that it is not sufficiently established how far
the power of such a majority extends beyond the choice of the instrument, namely the Administration, into the details of its conduct. I admitted his doctrine that the freedom and independence of Members of
Parliament must be maintained: and held only on the other hand that
the character of the Government itself, of which it must itself be the
judge was equally essential to the power of the party. That the prece-
dents of old times scarcely applied because Government as a whole was

now so much weakened, and especially Conservative Government in the face of Whig-Radical opposition, that perhaps the freedom of relation between Ministers and their supporters *must* now be more limited in order to give to the entire body the compactness necessary to enable it to make way. I also mentioned the case of the Ecclesiastical Courts Bill of this year compared with that of last year as a distinct proof that the course of the Government was very far indeed from being one of asking every thing from their friends and conceding nothing to them.

*June 17. 1844.*

## 168: ADD.MS 44777, ff. 194–195

June 17/20. 1844.
I went to Peel early in the day. He saw Sandon and Miles in my presence and he stated the argument for the course of the Government very mildly and clearly. We went over the commercial part of the question, with a view to his explaining it fully in the evening.

The Cabinet met at three and it was finally resolved to adopt the line which Peel disapproved on Saturday but almost advised Sunday and which Graham then considered to be attended with less evil than the alternative of resignation. This plan is a compromise between Sir R. Peel's original and extreme view, and the leaning of many members of the Cabinet—I think probably it would have appeared if a majority of the opinions had been successively declared—to make some concession to the vote of the House of Commons.

It was put by Lord Granville Somerset that some change not of an essential character might wisely be made in order to enable persons who were desirous to change their course to do so at least without indecency.

I considered the question of the renewal of the old duties for nine months, which I believe would have been upon the whole the best and most proper course after the adverse vote to have gone by after what Sir R. Peel said yesterday: and I only suggested whether it would be acceptable to our friends and answer the purpose contemplated by Lord Granville Somerset if we were to limit our Bill as it stands to nine months. Peel went so far as to say that that might be open to consideration if it were suggested and if it should seem likely to be beneficial in the course of the proceedings: but no more.

I heard his speech with great pain. The tone was hard, reserved, and introspective: and when he came to the part when he said it was his duty to consider what encouragement would be afforded by a concession from him to the renewal of similar conduct in future, and the formation of fresh combinations between friends and opponents against his policy, I had what in *Glynnese* is called a crup—I felt that injustice was done though unintentionally to honourable men and cordial friends, and also that the venerable dignity of a British Parliament was offended.

At the end of the speech we all felt ourselves out. The House seemed resolved into its primordial elements—persons conversed in knots—there was no tide of sympathy and common feeling in the debate—each man on our side expressed what was isolated and partial, the opponents firing in with skill to exasperate the inflamed or painful sentiment which in different degrees pervaded nearly the whole body of our friends. It was a grievous evening. Stanley spoke with not less tact than force and did all that man could do for a rally: some say the majority was owing to him. I determined [to take no part] in the course of the debate for I could not have assumed without gross indecency the ground that could hardly be taken by older and weightier men. Conversations with Members of Parliament subsequently convinced me that a deep wound had been inflicted upon the spirit and harmony of the party: that a great man had committed a great error.

Tonight he has done much, and offhand on Duncombe's challenge, to repair it. I am not sure however, that the cure is yet complete.

## 169: ADD.MS 44777, ff. 199–203

On Sunday the 7th [July 1844] Sir R. Peel sent to desire to see me on Monday morning. He opened the conversation by referring to the Railways Bill which smoothed the way—after the explanation on that subject he went to the question of Irish education. He referred to general topics, probability of collision with France, Irish dangers in case of a war, position of the Church in Ireland, position of the Queen with her confinement close at hand, her 'undisguised preference for a Conservtive Government' now notwithstanding the state of things which had formerly existed—his own obligation on no account to desert her at this moment—and his hope that I could find no ground of objection to his declaring in answer to Mr. Wyse that the Government could not adopt his motion—that they would, however, undertake to inquire into the whole subject matter of it (lay and ecclesiastical) during the recess, and would state at an early period of the next session whether or not they were prepared to adopt any practical measure.

I said that I was willing very much to place myself in his hands as to the language he might use: that my convictions as to the relation of my personal character to the question remained the same as they had been in the spring: that I thought I could not be an *author* of such a measure, and that if I were I could not thereafter expect to be taken for an honest man: that on the other hand I thought it would not be my duty to oppose it when proceeding from a Government which I knew adopted it as being on the whole the best means of defence for the Church of Ireland: that I considered the period for settling the question by joint endowment was gone by: that this step was in my view the commencement of a great transition, perhaps an inevitable one, but one of which there might be a question, admitting it to be inevitable, *who* should be the instruments to effect it: that I saw the amount of pressure and freely allowed that the maintenance of the Church in Ireland belonged to a view which was now in great measure antiquated and obsolete: that to me, however, it would become impossible to bear any efficient part in that maintenance if I concurred in the projected plan, no argument would remain really available for *me* after such participation. But having said all this with reference to the measure itself I was still very sensible of the evils of *any* secession upon such a question, and anxious to gain time at all events if practicable without dishonour, to go out in the recess rather than now, especially if possible to use the interval now to be gained for the purpose of disposing of myself in such manner so as not to go out upon that question.

He said that as a matter of honour he could not conceive how *more* could be required than to retire after a practical measure had been resolved upon: and he referred to the case of Wetherell as Attorney General.

I pointed out that in that case the Government were not publicly pledged to the consideration of the question. He admitted it but said that here the pledge would be only to a consideration which might have either an affirmative or a negative result.

I said that wishing to go to the very farthest point and by no means to stand upon any mere punctilio I would with his intimation of the nature of the explanation he was to give (which was not to be in *detail*) and of his view of the question of honour place myself in his hands.

At the Cabinet the substance of this conversation was more briefly repeated on both sides. Lord G. Somerset observed that he approved of the answer now to be given but he thought the greatest difficulties would be found to lie in the way of any practical measure.

I said that I was convinced the question of relations with the Court of Rome would present itself at the very outset and must be encountered.

(We had been on this in the previous conversation—and I found Peel's view was not to *recognise* the Pope's sovereignty without an *equivalent* but to proceed in the first place informally.)

At the Cabinet it was also agreed that the question of admitting Jews to corporations should stand over until next year—on account partly of Goulburn's position and mine—partly of the period of the session and the promise half made not to introduce new Bills of importance—partly on account of the other points of collision which have already arisen in the course of the year.

(At the conversation I had pointed out to Sir Robert Peel Easter next as the time at which so far as the affairs of my department are concerned they would leave me tolerably free to retire without causing inconvenience.

He also said at one time that it was the loss and not the consequences that he deprecated for he thought the necessity of some such measure would be generally acknowledged—but this was hardly consistent with what he himself said at other times, namely that the consequences of any disunion upon a religious question must be most formidable and must go far towards breaking up the Government.)

At this Cabinet we also discussed the Irish Charitable Endowments Bill. A letter from Dr. Machale to Sir Robert Peel deprecating the Bill was read and also one from the Bishop of Exeter to the Chancellor doing the same—the one apparently because the Bill does not recognise the Irish Roman Catholic hierarchy and priesthood and the other because it does. The Bill has in fact been carefully drawn by the Irish Attorney General and revised by the English, in order to avoid that recognition— I thought the Bishop of Exeter scarcely reasonable. On the other hand it was observed I think by Sir R. Peel and Graham that the two were exactly alike in their different positions: which I thought rather hard.

*July 16. 1844.*

Sir R. Peel also expressed great satisfaction at the results of our moderate commercial policy in the country which he said had surpassed all his expectations.                                                                            *July 17.*

## 170: ADD.MS 44777, ff. 204–205

July 19/20. 1844.

Last night on the education estimates Mr. Wyse opened his views. Assuming his principles and view of government to be sound, nothing could be more fair and moderate. There is however this rule for forms and principles of government: they must ever bear an analogy to the condition of the people, their inward tone and life. And to judge by our tone and life the higher theory however true in itself is no longer true to us—that is, it is an untrue representative of the result issuing from the concourse of wills and forces that make up our national system. That Government has a mind or is the presiding mind of the community is a doctrine which when the idea of mind and spirit become thoroughly dissociated one should perhaps wish extinct. How stands the case with us? Those who are farthest from Mr. Wyse for the most part are content to say, 'This is well, only give also to the Church Education Society.' And they do not perceive that they are here claiming State support after they have abandoned the only ground upon which *they* can be entitled to it. The only persons who really view the State as having a conscience which shall disapprove and exclude, fasten that conscience not upon the positive idea of the Church but upon the negation and repudiation of Popery. It seems then that the time is drawing near for a change of scenes and parts—and that this is indeed the commencement, or at least the recommencement of a great transition.

Sir Robert Peel said more in his speech last night, I am sure unintentionally, than he had indicated to me. Partly the general tone was different by some shades: but chiefly by introducing a favourite doctrine of his from which I dissent that as to the Maynooth grant no question of principle remains for if violated at all principle is violated as much by the present grant as it could be by a further one. There was nothing, however, that would justify my interposing in the debate nor was I challenged by any one.

I think he felt he had said too much for he explained and in doing so restrained his statement within the very limits which I had expected: viz. announcing that Government admitted the academical education of Ireland to be insufficient and would consider the means of enlarging it for all classes of the community: that they would also take into view the state of Maynooth and would at an early period of next session declare whether they were prepared or not to propose any measure upon the subject.

## 171: ADD.MS 44777, ff. 206–209

The Cabinet met on Tuesday the 19th [November 1844].

Sir J. Graham stated that O'Connell had been singularly cautious since the judgment in his favour and was evidently much at fault. He detailed the communications of the Lord Lieutenant with parties on the subjects of Maynooth and collegiate education: and read Lord Heytesbury's letter describing how Drs. Murray and Crolly at an interview declared in favour of a modification of the visitorial system of Maynooth—and Dr. Machale violently against any change—reporting also as in his own favour the resolution of the Roman Catholic prelates at their Convocation.

The papers were circulated—and we met again on Friday the 22nd. We discussed only collegiate education.

Colleges of a neutral character are to be founded and endowed by Act of Parliament: the Crown being Visitor—at Cork and Belfast the professorships are to embrace all the usual branches except theology. Thus far all seemed to agree.

But even here there is a difficulty with respect to religion. Sir R. Peel proposed that facilities should be given for the endowment of professorships of theology by individuals—and that there should be lectures within the walls of the college. If then the Socinians should propose to endow, was it to be allowed?

This question we resumed more fully today. Goulburn, Lord Haddington, Lord Wharncliffe were all sensitive on this subject, and disliked the countenance thus to be allowed to Socinianism: Lord Haddington stoutly contending, that persons of that profession were not Presbyterians.

Then it was pointed out that we give the *regium donum* to Socinians: and moreover, what I did not before know, that last year, one of the professors in the Belfast Academy having become Arian, the Ulster Synod applied to have him removed—the governing body of the Academy declined: the Ulster Synod applied to Government either to withdraw the salary and give it to one of their body, or to establish a new salary for one of their body. The Government chose the latter, and continued the salary to the Arian.

I lamented the difficulty but said if there was one thing amidst all the doubts on these subjects which is free from doubt, it is the utter incapacity of a Government to stand upon any mere doctrinal definitions, though it may deal with a Church, a totally different matter.

It was thought best on the whole that this power to accept endowments should be reserved in very general terms.

We then passed on to the question of Maynooth—and here it was observed as very important that the Trustees, memorialising with the authority of the Roman Catholic prelates, ask for an increase of the grant *upon the same terms* as those on which it is now given—thus striking at the root of the proposal to modify the visitorial power to which Sir J. Graham clings very much.

Sir R. Peel declared that though he thought it of great importance to obtain an effective visitorial power instead of the present nominal one, yet he considered the present state of the college so bad that he thought an increased vote to augment salaries and comforts would be of itself an advantage without any change in the conditions. However, he was for endeavouring to obtain such a change.

The Chancellor, Lord Wharncliffe, the Duke of Wellington and others gave their opinions that something must be done in which there was an universal acquiescence—and Peel said the time was now come for declaring the view of the Cabinet generally.

I had hereupon to *do the deed* over again.

I said I was precluded by considerations of personal honour from taking part in such a plan as a member of the Government: that I had so tied myself by the virtual pledge of my deliberate writings as to have no choice: that I had advocated a system which was daily becoming more and more impracticable: that its being so might be a good reason for the adoption of another, but yet not for my being a party to a design for departing in an important measure from the old one.

In answer to Lord Stanley who seemed to assume I thought myself bound to oppose the change, I said that I was by no means so: that if I were obliged now to say either I was bound to oppose it or bound not to oppose it, the latter was much nearer to my mind upon that question—that I could well conceive the pressure, was by no means sure that the measure could be avoided, considered the other members of the Government to stand in a position quite different from mine and to be free to take their course—but that in order to answer that claim which public opinion urges upon every man for decency and consistency, I felt it absolutely necessary to place myself in a position of independence where any conclusion I might form would be free from all just suspicion: and that I was certain that if I did otherwise I should inflict far more injury on the Government by destroying all just confidence in my character, than the little service which in any other respect I might be able to render.

*Deus adjuvet!*[1] The passage is a critical one.                    *November 25. 1844.*

## 172: ADD.MS 44777, ff. 212-215

January 14. 1845.

On Friday, December 6 (the day before I went to Newark) was held the last autumn Cabinet. On that day I was prepared for my catastrophe. Sir Robert Peel had declared in our discussions at the last preceding Cabinet that he thought the Maynooth grant ought to be enlarged and the state of the college improved even if the *terms* as to visitation should remain entirely unaltered. (The memorial of the Irish Roman Catholic prelates requests an increase upon the same terms as those now existing: and at the late interview with the Lord Lieutenant Dr. Machale declared that he in the name of the majority or of the whole body of the prelates would not accept an enlargement upon any other terms.) Sir Robert Peel had also declared that the Irish policy of the Government ought to be announced at the opening of the session. And as the Maynooth memorial was now before us I thought the time was come. But at the meeting on this Friday Sir Robert Peel recommended that Sir J. Graham should *first* settle the Charitable Bequests Commission—then the Collegiate Education Bill—and then take Maynooth. This therefore postponed the matter.

It was with a reference to this conversation in the Cabinet that I wrote to Sir R. Peel on the 2nd of January[2]—on the 9th I arrived in town and saw him. He expressed his desire that I should postpone taking any step until we came to a positive issue. He said a Maynooth Bill was in preparation—he did not know when it would be ready. He had not intended to imply that a declaration of intentions with regard to Maynooth should be made absolutely at the opening of the session: but that it should be made early. He hoped I had no disinclination to continue to act and advise upon the matters of Government. I told him my motive for writing was for fear that if I delayed longer, and suffered him to remain possibly under some notion that my mind had changed,

---

[1] 'May God help me!'
[2] Parker, *Sir Robert Peel*, iii, 163-164.

my resolution might come upon him by surprise and at a time more inconvenient than the present—with every day, as the preparations for
the session advanced, the inconveniences of my retirement would increase as regarded the business of the department. He replied that he
would be wholly responsible for that—that I had given the fullest and
fairest notice—and he should not have a word to say when I felt that
my time was come. I expressed a great anxiety to continue to aid in
public business as long as I could: more especially with reference to the
sugar duties, a matter in which I felt myself more especially responsible.

He said, 'I wish to speak without any reserve, and I ought to tell you
I think it will very probably be fatal to the Government.' He explained
that he did not know whether the feeling among Goulburn's constituents might not be too strong for him: that in Scotland as he expected
there would be a great opposition: and he seemed to think that from the
Church also there might be great resistance and he said the proceedings
in the diocese of Exeter showed a very sensitive state of the public mind.
I told him that I thought the feeling of the Church was not moving in
that direction: that the desire to fetter the proceedings of the Government towards other communions was rapidly diminishing—that the
anxiety rather was for some relaxation of the restraints incident to the
connection of the Church with the State. He made no answer.

I assured him that I viewed the matter as one of personal pledge:
that it was wholly unconnected with any thing like alienation of feeling:
and that I could not doubt that the Government having adopted the
measure the best thing that could happen would be its being carried.

The Cabinet of Thursday the 11th [January 1845] discussed the bill
for colleges in Ireland. *The* question was the position of the voluntary
theological lectures in the intended colleges. Sir R. Peel was desirous to
declare strongly the expediency of encouraging religious instruction:
I doubted whether an abstract declaration of its value, construable as
having reference to so many modes of religion alike would be of value—
the feeling rather seemed to be that we must let the theological department *sit loose*.

This day they have been upon the drainage and health of towns. Sir
R. Peel said what is now called the condition of the people question will
press very much in this session, Lord John having given notice of a
motion upon it. Whatever may be the difficulties—however it may be a
law of civilisation that the extremes of wealth and poverty should increase together—some effort must be made, and he advised laying upon

the municipal bodies with or without others the duty of improving the habitations of the people, under penalty of exposure, thinking that the power of general opinion would secure their fulfilment of the duty.

*January 14. 1845.*

## 173: ADD.MS 44777, ff. 216-218

The records of my official catastrophe need not be prolix.

On Tuesday, January 28 [1845] Sir R. Peel sent for me, and told me he had just offered my office to Sandon, who seemed disposed to accept it, but was staggered on hearing that I had resigned because of May-nooth, because of his constituents; and especially because he had pledged himself to a grant in favour of the Church Education Society of Ireland. Monday morning, said he, came the final answer, which he promised to send for my perusal: it was *no*. 'And that was a great blow.' He then said he had done he thought the best in his power by making Dalhousie President and Cardwell Vice-President—he added he was desirous to inform me exactly of what he had done.

Since that time I have had, besides many letters, conversations with Goulburn, Lincoln, Lord Ripon, Lord Haddington, Lord Aberdeen, Duke of Buccleuch, Sir J. Graham, Lord Granville Somerset, Herbert, Dalhousie: one and all of whom have spoken to me in a spirit of confidence and friendship: and I really hope that this painful operation has been effected with as little disruption of feeling, with as much reciprocal assurance of good motives and intentions, as was possible.

Today I went to see Sir R. Peel, to make some suggestions as to matters of business connected with the department. I have great gratification in finding his manner quite unchanged. *He* has never (I think justly) made allusion to the future: Lincoln, Dalhousie, and today Lord Aberdeen, have spoken of the separation as a short one: to which I could only answer 'sufficient for the day' and that no man is master of events in public life, nor can answer even for himself.

Sir R. Peel asked me today what I intended to do tomorrow on the Address. I adverted to the speech and he recited to me the part of it relating to trade, and part about education in Ireland. I said, and he seemed to assent, that probably some explanation would be required from me: but that I should endeavour to be as brief as possible—on the ground that the matters which had caused my retirement were not yet before the House. That I was desirous to avoid pledging myself to any course upon the measures themselves—and would endeavour to keep much within the compass of my last letter to him: [1] he was very anxious I should state there had been a perfect concurrence between us as to matters of trade: I said I had intended to state distinctly that the cause I assigned for retirement was the sole cause. I was also desirous to let it be known that I could not join in any opposition connected with what was termed the 'no Popery' cry: and that it was no measure relating to the Church which had caused my retirement, as a notion of that kind seemed to have gone abroad.

He thought I should ask an audience of the Queen on my retirement: and accordingly at the Palace today he intimated and then the Lord in Waiting, as is the usage, formally requested it. I saw the Queen in her private sittingroom. As she did not commence speaking immediately after the first bow, I thought it my part to do so: and I said, 'I have used the boldness to request an audience, Madam, that I might say with how much pain it is that I find myself separated from Your Majesty's service, and how gratefully I feel Your Majesty's many acts of kindness.' She replied that she regretted it very much and that it was a great loss. I resumed, that I had the greatest comfort I could enjoy under the circumstances, in the knowledge that my feelings towards Her Majesty's person and service, and also towards Sir R. Peel and my late colleagues were altogether unchanged by my retirement. After a few words more she spoke of the state of the country, and the reduced condition of Chartism, of which I said I believed the main feeder was want of employment. At the pause I watched her eye for the first sign to retire—but she asked me about my wife before we concluded—then one bow on the spot and another at the door, which was very near, and so it was all over.

Certainly I must say that from Her Majesty downwards I have received the greatest kindness which with a clear and resolved conscience within makes a sense of support for which I can never enough thank God and deplore my own unworthiness.                    *February 3. 1845.*

## 174: ADD.MS 44777, ff. 219–228

During discussions on the Maynooth project I have had conversations of which I make the following notes.

Before the day for the second reading Mr. Rochfort Clarke, the

---

[1] Parker, *Sir Robert Peel*, iii, 166–167.

Editor of the *Record*, came to me and said he understood I was to oppose the Bill and hoped I would present the St. Martin's petition. He considered that all differences among Protestants, even including Puseyites, should be laid aside and their united efforts applied to resisting a measure which went to the endowment of Anti-Christ, the great apostasy. He held forth at length upon these subjects, with a perceptible shade, I thought, of egotism.

I told him that I intended to support the Bill: as I conceived that no religious ground of opposition could be maintained in practice: declining any question open to dispute I put it to him that the favour of the State includes Unitarians, and that while such is the case (and I do not see how it can cease to be the case) on what plea can we exclude the Roman Catholic communion.

He said he objected to all Acts of endowment for any body other than the Church: but that he drew a distinction between a case of essential difference like that of the Church of Rome and difference lying only in matter which pertains to the 'further perfection' of a Church such as that between us and the Kirk. He had no tolerable plea for the case of the Unitarian Presbyterian.

Sir Robert Inglis came soon after and put with delicacy his inclination to know my intentions. I explained them. He said I had taken away one of his main hopes. Mr. Ward would move his amendment (for taking the money from the Church): on the question 'that the words proposed' etc. the opponents of the Bill would vote with the supporters of Mr. Ward: the Government would be left in a minority: they would resign the next morning: and his hope was that I!! might be sent for. I told him that quite apart from any question of incapacity, I must deprecate any issue of the kind: that I had doubted the wisdom of the introduction of *this measure as it stands*, and had rather preferred letting the Irish Church question stand entire: but that after its introduction I was clear as to my course, and that not from *fear* of what might take place in Ireland but because I thought this country could not adopt a policy such as could warrant in reason a resistance to this Bill. At the same time expressing the belief that we were on a downward course: and that this was a great step in the descent, although a legitimate consequence from the facts of our condition.

After I had spoken I asked him whether my speech was worse than my private conversation with him: he said no they exactly corresponded —he could not, however, reconcile them with my book.

Kinnaird came in the next day and said that my resignation had now made the case much better instead of worse for the Romist cause, as it gave much greater weight to my support of the Bill than if I had remained in office and been a party to the proposal.

Hope wants more explanation. Parties do not understand, he says, whether I repent of my book—or if not why I have left it—(?) or why meaning to support the Bill I disturbed the public mind by quitting office.

The Bishop of London says he cannot consent to the Bill, but will not vigorously oppose it—although he sees what is coming, and what this will introduce. I think he means, not only payment of the Roman Catholic priesthood, but appropriation of the Church revenues for the purpose.

I was sorry to find the Government were not pleased with my speech: I believe because I represented the Bill as bringing nearer the payment of the Roman Catholic priesthood. This of course was not likely to make the measure more palatable to the people of England. Which did not occur to me. Yet if it had I do not think I could have withheld the sentiment: if as I believe it be both true and likewise most important.

Blackstone said to me, 'You gave us a licking'—I said surely my speech was as pacific as it could be—he replied—'Oh I mean in the division, not your speech; you licked yourself more than any body else.' Smart enough. I merely answered, 'I am not uneasy on that score.'

The Bishop of London in his conversation said he wished the thing had been done by the Irish nation before the Union—as their own act. From this expression I think perhaps he only looks now to the payment of the Roman priests from the Consolidated Fund.

Sir R. Inglis told me that in 1826 (or 7) he advised Sir R. Peel to send the Duke of Cumberland to Ireland as Lord Lieutenant, and thirty thousand men, and *thus* to take a stand against the Emancipation. I did not think such counsel could have proceeded from such a quarter if the information had not been original. *April 29. 1845.*

Dr. C. Wordsworth called on me to recommend that I should take my stand in Parliament on the Church and State theory of Hooker: contend that all men were still members of the National Church, and wait for the time when they should be so. This he said would hold out a rallying point to the country and a strong combination of sentiment would gradually gather around it.

I told him I had long made up my mind not to pursue a political career governed by such a rule. That it was the corruption of individual convictions which was now lowering the tone of law—that this process could only be reversed by reforming individual convictions, and this is the work of religious agency addressed to the private conscience not of the State and its Acts of Parliament: that all which can be done there is to check the course of evil and to do such good, as the actual relations of the Church to our civil institutions may place within reach. That the State has repudiated the Church as its single wedded wife: the best that now remains is that she should have the special honour accorded to a wife among concubines. That our great difficulty was the want of a *religious conviction* on the duty of unity.

I told Fremantle at the Queen's ball, 'Well, you have put the pick into the wall—it will not end here'—he asked me if I was prepared to go farther—but we were parted after I had just had time to say I hoped we should decide something beyond the demands of the moment.

On Wednesday I met Stanley at Bunsen's: and told him also that it seemed to me we were standing upon a new era of ecclesiastical legislation: that the one remaining strong, practical argument for the Church in Ireland was in my view that the Roman Catholic Church was not in a disposition to accept the *conditions* of endowment. He said he did not see *who* was to do the work—i.e. alter the arrangement of Church property in Ireland.

I saw Sandon this morning and opened with him the same subject. I argued against his doctrine of restitution—which he stated that he had stated to be *quasi* restitution, and in the nature of redress or compensation rather than restitution in a strict sense. I told him that I thought social justice bore very strongly on the question of Church property in Ireland when the principle of adherence to the Church on the ground of its religious character and claims in Ireland has been compromised. But he said he thought we must consider the title of three centuries a good and sufficient title.

I do not think this argument has force enough for its end.

Tonight I have had a farther conversation with Lincoln: and we very freely exchanged our sentiments, beginning with my position at Newark, in respect to which we were agreed that I could not move from my seat unless in the event that it should be distinctly alleged by the Duke or by my constituents that they had been *misled* by me.

From thence I passed to the question—I hold that this concession would lead us very far—that I still retained my doubts as to the wisdom of separating this subject of Maynooth from the more general question in Ireland—that my feeling had always been, we were to support the Church in Ireland on the ground of religious truth and duty but that if we were driven from that ground there was no other argument so powerful in its favour as the argument of the poverty and the numbers of the Roman Catholics against it—that I had not arrived at definite conclusions but was endeavouring to work them out—and that at all events I became from day to day more disposed to say whatever we do let us at least not act only for the moment but take up our ground with some view to a permanent policy. That if our party were to go on doling out concessions at intervals of a few years, as long as any thing remained—the effect would ultimately be the most fatal to the characters of public men—the most calculated to deprive concession of all its value—and the most inimical to the general stability of the institutions of the country. And that worst of all, however we know the motives of Sir R. Peel to be most pure, yet in history these concessions proceeding from the leaders of our party and effected *by virtue of a power obtained under other anticipations*, would stand in history as a series of betrayals—and it is intolerable to move forward without resolving against such a course. That at present I found a *good* parliamentary argument in the fact that the Roman Catholic Church is not ready to submit to the restraints of an establishment. That I would rather make a plunge now or soon, than keep the country in slow torture. That this question led on to many others. The Church had paid for money, in liberty—that when the endowments are withdrawn liberty must be enlarged—that I grieved to see, for instance in Stanley's speech of last night, signs of a disposition to make the yoke of the Church heavier, while its temporal privileges are according to all reasonable anticipations likely to be reduced—that we must not be bound to go on with 26 bishops till the Day of Judgment. That therefore any settlement in Ireland (independently of the fact that it would probably pass into Scotland, and through Scotland perhaps into England) would be a very large measure, involving much legislation, and conferring freedom in exchange for the abstraction of property—that it was most essential such a balanced measure should be adjusted by persons who would deal fairly by the Church—that I feared Lord John Russell with his party though I should not fear him alone—but for this, I should think it most desirable that the work should be done by the party opposed to us.

Lincoln agreed that this must go farther—that the Romish priests never would be paid out of the Consolidated Fund—and generally took the same view. He said he in his speech had been most anxious to indicate a disposition to go farther—but that he had thought it hardly fair to the Government. That Herbert had the same view with him, and purposely abstained on Ward's motion from any argument on the Irish Church. That he had told Graham he could not take a strong line against Ward's motion—that Graham felt himself irrevocably committed. That he thought Peel would be forced forward by the younger members of his party to touch the property of the Church of Ireland.

*May 3. 1845.*

## 175: ADD.MS 44777, ff. 229–232

At Sir R. Peel's on the 12th of July (dinner) I had some interesting conversation with him regarding the state of public business and the personal position of those who carry it on. I had congratulated him upon appearing to bear his labours not worse than in former sessions in Parliament. He shook his head and complained of the pressure of a sense of *fatigue* upon the brain, I mean a physical sensation. He then spoke of the immense multiplication of details in public business and the enormous tax imposed upon available time and strength by the work of attendance in the House of Commons. He agreed that it was extremely adverse to the growth of greatness among our public men: and he said the mass of public business increased so fast that he could not tell what it was to end in and did not venture to speculate even for a few years upon the mode of administering public affairs. He thought the consequence was already manifest in its being not well done.

It sometimes occurred to him whether it would after all be a good arrangement to have the Prime Minister in the House of Lords—which would get rid of the very encroaching duty of attendance on and correspondence with the Queen.

I asked if in that case it would not be quite necessary that the Leader in the Commons should frequently take upon himself to make decisions which ought properly only to be made by the head of the Government. He said certainly and that would constitute a great difficulty.

That although Lord Melbourne might be very well adapted to take his part in such a plan, there were he believed difficulties in it under him, when Lord J. Russell led the House of Commons.

That when he led the House in 1828 under the Duke of Wellington as Premier he had a very great advantage in the disposition of the Duke to follow the judgments of others in whom he had confidence with respect to all civil matters.

He said it was impossible during the session even to work the public business through the medium of the Cabinet, such is the pressure upon time.

I observed that I had been reading the speculations of a writer named Anstey on the constitution who made it his great grievance that the country should be governed not by the Privy Council but by an arbitrary or informal committee of it: and recommending it as a cure for all our evils that we should recur to the Privy Council as the instrument of government, of which individual Ministers should be the servants. That it was very singular to find the speculatist arguing that we should go back from Cabinet to Privy Council at a time when the imperious necessity of affairs made it almost impossible to maintain the degree of concert implied in the system of government by a Cabinet and drove back the weight more and more upon individuals and one in particular.

It was on my lips to observe to him that the frame of his government was so adjusted as to impose upon him a maximum of parliamentary labour: for it is a singular combination of arrangements under which two Secretary of State's departments, the Board of Trade, and the India Board, have no Cabinet Minister to represent them in the House of Commons—but it occurred to me in time, that this would be justly construable into—why do you not invite others, e.g. myself?

He complained in particular of the mass of dispatches he was required to read without having so much as an ostensible fragment of time at his disposal for them.

It was pleasant to me to find and feel by actual tact as it were (though I had no suspicion of the contrary), his manner as friendly and as much unbent as at any former period. *August 14. 1845.*

## 176: ADD.MS 44735, f. 20

I quitted the Government because I did not think it fit that even if I had made up my mind which I had not done to the wisdom of the measure I should be a party to the proposal of it in Parliament.

I have supported the Bill because (the measure being now submitted for adoption or rejection in Parliament) I am convinced that the welfare of the country requires me to vote in its favour.

There is no inconsistency so far as I am aware between these two propositions.

But it is said that my support of the Bill is inconsistent with the principles of the work which I have published.

The principles of that work, bearing upon the present subject, were these: first that there is a particular view of national religion which is most accordant to the nature of a State and to the relation between governments and the governed: secondly that we ought to defend that system of State religion, in our own case, although it had then already been altered, from further alteration, so long as the general sense of the nation would warrant it.

I never held that it was to be adhered to by the State irrespectively of the convictions of the people and their religious divisions.

I did hold, and still hold, that in itself it is a misfortune, though relatively like many other acts it may be right.

(1) These were the *principles* of the work as it originally appeared: but they are more clearly developed in a larger edition of it, published above four years ago, which I set myself to prepare when I found that it had been misconstrued.

(2) Even if I had apparently propounded any view of State religion as unalterable, I might have paused before urging it to the point of causing convulsion in the country: first because I am not clearly convinced as to the lawfulness of force in such a case, secondly because I believe the result would probably have been concession larger in degree and both ineffectual and ignominious in its character.

(3) What I now hold is that the convictions of the country either as estimated by the actual practice of the State, or as by the arguments used in opposition to this Bill, will justify me in resisting it.

On this principle I acted in the Canada Clergy Reserves Bill of 1840.

*September 18. 1845.*

# INDEX

Abercromby, James, M.P. (1839 1st Lord
Dunfermline), 45, 108
Aberdeen, George Hamilton Gordon, 4th
Earl of, 46, 80, 91, 92, 109, 119, 127,
132, 162, 183, 192, 206, 273
asks for WEG as under-secretary
(1835), 42–3
conversations with WEG (1835), 47–8,
50–1; (1836), 72–5
WEG on, 47, 67, 72
on Church affairs, 49–50, 105–6
and the Queen's speech (1841), 153–5
and commercial treaty with Portugal,
184, 190, 220–1, 223, 224–5
and Church of Scotland, 212–13
on Canning, 219
and Stade duties, 220, 221, 226–8
and Maynooth grant, 233
and relations with the Papacy, 240
and Factory Bill (1844), 250, 252
and sugar duties (1844), 261
Acland, Sir Thomas Dyke, 10th Bt.,
M.P., 86, 129
Acland, Thomas Dyke, M.P. (1871 11th
Bt.) his first speech, 89
Adelaide, Queen
WEG on, 120
Albert, Prince Consort, 120, 161, 228
on duelling, 219
on Portuguese commercial treaty, 220,
222–3
Ali Murad, amir of Khairpur, 220
Allen, Joseph, Bishop of Ely, 139
Althorp, John Spencer, Viscount (1834
3rd Earl Spencer), 62, 73, 84, 114,
138
Andrews, Newark voter, 13
Anson, George Edward, secretary to the
Prince Consort, 162
Anstey, Thomas Chisholm, 280
Arbuthnott, John, 8th Viscount, 38
conversations with WEG (1836), 73–5
Ashburnham, Bertram, 4th Earl of, 91
Ashburton, Alexander Baring, 1st Lord,
132, 159

on Corn Laws, 185
*see also* Baring
Ashley, Anthony Ashley Cooper, Lord
(1851 7th Earl of Shaftesbury), 49,
94, 106, 139, 251
conversation with WEG (1837), 76–9
WEG on, 78–9
Ashley, Lady (née Lady Emily Cowper),
76

Baring, Alexander, M.P. (1835 1st Lord
Ashburton), 37, 39
*see also* Ashburton
Baring, William Bingham, M.P. (1848 2nd
Lord Ashburton), 147, 252
Baring Wall, Charles, M.P., 138–9, 183
Barnave, Antoine Pierre Joseph Marie,
86
Beckett, Sir John, 2nd Bt., M.P., 253
Bedford, John Russell, 6th Duke of,
71
Beresford, Lord John George, Arch-
bishop of Armagh
on Irish tithes, 109–10
Berryer, Antoine Pierre, 90
Betts, Newark voter, 17
Blackstone, William Seymour, M.P.
on WEG's resignation speech, 276
Blomfield, Charles James, Bishop of
London, 28, 29, 119, 124, 187, 195,
196, 202
on Maynooth grant, 276
Boler, William, Newark voter, 16
Bonham, Francis Robert, M.P., 94
Brodie, J., candidate for Elgin Burghs in
1835, 73
Brougham, Henry Peter, 1st Lord, 36, 39,
41, 45, 97, 162, 212, 213
Peel on, 62
WEG on, 71, 102
his bill for suppression of the slave
trade, 218, 219
Bruce, Lord Ernest Augustus Charles
(1878 3rd Marquess of Ailesbury),
161

Printed in England for Her Majesty's Stationery Office
by McCorquodale Printers Ltd., London

HM 5014   Dd 502037   K20 11/72   McC 3309